Reflecting His Glory

From Conformity to Transformation

Andrea Lennon

True Vine Ministry
Conway, Arkansas

Published by Morfx Press,
a division of Missional Press
149 Golden Plover Drive
Smyrna, DE 19977
www.missional-press.com
www.morfxpress.com

ISBN-10: 0-9825719-2-5
ISBN-13: 978-0-9825719-2-7

Printed in the United States of America

Unless otherwise indicated, Scripture quotations are from the Holy Bible, NEW INTERNATIONAL VERSION, copyright 1973, 1978, 1984 Biblica. Used by permission of Zondervan. All rights reserved.

Scripture quotations marked AMP are taken from the Amplified Bible, copyright 1954, 1958, 1962, 1964, 1965, 1987 by the Lockman Foundation. Used by permission.

Scripture quotations marked HCSB are taken from the Holy Bible, Holman Christian Standard Version, copyright 2003, 2002, 2000, 1999 by Holman Bible Publishers. Used by permission. All rights reserved.

Additional copies of this book can be ordered at www.andrealennon.net or www.morfxpress.com

Cover Photo by Sam Raynor of Grace Shall Reign

Lennon Family Picture provided by Amy Jones of Amy Jones Design

I dedicate this book to my husband, Jay, and children, Jake and Andrew. God has allowed me the privilege to be your wife and mother. I love you with all my heart. Thank you for your constant love and support. The road to this point in our lives has not been easy, but it has been good.

To the countless family and friends who invested time and resources into this project: thank you for embracing the call to come alongside me in the development and completion of *Reflecting His Glory*. May God richly bless you with His presence in your daily life.

Finally, and most importantly, thank You, Jesus, for redeeming my life. In response, I surrender myself to You. May my life reflect You– for Your glory alone!

Contents

About the Author

Andrea Lennon was born in Searcy, Arkansas, in March 1976. She spent the first few days of life in a hospital waiting for her parents, James and Sandra Morris, to pick her up for adoption.

From a very early age, Andrea loved going to church and felt at home with the people of God. As a six-year-old, Andrea received Jesus Christ as her personal Lord and Savior during a revival at First Baptist Church in Paris, Arkansas. God called Andrea to serve Him in ministry when she was eighteen, but Andrea did not respond to His call at that time.

In 1996, Andrea married Jay Lennon; after a year of marriage, they settled in Conway, Arkansas. They established a routine of going to church on Sunday and living like the world the rest of the week. This went on for some time but soon became unfulfilling. Both Jay and Andrea knew something was missing in their lives. It did not take them long to figure out that it was not something but Someone—the Lord Jesus. Jay and Andrea began seeking the Lord, and soon their lives changed radically. During this time, God called Andrea a second time to serve Him in ministry, and, praise His name, she responded yes!

Andrea always knew she was called to teach women the Word of God. In the fall of 2005, Andrea began leading women's ministry events. Since that time, Andrea's passion for teaching God's Word has grown. Andrea's desire is to honor the Lord by living out His Word in her own life and then challenging other women to do so as well.

In 2007, Andrea established True Vine Ministry for the purpose of reaching and discipling women in Jesus Christ. The Lord has faithfully opened doors at home and abroad for her to do this. Today Andrea praises God for the opportunities to invest in the lives of women.

Jay and Andrea Lennon live in Conway, Arkansas, with their sons, Jake and Andrew.

Before we begin…

My sweet friend, I count it a privilege to greet you in the name of our Lord and Savior Jesus Christ who left heaven, became man, lived a perfect life, died for our sins, and conquered death so that you and I can live in the freedom only He provides. As this study begins, I humble myself before you and our Heavenly Father and establish His authority over my life.

Even though I may never physically meet you, we have an undeniable connection through the blood of our Lord and Savior Jesus Christ. On the basis of His blood I say with all sincerity, "I love you, and it is my honor to serve you."

The very fact you made a decision to take part in this study is nothing short of God at work in your life. God in His infinite wisdom and design saw fit for you and me, along with others, to join together in the study of His Word. I find this a blessing that I do not take lightly. Much of what I share with you in this study is personal. It is what God through His Holy Spirit has taught me in my personal walk. I will admit I have learned the lessons the hard way but always with a loving Heavenly Father drawing me to Himself.

Over the next seven weeks we will explore the topic of *reflecting His glory*. **The goal of this study is for us to grow to think like Jesus, act like Jesus, and ultimately reflect the glory of Jesus Christ in every area of life.** Did you catch those last few words? *Every area of life.* Often in our walks with God we reflect the glory of Christ in limited areas that are easily seen and measured. The goal of this study, however, is to dig much deeper into our personal walks with God. This study will provide an opportunity to explore deep emotions, personal thoughts, and everyday actions we wish would disappear. As we progress, we will see that although these areas do not disappear, they can be transformed through the power of the cross.

Reflecting His Glory: From Conformity to Transformation is designed for individual or group study. If you are working through this study alone, enjoy the special time with your Heavenly Father. If you are working through this study as part of a group, utilize the discussion questions that are indicated with the ✿ . Additional help for groups can be found at www.andrealennon.net. Well, we have much to cover and only seven short weeks to cover it, so I challenge you to join me in the study of God's Holy Word.

For **His** Glory!
Andrea Lennon

Reflecting His Glory

Week 1: "Do Not Conform to the Pattern of this World…"

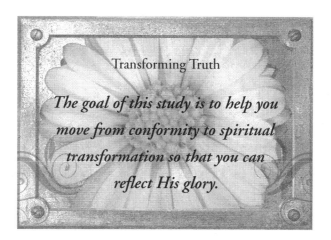

Transforming Truth

The goal of this study is to help you move from conformity to spiritual transformation so that you can reflect His glory.

Day 1: Overview of *Reflecting His Glory*

Welcome to Week One of *Reflecting His Glory*. I am so excited to jump into the study of God's Word! Let's not waste another moment. Join me as we begin in prayer.

Precious Heavenly Father,

It is with humble hearts we come before You and say, "What a mighty God we serve!" O Lord, You are far beyond our ability to comprehend, and words seem so inadequate to express our love and devotion to You. Lord, as we begin this journey, may it be to Your glory and honor. Take our lives and transform them by the power of Jesus Christ. Help us to be brave and explore areas of life that need exploring; may we have the desire to change areas that need to be changed. Lord, more than anything, may we look to You so that we can reflect You. We love You and place our lives before You. We ask You to do an incredible work in our midst for Your glory and Your honor. Amen.

Romans 12:2 will serve as our focus passage for this study:

Do not conform any longer to the pattern of this world, but be transformed by the renewing of your mind. Then you will be able to test and approve what God's will is—his good, pleasing and perfect will. (Romans 12:2)

Each week during our times of personal study we will take a portion of this verse and examine it in order to gain **Transforming Truths** for life. While we will look intently at Romans 12:2, this verse serves as just a starting point for our time in the Word. Our journey will take us to the Old and New Testaments, and we will look at the lives of several individuals from the Bible.

The outline for our study is listed below:
- Week 1: "Do not conform any longer to the pattern of this world…"
- Weeks 2, 3, and 4: "…but be transformed…"
- Week 5: "…by the renewing of your mind…"
- Weeks 6 and 7: "…Then you will be able to test and approve what God's will is—his good, pleasing, and perfect will."

Today we begin by familiarizing ourselves with Romans 12:2 as we:
- Gain initial thoughts about the verse
- Identify important facts about Roman culture
- Compare Roman culture to contemporary American culture
- Explore the relevance of the Word of God for our lives.

Initial Thoughts about Romans 12:2

Please read Romans 12:2 several times and answer the questions below.

Do not conform any longer to the pattern of this world, but be transformed by the renewing of your mind. Then you will be able to test and approve what God's will is—his good, pleasing and perfect will. (Romans 12:2)

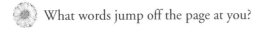 What words jump off the page at you?

_____

_____

_____

🌼 Why do you think these words grab your attention?

_____

_____

_____

_____

Two specific commands are listed in Romans 12:2. Please list the commands below.

1. _____

2. _____

🌼 What is the promise to claim if the commands are followed?

_____

_____

_____

_____

When I look at Romans 12:2, several words jump off the page at me. Words like *conform*, *pattern*, *transformed*, *renewing*, and *will* are just a few. As our study unfolds, we will discover that each of these words becomes a cornerstone concept and key to understanding how we are to forsake conformity and pursue the spiritual transformation that allows us to reflect the glory of Jesus Christ.

Romans 12:2 contains two commands:
1. **Do not conform to the pattern of this world**
2. **Be transformed by the renewing of your mind.**

In these commands, the apostle Paul provides two crucial instructions for every believer who longs to reflect Jesus Christ. The first instruction deals with conformity to the world's pattern. The second instruction deals with the concept of transforming our minds. When followed, these commands provide a path for testing and approving the good, pleasing, and perfect will of God.

Important facts about the Roman culture

In order to gain a proper context for Romans 12:2, please read each statement below. Each statement provides a glimpse into the Roman culture of Paul's day. As you read each statement, let the information sink into your heart and mind.

- Rome was the capital of an empire that stretched from Britain to Arabia.[1]
- Rome was wealthy and cosmopolitan.[2]
- Rome served as the diplomatic and trade center of the then-known world.[3]
- Rome had a large and flourishing Christian community at the time Paul wrote this book to the saints at Rome.[4]
- Rome was celebrated for its impressive buildings and thoroughfares; the famed system of Roman roads fanned out from the city, connecting it with distant provinces.[5]
- Rome had spread far beyond its fourth-century BC walls and lay unprotected, secure in its greatness.[6]
- Rome had both civic pride in its architecture and shame for its staggering urban social problems.[7]

Similarities between Roman culture and modern American culture

Using the information provided above, what similarities do you see between the Roman culture and today's American culture?

_____

_____

_____

Why are these similarities important to our study?

_____

_____

_____

_____

The similarities between the Roman culture of Paul's day and today's American culture are quite impressive. A few of the similarities include **resources, wealth, power, influence, strong Christian presence,** and **an unequal social system.** I find these similarities important because they remind me of the incredible relevance of the Word of God and, more specifically, the insight gained from studying the Word of God. Dear friend, may we never lose sight of this crucial fact: Paul wrote the letter of Romans to provide teaching for believers in Rome, and God preserved the letter so believers today can live their lives based on the Word of God, which provides wisdom, clear instruction, standards, and examples of how to live.

The Relevance of the Word of God

Isaiah 66:2 states: "I will look favorably on this kind of person: one who is humble, submissive in spirit, and **who trembles at my word**" (HCSB, emphasis added). This verse brings to light a critical factor in *reflecting His glory*—a reverence for the Word of God. The Bible is God's living, active Word and serves as the primary way God speaks to His people. Throughout the Old and New Testaments we see the necessity of the Word of God in a believer's life. We also see what happens when God's people neglect His Word.

As believers, we must look to the Word of God as our rulebook, guide, and standard for how we live. Listed below are references from **Psalm 119**. Each passage speaks about the importance of God's Word. Please read the verses and record what you learn about the relevance of the Word of God when applied to your life.

Vss. 1–2

Vss. 9–11

Vs. 45

Vs. 66

Vs. 165

The Word of God amazes me! Scripture teaches that through the study of God's Word we can experience blameless, pure, free, knowledgeable, discerning, and peaceful walks with God. Oh, how we need a love for the Word of God! Without a doubt, God's Word should be the standard for the Christian walk. Oftentimes believers in Christ lose sight of this fact and turn to the world in order to gauge success or failure. However, God's Word remains the fixed point of our lives for all who believe—even when we fail to recognize it.

What role does the Word of God play in your daily walk with God?

_____

_____

_____

_____

_____

_____

Do you desire for the Word of God to be your rulebook, guide, and standard for how you live?

_____

_____

_____

_____

_____

_____

I hope you answered yes! You and I will never *reflect His glory* unless we commit to following His plan.

Conclusion

As today's lesson comes to a close, please think about the concept of *reflecting His glory*. Do you desire to reflect the glory of Jesus Christ in every area of life? Do you want to move from conformity to this world to spiritual transformation?

Please journal your thoughts in the space below.

_____

_____

_____

_____

_____

If you answered yes to the above question, you need to understand that you just invited Jesus into every situation, circumstance, activity, thought, feeling, desire, and attitude going on in your heart and life. Do not fear! We serve a loving, gracious God who has the answers because He *is* the answer. In the space provided below, please journal a prayer to our Lord expressing your fears, anxieties, hopes, and dreams about living a life *reflecting His glory*. God bless you, my dear sister and new friend!

_____

_____

_____

_____

_____

_____

_____

_____

_____

_____

Reflecting His Glory

Week 1: "Do Not Conform to the Pattern of this World…"

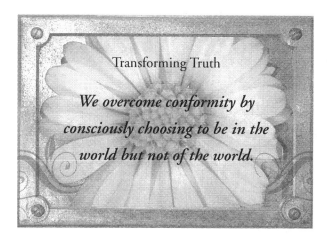

Transforming Truth

We overcome conformity by consciously choosing to be in the world but not of the world.

Day 2: Being *in* the World not *of* the World

Welcome back! Yesterday we introduced our focus passage and saw the importance of the Word of God in our lives. Today we are ready to begin our in-depth study of Romans 12:2. For the rest of this week, we will study the phrase, **"Do not conform to the pattern of this world."** During our time in the Word, we will examine the struggle each of us faces when it comes to allowing the things of this world to determine how we live.

Please join me in prayer.

Father, how we praise Your holy, righteous, and powerful name. To You be all glory and praise. Lord, as we examine the issue of conformity, please expose the sin in our hearts. Show each of us the areas of life where we have allowed the world to shape and mold us. Oh, how we want to deal with every habit, thought, action, and belief that does not conform to You and Your likeness! Lord, may we be grieved over the sin in our lives and have our hearts desire to return to You. Teach us this day for Your name's sake. In Jesus' name, amen.

As we begin, let's review Romans 12:2. Please read the verse carefully.

Do not conform any longer to the pattern of this world, but be transformed by the renewing of your mind. Then you will be able to test and approve what God's will is—his good, pleasing and perfect will. (Romans 12:2)

In your own words, please define the word *conform*.

_____

_____

_____

As you read Romans 12:2 and think about the word *conform*, what truth do you think Paul is trying to communicate?

_____

_____

_____

According to Webster's dictionary the word *conform* means "to be similar or identical to; to be in agreement or harmony with; to give the same shape, outline, or contour."[8]
So in other words, Paul was instructing us:

- Do not be similar or identical to this **world**
- Do not be in agreement or harmony with the **world**
- Do not try to have the same shape, outline, or contour of the **world**.

Of the three explanations listed above, does one provide you with a sense of freedom?

_____

_____

_____

In contrast to the sense of freedom, does one of the explanations listed above provide a difficult challenge for you to overcome?

_____

_____

_____

For me to know that I do not have to measure up to the same shape, outline, and contour set forth by this world provides a great sense of hope and freedom. On the other hand, to know that I am not supposed to be similar or identical to the world provides a great challenge because my flesh simply wants to be like everyone else!

The *in* and the *of*

Today we will examine what the Word of God teaches on the issue of conformity. We will do this by looking at New Testament passages addressing the difference between being *in the world* and being *of the world.* Below you will find a list of passages speaking about each condition. Please look up each verse in the New International Version of the Bible and fill in the appropriate blanks. (The verses are provided at the end of the lesson if you do not have access to an NIV Bible.) Once you fill in each blank, please summarize the New Testament teaching in the space provided.

To be *in* the world:
- John 1:10
"He was _____ the_____, and though the _____ was made through him, the _____ did not recognize him."

_____

_____

- John 9:5
"While I am _____ the _____, I am the light of the _____."

_____

_____

- John 13:1
"It was just before the Passover Feast. Jesus knew that the time had come for him to leave this _____ and go to the Father. Having loved his own who were _____ the _____, he now showed them the full extent of his love."

_____

_____

- John 17:11

"I will remain _____ the _____ no longer, but they (the disciples) are still _____ the _____, and I am coming to you. Holy Father, protect them by the power of your name—the name you gave me—so they may be one as we are one."

_____

_____

- 2 Corinthians 10:3

"For though we live _____ the _____, we do not wage war as the _____ does.

_____

_____

From the verses above, please summarize the New Testament teaching on living *in* the world.

_____

_____

To be *of* the world:
- John 17:14

"I have given them your word and the _____ has hated them, for they are not _____ the _____ anymore than I am _____ the _____."

_____

_____

- John 17:16

"They are not _____ the _____, even as I am not _____ it."

_____

_____

- 1 Corinthians 2:12

"We have not received the spirit _____ the _____ but the Spirit who is from God, that we may understand what the Spirit has freely given us."

_____

- James 4:4
"You adulterous people, don't you know that friendship with the _____ is hatred toward God? Anyone who chooses to be a friend _____ the _____ becomes an enemy of God."

_____

_____

- 1 John 4:5-6
"They are from the _____ and therefore speak from the viewpoint _____ the _____, and the _____ listens to them. We are from God and whoever knows God listens to us; but whoever is not from God does not listen to us."

_____

_____

From the verses above, please summarize the New Testament teaching on being *of* this world.

_____

_____

_____

It is clear from the passages above that believers are to be *in* the world but not *of* the world. Although this may seem like an insignificant distinction, Scripture teaches there is a major difference. We find this difference in the understanding of the two small prepositions.

First let's examine the preposition *in*. Please read the Greek definition below.

English word: *in*

Greek word: *en*

Root: a primary preposition denoting fixed position in place, time, or state—a relation of rest intermediate between.[9]

When looking at this definition and more specifically the root meaning of the word, two points are important to understand. First, the word *in* communicates a place of fixed position specifically in regards to location, time, or state. In other words, this term is used to describe a temporary location—one that occurs at a specific place and only for a specific time. Second, the word *in* describes a location that is between one place and another.

If I were speaking Greek, I would use this word to say, "I am *in* the grocery store" or "I am *in* the movie theater." By using this format, I clearly communicate a place of location or position as well as the notion that while I am *in* the grocery store right now, I will not always be *in* the grocery store.

What an important definition for us to understand if we desire to reflect His glory! Using the definition and thoughts provided above, please describe a life that is **in this world.**

_____

_____

_____

_____

Now let's look at the preposition *of* and see what we can discover. Please read the Greek definition below.

English word: *of*

Greek Word: *ek*

Root: a primary preposition denoting origin, the point whence action or motion proceeds from, out of place, time, or cause, literal or figurative.[10]

This is a much different term. The root meaning of this term denotes a place of origin, a point where action or motion proceeds from. To fully understand this truth, we must understand the word *origin.* According to Webster's dictionary, the word *origin* can mean *"the point at which something begins its course or existence and applies to things or persons from which something is ultimately derived; it often refers to the causes operating before the thing itself comes into being.*[11]

In other words, *origin* carries the meaning of something being born out of a situation or circumstance existing long before it came into being. Thus individuals find their identity from the situation or origin of their birth.

Again, if I were speaking Greek, I would use this word to say, "I am *of* the Smith family." Using the word *of* in this manner communicates the fact I came from the Smith family; I gain my identity from a group of people named Smith.

When thinking about Jesus' teaching regarding origin, we must understand that this world is not the point at which we began our existence. Additionally, this world is not the point from which we were derived. Long before our tiny fingers and tiny toes entered this world, we were in the mind of God. The Bible teaches that God sees us, knows us, and loves us. The world we live in did not form us in our mother's womb—God did!

Why would Jesus warn His followers against being *of* this world?

_____

_____

_____

Application

The concept of being *in* **this world** but not *of* **this world** challenges me daily. My flesh desires to live the comfortable, easy life this world tells me I deserve. The home, the car, the finances—you name it, I want it! Yet at the same time, I have a passion to reflect the glory of Christ and a deep desire to live a life free from the weight of this world.

How about you? Do you struggle with the things of this world?

_____

If so, please describe your struggle.

_____

_____

_____

The Word of God makes it clear that when we view ourselves as being *in* the world, we understand this world is only a place of temporary position. This world is where we live, where we move, and where we function, but it is not where we find our identity. No, my dear friend, this world is not our home. As members of the body of Christ, we do not derive our existence from anyone or anything outside of the Lord Jesus Christ. When we try to gain our identity from anything other than Christ, we immediately move from being *in* this world to being *of* this world. When this occurs we always conform to this world. Why? Because when we are *of* something, we find our origin in that thing and as a result our meaning, purpose, and relevance are gained from that object. When this occurs, conformity becomes the reality of our lives as we willingly forfeit our potential to *reflect His glory.*

Do you see how being *of* this world produces conformity to this world? If so, please explain.

_____

_____

_____

Conclusion

As we close, let's look at today's Transforming Truth that states: "We overcome conformity by consciously choosing to be *in* the world but not *of* the world." In all honesty, between you and your Heavenly Father, are you *in* the world or *of* the world? Please explain your answer below.

_____

_____

_____

_____

My sweet friend, if you are like me, you probably answered that you act like you are *of* this world more often than not. If so, hang on. God through His Word will provide specific help as we continue to position ourselves to *reflect His glory*. Over the next days we will look at three specific steps to combat conformity. Each step will allow us to make necessary changes so we can be *in* this world but not *of* this world.

Please close today's lesson with a word of prayer and express both your desires and apprehensions when it comes to the issue of conformity in your life.

_____

_____

_____

Scriptures for "in" the world and "of" the world.

To be *in* the world:

- **John 1:10**
"He was in the world, and though the world was made through him, the world did not recognize him."

- **John 9:5**
"While I am in the world, I am the light of the world."

- **John 13:1**
"It was just before the Passover Feast. Jesus knew that the time had come for him to leave this world and go to the Father. Having loved his own who were in the world, he now showed them the full extent of his love."

- **John 17:11**
"I will remain in the world no longer, but they (the disciples) are still in the world, and I am coming to you Holy Father, protect them by the power of your name—the name you gave me—so they may be one as we are one."

- **2 Corinthians 10:3**
"For though we live in the world, we do not wage war as the world does.

To be *of* the world:

- **John 17:14**
"I have given them your word and the world has hated them, for they are not of the world anymore than I am of the world."

- **John 17:16**
"They are not of the world, even as I am not of it."

- **1 Corinthians 2:12**
"We have not received the Spirit of the world but the Spirit who is from God, that we may understand what the Spirit has freely given us."

- **James 4:4**
"You adulterous people, don't you know that friendship with the world is hatred

toward God? Anyone who chooses to be a friend of the world becomes an enemy of God."

• 1 John 4:5–6
"They are from the world and therefore speak from the viewpoint of the world, and the world listens to them. We are from God and whoever knows God listens to us; but whoever is not from God does not listen to us."

Reflecting His Glory

Week 1: "Do Not Conform to the Pattern of this World…"

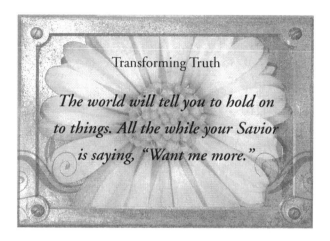

Transforming Truth

The world will tell you to hold on to things. All the while your Savior is saying, "Want me more."

Day 3: Combating Conformity: Recognizing the Pattern of this World.

Through the rest of this week, combating *conformity* will be our central focus. Today we will begin by examining the first step in combating conformity—recognizing the pattern of this world. Let's begin with a word of prayer.

Dear Lord,
We praise You this day for who You are. You are holy, and the very fact that You are holy causes us to deal with the issue of conformity. Lord, forgive us for the times we fail You and for the times when we set this world up as our home. May we always remember that our true home is with You. We thank you for Your love and Your grace that continually meet us where we are. Lord, today, meet us in Your Word and challenge us to love You more than anyone or anything. Give us spiritual eyes to see how we conform to the pattern of this world. May we want *NOTHING* and *NO ONE* more than we want you! In Jesus' name, amen.

Please read Romans 12:2 and circle the word ***pattern*** in the verse.

Do not conform any longer to the pattern of this world, but be transformed by the renewing of your mind. Then you will be able to test and approve what God's will is—his good, pleasing and perfect will. (Romans 12:2)

We often overlook the word *pattern* when we study Romans 12:2. However, if we want to adequately deal with the issue of *conformity*, we must also deal with the concept of *pattern*. Why? Because the *pattern* of this world produces *conformity* to this world. Our key verse teaches this truth. "Do not conform any longer to the ***pattern*** of this world." Face it. The world we live in has a pattern. A *pattern* is a "form or model used for imitation."[12] A worldly pattern emphasizes certain outside characteristics, qualities, and possessions needed in order to achieve a certain standard of success. I will be honest. I struggle with the pattern of this world on a daily basis. Please allow me to share just one example from my life.

One afternoon I was chatting with friends while our children played together, and the topic of summer vacations came up. It was just a normal question posed by one of the women, "What is everyone doing for summer vacations?" One by one my friends took turns listing vacations from Sea World to Disney World and all stops in between. As I sat listening to them, it dawned on me that I had not planned a family vacation! Panic set in, and immediately I started thinking, "What can we do, where can we go, and how much will it cost?" I raced home, jumped on the Internet, and began planning a vacation on short notice and a tight budget.

Not long after I began, my husband Jay came home from work. Immediately he could sense something was not right. Our conversation went something like this:

"Honey, how are you doing?" Jay asked.

"Fine," I answered.

"What are you working on?"

"A family vacation."

"I thought we decided not to take a family vacation since we are going to San Antonio for our anniversary," he said, puzzled.

"Well, everyone else is taking a family vacation, and I was thinking we need to take one too. I do not want the boys to feel left out. Just think about Jake when he goes back to school in the fall and his friends ask him, 'What did you do over the summer?' Don't you want him to be able to have something fun to talk about?" I said defensively.

"Well sure, honey, but I do not think Jake will be too upset if he does not get to go on vacation this year. Besides, we can't afford to take two vacations," Jay replied.

"Well maybe, but most families take family vacations in the summer, and I thought we should too."

Slowly Jay backed off since he could tell I was determined to make this family vacation work. After a couple of hours of trying everything, I reluctantly left the computer and announced, "We cannot take a family vacation this year. We do not have the time or money. Maybe we can take a few days and go camping."

After the incident passed and I was back in my right mind, I started to think. What was going on here, and why did it affect me so much? I was so worked up over a family vacation that my heart beat a little faster and my temper grew short; I was willing to do anything to get my way. In the course of just a few hours, I went from not caring about having a vacation to just having to do something in order to feel like I was okay and providing for my children *like everyone else*. It took several days to process all the emotions coming out of the vacation experience, and today's study played a key role in my discovery process.

Perhaps you can relate to the story from my life. You too have experienced times when you were willing to do anything and everything in order to be like everyone else. During these times, we must understand that something significant is taking place. Quite simply, we are asking this world, "What must I do or what must I possess in order to fit in?"

The world's pattern can produce struggles in many areas of life. For example, some people struggle with choices about:
- **Their home**—what size, what neighborhood, what décor?
- **Their clothes**—what size, what brand, how stylish?
- **Their vehicle**—what type, how new, how full of extras?
- **Their children's education**—public, private, or home school?
- **Their lifestyle**—full-time homemaker, or work part-time or full-time?
- **Their appearance**—are they in shape, out of shape, or beyond any shape?

- **Their family**—what relationships, priorities, and activities?
- **Their desired overall quality of life**—what do they think they "need" in order to feel successful and make an impact on this world?

The areas listed above, along with a host of others, make up the worldly pattern you and I face—and every day this world is trying to sell its pattern to us. Unfortunately, every day we are buying into the pattern and setting ourselves up for failure when it comes to reflecting the glory of Christ.

What is the greatest pressure you face when it comes to feeling like you need to be something or possess something in order to fit in?

_____

_____

_____

_____

The Rich Young Man

Today as we open God's Word, we are going to study an individual who struggled with the pattern of this world. He, like many of us, bought into the world's model for success and so set this world up as his standard. Please read Mark 10:17–22.

What question did the rich man ask Jesus in verse 17?

_____

_____

_____

_____

In verse 19, how did Jesus respond?

_____

_____

_____

_____

In verse 20, how did the rich man respond to Jesus?

_____

_____

_____

_____

In verse 21, what feeling did Jesus have for the man?

_____

_____

_____

_____

In your opinion, why is it significant that Jesus loved this man?

_____

_____

_____

_____

According to Jesus, what did the rich man lack? (vs. 21)

_____

_____

_____

_____

How did the rich man respond to Jesus' invitation? (vs. 22)

_____

_____

_____

_____

What can you conclude from the rich man's response?

_____

_____

_____

_____

As we think about the pattern of this world, let's explore this passage and see what we can learn.

Verse 17 begins with the rich young man falling at Jesus' feet and asking the question, "What must I do to inherit eternal life?" Jesus, who knew the rich man's heart, answered him by listing the specific commandments. The rich man declared his right standing in verse 20, stating, "All these I have kept since I was a boy." I imagine relief flooded the man as he stated his response. You see, he had just asked Jesus a life-or-death question, a question so crucial that eternity hung in the balance. I believe this man felt the weight of the world lifting off his shoulders as he thought he measured up to Jesus' standards. However, the rich man was wrong.

While I believe the rich man felt relief, Scripture states Jesus felt something quite different. Jesus felt love. Amazingly, even when the rich man got it so wrong, Jesus got it so right. Verse 21 states, "Jesus looked at him and loved him." What a powerful message Jesus sent! Even when the rich man worked hard in order to justify himself before Jesus, Jesus' love remained true. I find this significant because it reminds me of how undeserving I am of God's mercy and grace. It also reminds me that the love of Christ is not earned but rather given to those who believe. What a loving Savior we serve!

The rich man did not experience relief for long. Jesus quickly brought him back to reality. Jesus explained to the man that he lacked one thing—the willingness to give up all he had in order to follow the Lord. How did Jesus convey this truth? He challenged the man to sell the worldly possessions that meant the most to him, give the money to the poor, and follow Christ. The rich man's response tells it all. His face fell, and he turned and walked away.

I do not know about you, but I find this passage of Scripture challenging. This man looked into Jesus' face and had to choose between his "dream" or Jesus. The challenge was to give up financial resources—giving up security, prominence, and self-sufficiency, the very things the world told the rich man to achieve. For us, it could be anything that we draw our security and significance from—our wealth, our appearance, our family, our career. How do we respond when we realize that following Jesus will require giving up something we've worked very hard to possess? There is no doubt the rich young man bought into the pattern of this world; as a result, he lost the opportunity of a lifetime, trading eternal reward for momentary comfort.

I wonder if you can relate. Do you struggle when it comes to conforming to the pattern of this world? Does your desire for security, prominence, and self-sufficiency get in the way of knowing Jesus? Perhaps your struggle is different from that of the rich young man. Maybe you struggle with holding onto a past relationship, a man-made dream, or a desire to be someone or something you are not. No matter. One thing is certain. Everything in this world will tell you to hold on to it for dear life. All the while your Savior is looking into your face with so much love He can hardly contain Himself and saying, "Want me more."

So the question before you is, "What is holding you back from knowing Jesus more?"

_____

_____

_____

_____

_____

_____

_____

Conclusion

As we close today, I want you to imagine yourself in the rich man's position, humbled at the feet of Jesus asking this question, "Lord, what does it take to know You more?" Then imagine Jesus looking into your eyes with so much love His heart is physically moved when He answers by asking you to give up the very thing you worked so hard to possess. My precious friend, what will your response be?

What are you holding on to that is keeping you from knowing Jesus more?

_____

_____

_____

Are you willing to give up your man-made dream so you can *reflect His glory*?

_____

_____

_____

_____

If so, close with a prayer and commit to follow Jesus no matter what the cost.

_____

_____

_____

_____

_____

Reflecting His Glory

Week 1: "Do Not Conform to the Pattern of this World…"

Transforming Truth

Sin is serious because it hinders our fellowship with God.

Day 4: Combating Conformity: Recognizing the Sinfulness of our Hearts

Yesterday, we examined the first way to combat conformity in our lives. This involved recognizing the pattern of the world. Today, we are going to look at the second way of combating conformity: recognizing the sinfulness of our hearts.

As I type this lesson, I find my heart heavy simply because today's subject is one I know all too well. To be very upfront with you, I have firsthand experience with this subject. Today we are going to look at the reality many of us face—the reality of living life from the *scattered place*. For the purposes of this study, we will define the *scattered place* **as a place of compromise reached by striving to imitate the pattern of this world instead of the pattern of God.** As Scripture will show, the sinfulness of our hearts always causes us to live our lives from the scattered place. Therefore, we are going to dig deep and look at the cause and effect of sin in the believer's life. Let's pray.

Dear Lord,

As we come to You this day, we come with heavy hearts. Lord, we know that we are sinful. Scripture teaches that we were sinful from the moment of our births. Help us to recognize the sins that keep us from reflecting You. Show us the areas of life where we live from a scattered place. Lord, place in our hearts a desire to return to You. In Jesus' name we pray, amen.

I would like to introduce the concept of the scattered place by telling you about a phone conversation I had with a friend of mine. It was during one of those priceless moments when our children were occupied and we had a chance to open up and share with one another. My friend related some of the struggles going on in her spiritual life and stated that she felt like her spiritual life was in neutral. Her times of prayer and studying her Bible, when they occurred, were average at best. Her desire to go to church had also dwindled. No doubt my friend was at a spiritual low. She said, "Andrea, I do not know what it is like to be where you are in your relationship with God." Then she took it one step further when she said, "I do not know if I want to go there."

Wow! It blew me away. My friend expressed what so many of us feel: "Lord, is my walk with you really worth it?" As my friend talked, my heart broke. She was just giving up, right in front of me. I felt so helpless, so afraid, and so inadequate to be the one with whom she shared her feelings. I quickly pulled my thoughts together and told my friend how much I loved her and how I wanted her to know and experience God's best. We said a few more things and hung up.

Following our conversation, I immediately ran to my room, fell on my knees, and prayed for my friend. I cried out to God on her behalf. "Oh how I want her to know You, Lord, to know the intimacy You offer. If she could just get a taste of You, she would never want anything else." I knew to cry out for my friend because I had experienced similar feelings. Not too many years earlier, I found myself in her position saying the exact same things, wondering if a life of defeat and mediocre Christianity was all I would ever achieve. I remember asking God, "Is this all there is to my relationship with You? Because, honestly, this is not working."

With my friend heavy on my heart and all the feelings from my past fresh on my mind, I opened my Bible to Deuteronomy 4 and read an amazing passage of Scripture. This passage of Scripture spoke to where I had lived many years of my life—a place I believe many others live as well. The Bible describes this place as the *scattered place*.

The Scattered Place

Please read Deuteronomy 4:25–28 and note the word *scatter*. After you read the passage, answer the questions below.

In verse 25, when did Moses state these things would happen?

_____

_____

_____

What sign would show the people had become corrupt?

_____

_____

_____

What would be the consequence the people would receive for turning away from God?

_____

_____

_____

What would the people worship while living in the scattered place?

_____

_____

_____

In your opinion, what would be the root issue in the children of Israel's life leading them to live life from the scattered place?

_____

_____

_____

What a powerful warning God, through Moses, gave to a specific group of people for a specific time in history! Let's examine four key points introduced in this warning and discover what each point meant **THEN,** to the Israelites, and what it means **NOW,** to us today.

1. **The Promised Land:** In this passage, the Israelites were sitting on the outskirts of the land God had promised to give them, and Moses was instructing them about what would take place once they entered and possessed the land. Remember, Moses had rebelled against the Lord and was not permitted to enter the land. Because Moses knew he was not going into the promised land, he called the people together in order to give final warnings and instructions. The bulk of these instructions dealt with taking and possessing the land. Please read the brief summary of the Israelites' journey to the promised land. This will help you discover the significance of the promised land **THEN** and **NOW.**

THEN

In Old Testament times, **the promised land was a place of physical rest and physical abundance, a prime spot of land flowing with milk and honey.** God promised this land to Abram and his descendents in Genesis 12, and in Genesis 15 God entered into a covenant with Abram ensuring Abram's descendants would inherit the land.

In Exodus 3, God raised up Moses to lead the Israelites out of Egypt and into the promised land. Once the people were on the outskirts of the land, God instructed Moses to send twelve spies into the land. Numbers 13 records that once the spies entered, they were overwhelmed by the goodness of the land. Unfortunately, the spies were also overwhelmed by the greatness of the inhabitants. As a result, the spies, except for Joshua and Caleb, returned to camp claiming the nation could not take possession of the land. As this report spread, the Israelites rejected Moses's leadership. They also rebelled against God's plan to bring them into the promised land.

The anger of the Lord burned against the Israelites, so God informed them that He would do to them exactly what He heard the people say (Numbers 14:28). (Makes you want to be cautious with your words!) Therefore, the nation wandered in the desert for forty years providing time for the disobedient generation to die. In the place of the disobedient generation, God raised up the next generation to take possession of the land. This new generation becomes the focus of Moses's final warnings and instructions in Deuteronomy 4:25–28.

NOW

Today the concept of the promised land is not seen in a physical location but a **spiritual location**. This truth is taught as believers are called to be *in* the world but not *of* the world. Although our ultimate place of rest is in heaven with Jesus, we learn from the New Testament that we do not have to wait until glory to experience God's peace and rest. Through Christ Jesus, peace is available right now! The New Testament concept of the promised land is accessed when the following two qualities are evident in life.

- **The first quality is *spiritual rest* or peace with God through Jesus Christ.** Romans 5:1–2 states: "Therefore, since we have been justified through faith, we have **peace with God through Jesus Christ,** through whom we have gained access by faith into this grace in which we now stand. And we rejoice in the hope of the glory of God."

  According to Romans 5:1–2, how do we have peace with God?

  _____

  What does it mean to you to have spiritual rest or peace with God in your life?

  _____

  _____

  _____

- **The second quality is *spiritual abundance* evidenced by spiritual fruit produced in and through a believer's life.** In John 15:8 Jesus states: "This is to my Father's glory that you bear much fruit, showing yourselves to be my disciples."

  According to John 15:8, what brings the Father glory? _____

  As we bear fruit, what does it show? _____

  According to Galatians 5:22–23, what fruit is displayed in a believer's life when living in the New Testament promised land?

  _____

  _____

  _____

If you are in Christ, you have come to the point of acknowledging your desperate need for a savior. Thus, you have taken the first step to entering God's rest. However, for many, the second step becomes the point we fail to recognize and apply to life—spiritual abundance evidenced through spiritual fruit bearing. John 15:8 clearly states that spiritual fruit in the believer's life brings the Father glory and shows that a person belongs to the Father. From Galatians 5:22–23, we understand that spiritual fruit occurs as we express love, joy, peace, patience, kindness, goodness, faithfulness, gentleness, and self-control.

To put it simply, you and I live in the New Testament promised land when we surrender to the lordship of Jesus Christ and, as a result, bear His fruit and not our own. This truth teaches that amidst the most challenging situations in life, spiritual fruit can be produced. As you and I surrender to Jesus, we can display love in unlovable situations, peace during difficult storms, and kindness when our insides really want to display anger. Through Christ, spiritual fruit becomes the outward evidence of the inward change that flows from the New Testament promised land experience.

2. **Moses's Warning**: Moses's instructions in Deuteronomy 4:25–28 to the Israelites were clear: "Once you get into the land . . . be careful!" These instructions were relevant **THEN**, and they are still relevant **NOW**. Let's see how.

THEN

Verses 25 and 26 of Deuteronomy 4 state: "After you have had children and grandchildren and have lived in the land a long time—if you then become corrupt and make any kind of idol, doing evil in the eyes of the LORD your God and provoking him to anger, I call heaven and earth as witnesses against you this day that you will quickly perish from the land that you are crossing the Jordan to possess."

In these verses Moses communicates one thing: Once you have settled in the land and have lived there a long time, **be careful.** In essence, Moses is saying, "Once you have moved in, established your daily routine, had children and grandchildren, driven out a few giants, and had the newness of the entire situation wear off, **beware!** Why? It is at that time you will be tempted to become corrupt."

In your opinion, why would Moses give this instruction?

_____

_____

I believe Moses gave this warning for two reasons. First, once the Israelites were settled in the land it would become easy for sin to creep into their lives unnoticed. Second, the longer the Israelites lived in the land, the greater the temptation would be to allow their walks with God to fall into a cycle of comfort and routine.

NOW

Today the same possibilities exist. As believers we must guard our lives from the trap of sin and routine. A contemporary version of Moses's instructions could read, "Once you have accepted Christ, established your daily walk with God, allowed some spiritual fruit to grow in your life, and overcome significant challenges in your life, beware!" Why would Moses say this? Because we can easily fall into the trap of becoming comfortable or routine in our relationships with the Lord, even while living in the place of promise and rest. When this happens, sin always finds its way into our lives, and often sin enters the picture through idol worship.

> 3. **Idol Worship:** According to Deuteronomy 4:25–28, the most likely way corruption would enter the nation's life was through idol worship. Idol worship was a real possibility **THEN** because the nation was entering a land filled with pagan worship to pagan gods. **NOW** idol worship presents just as much of a possibility as believers daily fight the desire to conform to the world.

THEN

Moses knew the hearts of the people; he knew they would be drawn to worshiping other things and other people once they were established in the promised land. Because of this certainty, Moses clearly states that one sign of the people's corruption would be idol worship.

Idol worship is placing anything or anyone before God. The root of idol worship is sin; it would be demonstrated as the people turned from God and embraced man-made standards for success. Do not miss this crucial point—**idol worship is sin**. Think about it. At the very heart of idol worship is valuing something or someone more than we value God. As we value something or someone more than God, we set that person or thing up as our god. When this occurs, sin enters our lives, and our relationship with God is affected. We know this is true because sin has always been the number one deterrent to the tangible presence of God in a believer's life.

NOW

Today we struggle just as much with idol worship. Daily, believers in Christ move about and function in this world and, as a result, fight the ever-present tendency to worship man-made things. Oftentimes we fail to call idol worship what it is and instead explain away the sin in our lives by saying:

- "It's not really that bad."
- "Everyone else is doing it."
- "It is how I was raised."
- "Everyone has a vice. This is mine."
- "Compared to _____, I am not that bad."

Can you think of others?

-
-
-

However, in the eyes of a Holy God, sin is sin and always carries a consequence. We find the consequence for allowing sin to creep into life both in the Old Testament and New Testament in the principle of the scattered place.

4. **Scattered Place:** Once sin entered the picture through idol worship, Deuteronomy 4:27–28 states: "The Lord will scatter you among the peoples." God would remove the people from the place of promise and rest to a scattered place. The scattered place **THEN** was a physical location and involved moving from one location to another. **NOW** the scattered place is a spiritual location and involves losing spiritual sensitivity to call sin, sin.

THEN

In Old Testament times, the judgment of God for allowing idol worship into the nation of Israel involved the removal or scattering of God's people from the promised land. Remember, the scattered place was a place of compromise reached by striving to imitate the pattern of this world instead of the pattern of God. Once scattered, the people would experience an amazing thing. The Israelites would lose spiritual sensitivity and turn to man-made gods of wood and stone, gods that could not see or hear or eat or smell. Sadly, the children of God would look to these "gods" in order to gain life, meaning, purpose, and protection.

NOW

Today, idol worship in a believer's life has the same consequence. When we allow sin to go unnoticed in our lives by creating idols and placing those idols before God, we will also find that we live our lives from the scattered place as we strive to imitate the pattern of this world instead of the pattern of God. Paul gives a strong warning regarding this subject in 1 Corinthians 10:1–12.

Please read 1 Corinthians 10:1–12 and answer the following questions.

In verse 5, what did Paul state was the consequence for Israel's disobedience?

_____

_____

In verse 6, why did Paul state these things happened? _____

In verse 7, what was Paul's strong warning to you and me?

_____

Fill in the blanks using verses 11 and 12. (Please use the New International Version.) "These things happened to them as _____ and were written down as _____ for us, on whom the fulfillment of the ages has come. So, if you think you are _____ _____, _____ _____ that you don't fall."

Do you see the amazing similarities between the Old Testament and New Testament tendencies to allow sin into our lives? Today, as New Testament believers, we face the same struggle the Israelites faced. We too have the have the ability to live our lives in such a way as to turn to and focus on man-made things that cannot see or hear or eat or smell, and yet we look to these things in order to gain life, meaning, purpose, and protection. When this happens, sin abounds in our lives, and our spiritual sensitivity is compromised. In response to this tendency, we hear from Deuteronomy 4:25–28 and 1 Corinthians 10:12, "Be careful!"

Application

I get chills just thinking how often I allow the same process to happen in my life.
- **Promised Land:** I am living in the place of promise and rest in my relationship with God. I experience spiritual rest through Jesus Christ and spiritual fruit like love, joy, peace, patience, and kindness, even when I face difficult situations and circumstances.

- **Warning:** I am walking faithfully with the Lord when I ignore Scripture's warning to be careful of complacency. Whether suddenly or slowly, I compromise and allow sin to control my life. I start conforming to the world's pattern.
- **Idol Worship:** When this happens, I lose my focus on God and slowly allow other things in life to become more important than my relationship with the Lord.
- **Scattered Place:** Before long, I find myself in a place where all I can do is react to situations of life. All the while, I try to maintain some kind of handle on things. Yet, I am scattered and looking to the things of this world (that cannot see or hear or eat or smell) in order to provide meaning and purpose for my life.

Do you see the relationship between the Old Testament principle of the scattered place and the New Testament reality of living life in conformity with this world? Please explain.

_____

_____

_____

What role do you think sin plays in believers missing out on God's best?

_____

_____

Describe a time when you know sin caused you to miss out on God's best for your life.

_____

_____

_____

Are you currently living in the scattered place? If so, please explain and close with a prayer expressing your desire to return from the scattered place to a place of promise and rest.

_____

_____

_____

_____

Reflecting His Glory

Week 1: "Do Not Conform to the Pattern of this World…"

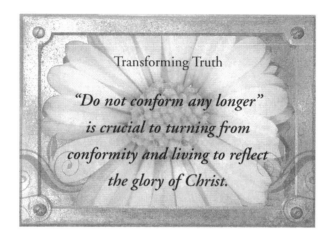

Transforming Truth

"Do not conform any longer"
is crucial to turning from
conformity and living to reflect
the glory of Christ.

Day 5: Combating Conformity: Choosing to Live for Christ

During our last two days of study we examined two ways to overcome conformity—recognizing the pattern of this world and recognizing the sinfulness of our hearts. Today we are going to look at the third way—choosing to live for Christ. Let's pray.

Dear Lord,

We're so grateful that You allow us to live our lives for You! Lord, may this truth bring peace, hope, and focus into our daily walk with You. We thank You that we do not have to muster up the strength to live for You on our own; You are faithful to supply all that we need for life and godliness. Help us this day to choose You. Truly, no greater choice exists. We love You and praise You. In Jesus' name we pray, amen.

Please read Romans 12:2 and circle the phrase noting an element of time.

Do not conform any longer to the pattern of this world, but be transformed by the renewing of your mind. Then you will be able to test and approve what God's will is—his good, pleasing and perfect will. (Romans 12:2)

Did you circle the phrase *any longer*? This phrase is critical to turning from conformity and living a life reflecting the glory of Christ. Please read Deuteronomy 4:25–28 and refresh your memory from yesterday's lesson. Then read verses 29–31 and answer the questions below.

From Day Four, what was the result of living life from the scattered place? (vs. 28)

_____

_____

_____

_____

In verse 29, we see the statement, "But if from *there...*" Where is *there*?

_____

What should we do from *there*?

_____

_____

_____

_____

What is the result of doing that (the above answer) from *there*? (vs. 29 and 30)

_____

_____

_____

_____

Thinking back to Day Four, we saw the result of living life from the scattered place displayed in losing spiritual sensitivity to call sin, sin. As a result, we live life looking to the things of this world to gain meaning and purpose instead of looking to God.

As we continue to look at Deuteronomy 4 in order to get help on dealing with the issue of conformity in our lives, we see an interesting statement in verse 29: "But if from there…." The *there* talked about in this statement is the scattered place. This statement communicates a vital fact—help is available for those living in the scattered place! What an incredible word we need to hear! So, how do we receive this help? How do we return from the scattered place? The Scripture teaches that deliverance from the scattered place requires two actions.

Step One: Seek God.

In order to return from the scattered place, you must seek God. Verse 29 states, **"But if from there you seek the LORD your God…."** The word used for *seek* in this passage means "to seek to find, to seek to secure, or to seek the face."[13] This definition is important because it implies a very specific kind of seeking.

When seeking God two options are available: **seeking the *face* of God** and **seeking the *hand* of God. Seeking the *face* of God is seeking God for who He is. Seeking the *hand* of God is seeking God for what He can do**. Both seeking options are described and encouraged in the Word of God. However, it is easy to fall into the trap of seeking God for what He can do and miss out on seeking Him for who He is. If we desire to return from the scattered place, we must move past seeking God for His hand alone and humble ourselves and seek His face.

For just a few minutes, I want you to think about your seeking process. How often do you truly seek the face of God? In order to examine the seeking process, let's study a familiar passage of Scripture found in Luke 15.

This passage tells the story of two sons and one father. Although the sons had different ways of relating to their father, they were equally his sons. One son (the prodigal son) loved the father but wanted his father's riches so he could leave home to spend the wealth on worldly living. The second son (the older brother) loved the father but also desired the father's riches. This son stayed close to home to try to secure his father's blessing in the form of material wealth. Throughout the parable, we see the father, who represents God, graciously meeting the sons where they were and inviting them to know him at a deeper level. As we think about our seeking process, we can know that if we long to have a meaningful relationship with our heavenly Father we too must long to know Him at a deeper level. Please read Luke 15:11–31. Then read the lists of each son's actions and attitudes followed by the section that describes the loving intent of the father.

Actions and attitudes of the prodigal son:

- The focus of this son was on what his father could do for him. This is shown in verse 12: "Father, give me my share of the estate."
- When the son received his share of the money, he set off for a distant country (vs. 13).
- When the son was in the distant country, the son squandered what the father had provided on a lifestyle that did not honor the father (vs. 13).
- In verse 14, the son began to be in need.
- When the son began to be in need, he first tried to solve his own problem by hiring himself out to the citizen of the distant country (vs. 15).
- When the son could not solve his own problem, the son came to his senses and set out to find his father (vss. 17–18).

These actions and attitudes reveal a *needs-based relationship*. When this son had a need or a desire and could not fulfill it on his own, the son ran to his father for help.

Actions and attitudes of the older brother:

- When the older brother enters the story, we see him in the field tending his father's business. Initially we might think the older brother understood the importance of seeking and serving the father and as a result chose a life that honored his father. However, we see a different attitude displayed in the older brother as the story unfolds (vs. 25).
- When the older brother came near the house, his true motives appeared. The older brother found out that his younger brother was home and that a party was going on in the younger brother's honor (vs. 28).
- The older brother refused to come in to the party (vs. 28).
- Since the older brother would not come in to the party, the father went out to talk to the older brother (vs. 28).
- The older brother stated his case. He said, "All these years I've been slaving for you and never disobeyed your orders. Yet you never gave me even a young goat so I could celebrate with my friends. But when this son of yours who has squandered your property with prostitutes comes home, you kill the fattened calf for him" (vs. 29). In this straightforward statement, the older brother made his feelings known to the father—he felt he had been wronged. He wanted to know

why he had not been rewarded for choosing to stay at home and serve his father. At the heart of this exchange, the older brother revealed why he had stayed at home and served his father.

The older brother's actions and attitudes reveal a *works-based* relationship. The older brother believed that his "right" actions could earn his father's blessing. If he stayed at home and did everything just right, he would receive the material reward.

The loving intent of the father:

- The intent of the father toward both sons was clear—restoration to himself. The father opened his arms to the prodigal son and welcomed him home. At the same time, the father opened his heart to the older brother and invited him to know him at a deeper level. We see this truth in verse 31. The father stated, "My son, you are always with me, and everything I have is yours." What can we learn from this verse of Scripture? One truth is essential: *The greatest reward God gives does not come in the form of material blessing. The greatest reward comes in the form of His presence in our daily lives.* This truth is vital to understand as we seek to return from the scattered place.

In the seeking process, we can fall into the trap of seeking God like the sons sought their father. We can seek God like the prodigal did—running to God only in times of need. Or we can seek God like the older brother did—trying to earn His blessing by doing all the right things. These two approaches amount to seeking God for His hand alone. This is true because our actions and attitudes focus on what God can do for us instead of who He is. To move past this tendency, we must embrace the seeking process described by the father in this parable. We must desire God's presence above anything that we think He can do for us. As we embrace this approach to seeking, we not only receive what God can do for us (His hand) but also experience who He is (His face) to us.

Why do you think it is important to seek God's face when you are living in the scattered place?

_____

_____

_____

We must seek the face of God from the scattered place for one simple reason. Seeking God's face breaks the cycle of sin in our lives by allowing us to focus completely on the Father. Remember, the very thing that causes believers to live in the scattered place is sin. As we refocus on the face of God, sin is exposed. Once exposed, sin can be confessed and turned from so that our love relationship with the Father is restored.

Of course, there are times when we seek God's hand through directed supplication as clearly taught in the Bible. However, before we turn to the hand of God, we first turn to the face of God. Why? *Seeking the face of God displays a great desire for God to be a part of each moment of our day—not just the moments when we have a tangible need in our lives.*

What is God challenging you to do when it comes to the way you seek Him?

_____

_____

_____

Step Two: Wholeheartedly Obey God

The second step to returning from the scattered place is wholehearted obedience. Deuteronomy 4:30 states, **"When you are in distress and all these things have happened to you, then in later days you will return to the LORD your God and obey him."** The word *obey* in this passage means "to yield." The definition of *yield* is "to surrender or relinquish to the physical control of another; to hand over possession of; or to surrender or submit (oneself) to another."[14] Without a doubt, the hardest aspect of my walk with the Lord is to yield to Him—to surrender, relinquish, or hand over control of my life to His possession.

How about you? Is yielding to God a challenge in your daily walk?

_____

_____

If so, what is the biggest challenge in your yielding process?

_____

_____

What areas of life is God calling you to yield?

_____

_____

_____

Yielding—surrendering or relinquishing control of our lives to our heavenly Father—is the true test when it comes to choosing to live for Christ. Will we follow Him? The answer to this question will determine if we return from the scattered place or if we will continue to live for the desires of this world. Dear friend, choose Christ!

Conclusion

Deuteronomy 4:31 provides the reason for the returning process. It reads, **"For the LORD your God is a merciful God; he will not abandon or destroy you or forget the covenant with your forefathers."** Isn't it good to know we serve a merciful God who will not abandon, destroy, or forget His children? I do not know about you, but knowing this challenges me to deal with the sin in my life, seek the face of God, and obey Him, no matter the cost.

Please close with a time of prayer. Take time to confess your sin, seek God's face, and commit to obey Him, no matter the cost.

_____

_____

_____

_____

_____

_____

_____

_____

_____

_____

Reflecting His Glory

Week 2: " ...but be transformed..."

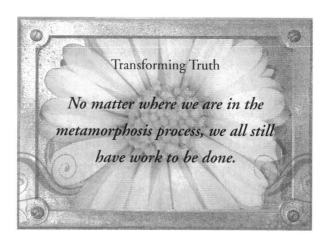

Transforming Truth

No matter where we are in the metamorphosis process, we all still have work to be done.

Day 1: Transformed—A Spiritual Metamorphosis

As we begin our second week of *Reflecting His Glory*, I hope and pray God has challenged you to look at areas in your life that need change. For the next three weeks we will examine the phrase **"but be transformed"** from Romans 12:2. Although this phrase holds just three words, we will discover that it conveys a powerful concept that is crucial to the reflecting process. Before we begin, please join me in prayer.

Dear Lord,
You and You alone are worthy to be praised. Lord, as we continue our journey
through Your Word, please teach us more and more about You. As we look at the
topic of transformation, may we begin to see the changes You have in store for our
lives. O Lord, show us how to be changed in order to look like You. May we settle

for nothing less than all of You working in and through our lives so we can reflect Your glory! By Your grace, may we move from conformity to spiritual transformation. (Please finish this prayer by placing your thoughts and desires before the Lord.)

Please review Romans 12:2. As you read the passage underline the word *transformed*.

Do not conform any longer to the pattern of this world, but be transformed by the renewing of your mind. Then you will be able to test and approve what God's will is—his good, pleasing and perfect will. (Romans 12:2)

When you think about *transformation*, what comes to mind?

_____

_____

_____

Thinking back over your life, list and briefly explain examples of real life transformations you have seen or experienced.

_____

_____

_____

_____

_____

Personally, I have seen physical transformations, spiritual transformations, home transformations, and even one transformation that did not transform! Now, before I confuse you, let me explain. I was required to take an art class in college. Going into the class, I was nervous because I am not an artistic person. The extent of my ability to express myself through drawing involves an occasional stick person standing outside a stick house with a stick tree in the yard. I fully anticipated that this class would challenge my artistic skills.

During the first day of class, the professor talked about the course and explained the final project—a transformation series. I was to draw an initial picture and "transform" it into something else, showing my work in three intermediate drawings.

I thought and thought about the project. What was I going to draw, and how would I transform the drawing into a different object? Finally, the day came when I had to begin working on the project. I selected as my original picture a whale. I thought it would be simple and easy to draw, so I drew what I thought was a decent whale. Next, I decided to transform the whale into a hot air balloon. Again, I thought these objects were similar in shape and size, so just a few lines would be required. I drew the hot air balloon and felt good about the results. Now came the hard part. I had to change a whale into a hot air balloon. In the course of three pictures, I did my best to achieve this goal. The results were pitiful!

On the day the projects were due, members of the class took turns presenting their drawings and allowing the class members to make comments. When it came time for me to place my drawing on the front easel, I had a sinking feeling in my stomach. The professor looked at the project and then looked at me. "So, class, what do you think?" he asked. Silence filled the room. Feeling very awkward and embarrassed, I tried to explain the project and show how I took a whale and transformed it into a hot air balloon. Finally, the professor let me off the hook and called the next person to the easel.

A few days later, I noticed the transformation projects hanging in the display cases that lined the art hallway. I quickly looked to find my project. Surprisingly, my project was nowhere in sight. When I walked into the class, one lone project deemed not acceptable for the hallway lay on the counter—mine!

As I think back on this, I cannot help but laugh. At the time, I was embarrassed and could not wait to get out of the class. Today, however, I realize the relevance of the story in my life. Now it is easy for me to see how much of the Christian life is represented in my art project.

As believers, we have a clear-cut picture of our beginning in Christ. We can articulate the initial change that took place when we asked Jesus into our lives. Since we know from Scripture what we should look like when we see Jesus face to face, the ending picture is also clear. However, the middle portions of our lives—the pictures showing step-by-step change being worked out on a day-in-and-day-out basis—at times are fuzzy.

This reality can leave believers in Jesus Christ feeling awkward and embarrassed as we "stand" before the world and do our best to show through our actions and deeds how we are being changed into the likeness of Christ. And on the day of final judgment when we stand before the Creator of the universe and in essence present our lives to Him, we certainly don't want to experience the same sinking feeling.

As we think about the reality of transformation being worked out in our lives, we must ask ourselves a crucial question: "Where am I in the transformation process?" The apostle Paul, writer of much of the New Testament, knew about transformation. As we read Paul's letters, I believe we can see a clear beginning, middle, and end to the transformation process in his life. Let's take a look, and as we do, please keep in mind the characteristics of a transformation drawing—clear-cut beginning, clear-cut ending, and three pictures in the middle showing step-by-step change.

Paul's Beginning

We see the apostle Paul's beginning picture in a position of humility on the road to Damascus. At the time, Paul was called Saul, and he was persecuting believers. In fact, the very reason Saul was on the road to Damascus was to find men and women who believed in Jesus Christ. Once he found them, Saul had the authority to take these men and women to prison in Jerusalem. However, God had different plans for Saul's trip.

Please read Acts 9:1–18. In your mind, take a snapshot of Saul's beginning picture in Christ as described in verses 3–6. Then describe or draw your snapshot below.

- Snapshot 1:

Paul's Middle

During the middle portion of Paul's life, we see his on-going growth in maturity in Christ as he, under the inspiration of the Holy Spirit, pens thirteen New Testament books. Below, you will find three life examples displaying Paul's continual devotion to the transformation process. In these accounts, we see Paul growing in his boldness for the gospel, displaying peace during trying situations, and exhibiting a love for Christ.

- **Courage and Passion:** On Paul's first journey we see an interesting snapshot from Paul's life. **Please read Acts 13:1–12**. In this snapshot we see a sign of transformation as Paul confronts a Jewish sorcerer and false prophet named Bar-Jesus. The transformation this picture displays shows Paul moving from persecutor to protector of the church. You find the outcome of this transformation snapshot in verse 12: "When the proconsul saw what had happened, he believed, for he was amazed at the teaching about the Lord."
- **Contentment in Life:** One of my favorite snapshots from Paul's life shows that he chose to display contentment in the face of difficult life circumstances. Whether in prison, beaten, shipwrecked, hungry, or plagued by a thorn in his flesh, Paul made the choice to be content in all situations of life. Please read **Philippians 4:10–13**. In verse 11, Paul states, ". . . for I have learned to be

content." The word *learned* in this passage means "to study or be instructed." For Paul, contentment in difficult life circumstances did not come naturally. Paul, through the empowering of the Holy Spirit, learned to be content. From Scripture we note that contentment in Paul's life was not based on pleasant or easy life circumstances. Verses 12 and 13 teach that Paul knew what it was like to have plenty and be in need, to be hungry and be well fed. Paul refers to the ability to be content in all circumstances of life as a secret. Please write the secret in the space below.

_____

_____

_____

Paul's contentment was not based on material possessions or even a full stomach but rather on his desire to allow Christ to empower him. In verse 13 he declares, "I can do everything through him who gives me strength." This transformation snapshot displays Paul's peace in life—regardless of circumstances—as he found his complete sufficiency in Christ.

• **Confidence in God:** As we follow Paul's steps through the New Testament books, we see Paul had every right to place confidence in the flesh. Please read **Philippians 3:3–11** and list all the reasons Paul could have placed his confidence in the flesh.

_____

_____

_____

In these verses, Paul explains why he could have taken hope from the circumstances of his life simply because he met the world's standard for success. After all, Paul was well-educated, affluent, and highly motivated; he could have been on a "who's who" list in terms of religious practices. However, Paul realized every worldly benefit in life became a complete loss in comparison to knowing Christ. He states this best in verse 10: "I want to know Christ and the power of his resurrection." Paul demonstrated a sign of transformation in his life by turning aside from the confidence of the flesh and embracing one all encompassing purpose in life: "I want to know Christ."

Below, please describe or draw three pictures representing the three snapshots from the middle portion of Paul's life and ministry.

- Snapshot 2:

- Snapshot 3:

- Snapshot 4:

Paul's Final Condition

Paul's final snapshot is one of complete surrender as he nears the end of his life. He wrote to Timothy from a jail cell in Rome. Please read **2 Timothy 4:6–8**. In this passage we can sense and feel a tone of complete humility and peace as Paul nears his departure from this world to the next. What a sign of transformation in verse 7 as Paul states, "I have fought the good fight, I have finished the race, I have kept the faith." Can you hear the peace in Paul's writing? At this point in Paul's life and ministry he heard the voice of his heavenly Father calling him home. In response to this call, Paul did not fight his departure but embraced it as the final leg of a journey that began many years before on a dusty road to Damascus. Please explain or draw a picture of Paul at this point in his life.

- Snapshot 5:

Paul's life and ministry were truly amazing. In all five snapshots we see Paul looking more and more like Christ. Transformation was a part of his daily walk with the Lord. Nowhere in Paul's writing is the call to transformation more evident than in Romans 12:2. "Do not conform to the pattern of the world, **but be transformed...**"

The Call to Transformation

Now that we have a better grasp on the idea of transformation, let's turn our attention to Romans 12:2 and see what transformation means in the context of this passage. In Romans 12:2, the word *transformed* means "to be changed in form."[15] The Greek word used is *metamorphoo*. I know you can hear its similarity to a familiar word, *metamorphosis*. For the purposes of this study, we will define metamorphosis as follows (adapted from Wikipedia on-line encyclopedia.)

> *Metamorphosis* **is a process by which an animal physically develops after birth or hatching and involves significant change in form as well as growth, and differentiation; it includes a change of habitat or of habits.**[16]

In this definition of metamorphosis, we find four keys elements that must take place in order for metamorphosis to occur.

Please list the four key elements in the metamorphosis process:

1._____

2._____

3._____

4._____

Although this is a secular definition dealing with physical metamorphosis, we can see parallel principles that can be used to describe a spiritual metamorphosis. **Over the next three weeks we will examine what it means to have a spiritual metamorphosis by exploring the Scriptures' teaching on significant changes in form, spiritual growth, differentiation, and changes in habitats and habits.** Our study will be lengthy because of the importance of the subject. If you and I truly desire to *reflect His glory*, we must surrender to the metamorphosis process so that we can move away from conformity and be transformed into His likeness!

Conclusion

As we conclude today's lesson, think about your life in the area of spiritual metamorphosis. Where are you in the transformation process? Are you at the beginning stages, somewhere in the middle portion, or do you find yourself nearing the end?

Please take a moment and describe your current place in the process.

_____

_____

_____

_____

No matter where we are in the metamorphosis process, we all still have work to be done. I hope and pray you are ready to do the necessary work so that your transformation pictures will be pleasing in His sight.

Please journal your thoughts below and close by expressing your desire to live a life transformed by the power of Christ.

_____

_____

_____

_____

_____

_____

Reflecting His Glory

Week 2: "...but be transformed..."

> Transforming Truth
>
> *As Jesus walked on this earth He did amazing things—He healed, He loved, and He taught. Most importantly, He made a way to save us.*

Day 2: A Significant Change in Form, Part 1

Yesterday we introduced the concept of spiritual metamorphosis. I believe that in order to experience spiritual metamorphosis, four key elements must take place. These elements include **significant change in form, spiritual growth, differentiation**, and **changes in habitats and habits**. We will examine each of these elements in detail to see how they apply to *reflecting His glory*. Let's begin with the first key element in the metamorphosis process—**a significant change in form**.

In order to have a significant change in form, an individual must have a personal relationship with Jesus Christ that begins through the process of salvation. Today we will examine the process of salvation and ask the question, "Do I know for sure I will spend eternity in heaven?" Let's pray.

Father, we love You and we praise You. To You and You alone be all the glory both now and forever. I pray that You would speak to our hearts as we open Your Word of truth. Teach us about Yourself and bring those who do not know You into a saving relationship with Christ Jesus our Lord. Amen.

The New Testament story of Philip and the Ethiopian eunuch provides an example of a person who experienced salvation. Please read Acts 8:26–39 and answer the following questions.

Who appeared to Philip, and what instructions did he give in verse 26?

_____

_____

_____

Whom did Philip meet on the road in verse 27?

_____

What details are provided in Scripture about the life of the Ethiopian eunuch?

_____

_____

_____

Where had the eunuch been prior to meeting Philip, and what had the eunuch been doing?

_____

What was the eunuch reading when Philip approached?

_____

In your opinion, why is it important that the eunuch is returning from worship and reading the Scriptures when Philip meets him?

_____

_____

_____

In verse 35, what did Philip explain to the eunuch?

_____

_____

_____

What did the eunuch want to do in verse 36?

_____

Following the encounter with Philip, the eunuch left the scene with what kind of attitude?

_____

In this passage two crucial events take place—Philip's obedience to the leading and guiding of the Holy Spirit and the eunuch's salvation experience as he placed his faith in Jesus Christ. Philip was instructed by the angel of the Lord to go south to the road leading down from Jerusalem to Gaza. Philip obeyed the directions and met an Ethiopian eunuch. The eunuch was a high government official who feared God.[17] Scripture teaches that the eunuch had responsibility for the treasury of the Queen of Ethiopia. He had gone to Jerusalem in order to worship; he was traveling home when he encountered Philip.

When Philip and the eunuch met, Philip discovered the eunuch reading an Old Testament passage of Scripture from Isaiah 53. Philip asked the eunuch, "Do you understand what you are reading?" The eunuch responded, "How can I understand unless someone explains it to me?" With this invitation, Philip explained the passage of Scripture. Then the eunuch asked the question, "Who is the prophet talking about, himself or someone else?" Philip stated the prophet spoke of Jesus. Acts 8:35 records that "Philip began with that very passage of Scripture and told him the good news about Jesus."

What a powerful, life-changing truth for the eunuch to understand—Jesus was the long-awaited Messiah, and every verse in the Old Testament pointed to His coming. Once the eunuch recognized this truth, he placed his faith in the Lord Jesus Christ and, as a result, experienced a significant change in form—he moved from being spiritually dead to being spiritually alive. This change is evidenced in the fact that the eunuch asked to be baptized and went on his way rejoicing (vs. 36 and 39).

Salvation—Moving From Death to Life

When the eunuch placed his faith in the Lord Jesus Christ, a powerful thing took place. The eunuch took his first step in the spiritual metamorphosis process by experiencing a significant change in form. The significant change in form the eunuch experienced moved him from a position of spiritual death to spiritual life.

In order to understand the process, please look up the passages listed below. Once you have read the passages, please explain the process in your own words.

John 5:24

_____

_____

_____

Ephesians 2:1–5

_____

_____

_____

When we are physically born into this world we are dead in our sins and separated from God. Although we are physically alive because our hearts beat and our blood flows, our hearts and souls are separated from God. We are destined to spend eternity paying the debt for our sins; Romans 6:23 states, **"…for the wages of sin is death."** The word *wages* in this passage means "payment" and carries the idea of paying off an on-going list of wrongs. This list is so long that no person could ever accomplish this task on his or her own. The word *death* used in Romans 6:23 refers to eternal death and implies everlasting separation from God. From this single phrase we can know that apart from God stepping into our lives, no hope exists for overcoming the deep sin debt.

However, Romans 6:23 goes on to state: **"…but the gift of God is eternal life in Christ Jesus our Lord."** The Greek word translated as *gift* is *charisma* and means "a gift of grace or an undeserved benefit."[18] The benefit of receiving this gift is eternal life—the right to spend eternity in heaven with God because He has forgiven our debt of sin.

Think back to the story of the eunuch and how he moved from a position of spiritual death to spiritual life. The relevancy of his story challenges each of us to examine our spiritual position before the Lord. Acts 8 tells us some interesting details about the meeting between the eunuch and Philip. The eunuch was on his way home from worship, similar to how we might attend a church service. He was even reading Isaiah, the equivalent of how we read our Bibles. And yet the eunuch clearly stated that he did not understand the Scriptures and did not know what it meant to have a relationship with Jesus Christ.

I am afraid many individuals attend church regularly and read their Bibles, but they have little understanding of such a personal relationship with Jesus. A person in this condition may feel safe because she is doing what she thinks are the right things; deep in her soul, though, a longing exists that can only be met by God.

Today, if this describes you, please know that the opportunity still stands for you to hear the good news of Jesus Christ and experience a significant change in form. This change occurs as you understand and accept the same truth the Ethiopian eunuch received so many years ago. This truth is: **Jesus is the fulfillment of Old Testament prophecy; just like every Old Testament verse points to the coming of Christ, every New Testament verse reflects on the finished work of Christ.**

Bringing This Truth Home—Sharing My Decision for Christ

The best decision I ever made was to place my faith in Jesus Christ. At the age of six, I realized I could not pay the debt of my sin, so I confessed my sin and asked Jesus to save me.

Let me share a few of the details. Church was always a part of my life as I was growing up. Sunday morning service, Sunday evening service, and Wednesday activities were the norm at my house. This was never a problem for me because I loved church! Some of my fondest childhood memories took place at First Baptist Church in Paris, Arkansas. From a very early age, church was the place I felt most at home. Singing hymns, reading Bible stories, and being around God's people ministered to me from the beginning.

I always appreciated the moving of the Holy Spirit in my life and knew that my life only made sense with God in it. To my parents' credit, they let me know from an early age that I was adopted and that God had allowed me to be a part of their family. Sadly, I struggled with my adoption because I felt rejected. God slowly showed me that He had a plan for my life even if I did not understand the details.

At the age of six I entered into a saving relationship with Jesus Christ. My church was having a series of revival meetings with an evangelist, and it was kids' night. (Can anyone remember revivals and hot dog suppers?) Following the meal, the evangelist talked about sin and how it separates us from God. He also shared that Jesus died on the cross so that anyone who received His salvation could live in heaven with God. I remember sitting in my seat thinking, "I do not want to go to hell." Although skipping hell was heavy on my mind, a sense of sadness over the sin in my life was also heavy on my heart. As I thought about the fact that Jesus died for me, I felt His unconditional love, and it moved me. That night I remember praying to receive Christ.

As I think back on my salvation experience, I am overwhelmed with thankfulness to God. Because I was a young child, I did not fully understand the sovereignty of God to have me in that place, at that time, for that purpose, but today I praise Him.

Bringing This Truth Home in Your Life

Today as you think about your life and where you stand with God, you fall into one of two categories. In the first category are individuals who have **not** confessed their sins and asked Jesus to be Lord of their lives. The second category consists of individuals who have placed their faith in Jesus Christ and as a result will spend eternity in heaven with God.

If you are in the first group, I invite you to work through Application 1 and prayerfully consider your need for a Savior. If you are in the second group, I invite you to work through Application 2 as you reflect on your decision to follow Christ.

Application 1

Sweet friend, thank you for your honesty to admit that you do not have a personal relationship with Jesus. Oh, how I long to wrap my arms around you and let you know how much Jesus loves you. Right now you can experience that love as you give Him control of your heart and life. Follow the steps below and surrender to your need for a Savior.

- Step 1: Recognize and accept the sinfulness of your heart. Romans 3:23 states: **"For all have sinned and fall short of the glory of God."** This verse makes it very clear—all have sinned. We sin whenever we think a wrong thought, have a wrong motive, or do a wrong action. I think we can agree that everyone on this earth has sinned. Please take a few moments and confess the sinfulness of your heart. When you do this, take your time and really talk to God. Talk to Him like you would talk to your best friend. Tell Him everything you have ever done that you regret and wish you could take back. List the sins specifically and allow your heart to feel the weight of the debt for that sin in your life. Once you have confessed your sin, ask for God to forgive you for your sin.

_____

_____

_____

_____

_____

_____

_____

- Step 2: Believe that Jesus died in your place. Romans 5:6-8 states: **"You see, at just the right time when we were still powerless, Christ died for the ungodly. Very rarely will anyone die for a righteous man, though for a good man someone might possibly dare to die. But God demonstrates his own love for us in this: While we were still sinners, Christ died for us."** What an amazing truth! While you and I were powerless to do anything about our condition of spiritual death, God made a way and provided a perfect sacrifice to pay the sin debt in our lives. A little over two thousand years ago God sent His Son Jesus to earth. Jesus lived a perfect sinless life, and during His time on earth He was completely God and completely man. As Jesus walked on this earth He did amazing things. He healed people. He loved people. He taught people, and most importantly, He made a way to save people. Jesus died a cruel death so you and I can have eternal life—life that never ends and results in spending eternity in heaven with God. In the space below, thank Jesus for dying in your place and paying your penalty for sin.

_____

_____

_____

_____

_____

_____

_____

- Step 3: Confess that Jesus is your Savior and believe in Him. Romans 10:9 states: **"That if you confess with your mouth Jesus is Lord and believe in your heart that God raised him from the dead, you will be saved."** To *confess* means to admit, declare, or acknowledge. To *believe* means to put your faith in and implies complete and total trust. From Romans 10:9 we know that in order to have a personal relationship with Jesus, you need to admit, declare, or acknowledge Jesus as Lord and trust the fact that God raised Him from the dead. The importance of believing that God raised Jesus from the dead is seen in the fact that when Jesus came back to life, He demonstrated that He is God and that everything He said is true. As a result, the power of death has no hold on Him. Take a few minutes and record your prayer below. Confess Jesus as your Lord and Savior and place all of your trust in Him.

_____

_____

_____

_____

_____

_____

- The Result: By wholeheartedly following the steps above, you can know beyond a shadow of a doubt that God saved you and made you His child. John 1:12 states: **"To all who received him, to those who believed in his name, he gave the right to become children of God."** Sweet friend, you can rejoice this day because of the truth taught in this Scripture. When you place your life in Jesus' hand you receive the right to be God's child; once you are God's child, you are safe and secure in Him. Please close your time of prayer with thoughts of thanksgiving as you begin a new life in Christ.

_____

_____

_____

_____

_____

_____

- I encourage you to share your news with a friend, minister, Bible study teacher, or relative. Then quickly get involved in a church that teaches you how to grow in your relationship with Jesus Christ by focusing on the principles taught in the Bible. May God bless you as you learn to walk in relationship with Him. Please record the date of your decision in the space provided.

_____

Application 2
Thinking Back on Your Decision for Eternal Life

If you know that you already placed your faith in the Lord Jesus Christ and have experienced a significant change in form by moving from a position of spiritual death to spiritual life, then praise God for the work He has done in your life! Please take a few minutes and describe your salvation experience below. Be as descriptive as possible and include the date, time of year, place, people involved, first signs of conviction, and any other details that come to mind.

_____

_____

_____

_____

_____

_____

_____

_____

_____

_____

_____

_____

_____

_____

Conclusion

I praise God for the hope that comes in Jesus Christ alone. It is good to know that we do not have to pay the penalty for our sins. If we did, who could stand? To my new sisters in Christ, please know that I love you and that today there is rejoicing in heaven because Jesus lives in your heart. You made the biggest and best decision of your life, and I will be praying for you as you learn what this relationship with God means.

To my long-time sisters in Christ, thank you for taking time to reflect on your decision to follow Christ. It is easy to allow the busy-ness of life to get in the way of thanking God for the profound gift of salvation. Let's not let that happen.

Whether this is your first day as a sister in Christ or you have been one for many years, take a moment and thank God for the gift of Jesus Christ and the opportunity to experience a significant change in form through the process of salvation.

_____

_____

_____

_____

_____

_____

Reflecting His Glory

Week 2: " ...but be transformed..."

Transforming Truth

No matter where we are in our walks with God, we need a significant change in form.

Day 3: A Significant Change in Form, Part 2

In yesterday's study we examined what it meant to have **a significant change in form** occurring through the process of salvation. Today we will learn that accepting Jesus Christ as our Lord and Savior is only the beginning of the process of change. You see, once we are saved we have an ongoing call for **change in form** as we make it our goal to move from conformity to spiritual transformation.

Paul teaches about this truth in 1 Thessalonians 4:1. Paul states: "We instructed you how to live in order to please God, as in fact you are living. **Now we ask you and urge you in the Lord Jesus to do this** *more and more*" (emphasis added). The call to change in form is clear. We are to look like Him, act like Him, and reflect Him *more* and *more* in our daily walks with Him. As we do this, *reflecting His glory* becomes a reality in our lives. Please join me in a word of prayer. As you pray, I challenge you to commit yourself to the process of becoming *more like Christ.*

Father, we praise You for You are holy and worthy of all praise. We thank You for the privilege of knowing You—even more, for the privilege of being known by You. Lord, I pray that as we look at the issue of ongoing change in form, we will open our lives to You and invite You to shine Your bright light into every dark corner of our souls. Please expose the sin in our lives and enable us, through Your Spirit, to change. How we want to be transformed to be *more like You!* Give us the grace to reflect You in every area of life. In Jesus' name, amen.

God's Call: Ongoing Change in Form

The call for ongoing change in form is a call for believers to change from their former way of living—the life they lived before they knew Christ—and to embrace a new life in Christ. The book of Ephesians has much to say about this call. Please open your Bible to Ephesians 4:22–24. Read the passage of Scripture carefully, then write your initial observations about the phrases listed below.

- **"You were taught, with regard to your former way of life . . ." (vs. 22):**

  _____

  _____

  _____

  _____

- **". . . to put off your old self, which is being corrupted by its deceitful desires . . ." (vs. 22):**

  _____

  _____

  _____

  _____

- **". . . to be made new in the attitude of your minds . . ." (vs. 23):**

  _____

  _____

  _____

- **". . . and to put on the new self, created to be like God in true righteousness and holiness." (vs. 24)**:

_____

_____

_____

_____

This instruction from God's Word is the call to put off the old self (the life lived before knowing Christ) and to put on the new self (the life created to be like Christ). At the very heart of this passage, we see the call for ongoing change in form. Let's see what we can learn about being transformed to be more like Christ.

- **"You were taught, with regard to your former way of life . . ."**

We have a clear indication by the phrase "you were taught" that the recipients had previously received these instructions. Church history teaches that the apostle Paul wrote the book of Ephesians and that the believers in Ephesus were the primary recipients. Although strong indicators lead scholars to believe that the book of Ephesians was a circular letter (meant for several churches), there is no doubt Paul had a special place in his heart for these believers.

In Acts 19–20, we find details of Paul's time with the church in Ephesus. Paul's ministry was highly effective; he reached many people with the gospel of Jesus Christ. Further, we read that Paul invested in the lives of the Ephesians and taught them the significance of being transformed to reflect Christ's glory.

We see specifically in Acts 19:23–41 the effectiveness of Paul's ministry in Ephesus. Please read this passage of Scripture and describe the events recorded:

_____

_____

_____

_____

In this passage, a silversmith named Demetrius instigates a riot. Demetrius's profession involved fashioning and selling silver "gods" for the people to worship. As Paul ministered in Ephesus and people turned from idols to worship the true God, the business of making "gods" lost customers and as a result, lost money. Scripture records Demetrius's words in Acts 19:26–27:

"And you see and hear how this fellow Paul has convinced and led astray large numbers of people here in Ephesus and in practically the whole province of Asia. He says that man-made gods are no gods at all. There is danger not only that our trade will lose its good name, but also that the temple of the great goddess Artemis will be discredited, and the goddess herself, who is worshipped throughout the province of Asia and the world will be robbed of her divine majesty."

The Lord used Paul to make such a profound impact on his environment that the pagans felt the effects! Paul invested strongly in the people of Ephesus and with that investment came truly life-changing results.

The primary way Paul invested in the Ephesians' lives was by teaching them how to live after they received the Lord Jesus Christ. Ephesians 4:22–24 provides support for this claim. Let's examine the three things Paul taught the Ephesians to do:

1. **"To put off your old self, which is being corrupted by its deceitful desires."** Paul's first teaching was to "put off your old self." The phrase *put off* means "to get rid of or do away with." When thinking about putting off or doing away with the old self, Paul encouraged believers to get rid of the way of life they pursued before receiving Christ Jesus as Lord.

   Please make a list of old selfish ways that must be dealt with once we receive Christ Jesus as Lord.

   _____

   _____

   _____

   _____

   _____

Why do you think it was important for the Ephesians to deal with their former selfish ways of life?

_____

_____

_____

_____

Paul encouraged the Ephesians to deal with aspects of their old way of life; this could have included forsaking materialism, lust, greed, pride, idol worship, stealing, cutting, binging, purging—the list could go on and on! The reason Paul encouraged the Ephesians to deal with these old ways was that the old self was being corrupted. To *corrupt* means "to degrade with unsound morals or principles or to cause to rot or spoil."[19] The deceitful desires within the hearts of the Ephesian believers were causing corruption in their walks with God. This is true because the deceitful desires were contrary to God's desires and were hindering God's work in the believers' lives.

What a challenge we have before us today—to deliberately do away with the **sinful habits, personal agendas, selfish ambitions**, and **anything else** that gets in the way of knowing Jesus more. Why? Because these sinful habits, personal agendas, and selfish ambitions are corrupting our walks with God and ultimately getting in the way of our capacity to *reflect His glory*.

2. **"To be made new in the attitude of your minds."** Paul's second teaching was "to be made new in the attitude of your minds." The key phrase in this statement is *made new*. This phrase means "to renew again, make young again" and is used in this passage to represent the spiritual quality of the mind.[20] This crucial concept in the ongoing call for change communicates the call for renewing again and again and again.

When you think about doing something again and again and again, what activities come to your mind?

_____

_____

_____

_____

When I think about doing something again and again and again, I think of activities like laundry, housework, errands, paying bills, parenting, and relationship building. All of these things represent areas of my life that I will never be able to check off my list as being completed.

The same is true in our walks with God. When it comes to becoming like Christ, acting like Christ, and ultimately reflecting Christ, we never arrive. We are never done. We must be open to the idea of renewing again and again and again so we can look more and more like Him.

What was Paul encouraging the Ephesians to renew? The verse states the Ephesians were to renew the *attitude of their mind*. The word for *attitude* used in this passage represents the spirit within the person that influences the person's thoughts and actions. Paul makes this plea to the Ephesians because he understands that the spirit of the mind, when changed, radically alters the direction of our lives.

Today as we are open to the call for a change in form, an incredible thing takes place. The Holy Spirit transforms who we are at the very core of our being. This transformation process is an ongoing process because no matter where we are in our walks with God, we need a significant change in form. We need to be changed from the inside out!

3. **"And to put on the new self, created to be like God in true righteousness and holiness."** Paul's third teaching communicates how the Ephesians were to renew their minds and thus experience an ongoing change in form. Paul instructs them to "put on the new self, created to be like God in true righteousness and holiness." To *put on* means "to clothe yourself with" and carries the picture of sinking into your clothes.

When you think about sinking into something, what does that involve?

_____

_____

_____

To me, the idea of sinking into something occurs only as we surrender to that thing. I find it interesting that Paul instructs the Ephesians to sink into the new self. What a funny instruction for Paul to give! However, sinking makes perfect sense. In essence, Paul teaches, "Stop fighting who Christ made you to be—surrender to it!" Why would Paul write this? Because only as the Ephesians surrendered to who Christ created them to be would they give up control and allow themselves to be completely changed into the "new self." Just so the Ephesians would not wonder what the "new self" looked like, Paul provided a perfect description. The "new self" was created to be just like God—to be perfect and true in righteousness and holiness.

Application

The application for this study is straightforward. Each day we are called to be more and more like Jesus Christ. You can run from this call, or you can embrace this call. If you run, you will never experience the ongoing change in form which leads to being more and more like Christ. If you embrace this call, you will be changed into the likeness of Jesus Christ and *reflect His glory.*

As we think about this call, we must stop and take a hard look at our lives. We must ask the question, "Am I becoming more like Christ?" As you think about this question, I ask you to honestly answer the following questions.

1. What old, sinful ways still reside in your heart? Please be as specific as possible.

_____

_____

_____

_____

2. Do you really desire change in these areas of life?

_____

3. What must happen in order for change to take place in your life?

_____

_____

_____

_____

4. Are you ready to embrace these steps?

_____

I pray that you are ready to embrace the call to become more and more like Christ. Please close with a word of prayer asking the Lord to help you embrace this call every single day.

_____

_____

_____

_____

_____

_____

_____

Reflecting His Glory

Week 2: " ...but be transformed..."

Transforming Truth

Beware of measuring spiritual growth from a human perspective.

Day 4: Spiritual Growth—What it is NOT!

Today we continue our look at spiritual metamorphosis. We will examine the second key element in the metamorphosis process—the element of **spiritual growth**. As we explore spiritual growth, we will dispel many myths we have about this topic.

In your own words, please define *spiritual growth*.

_____

_____

_____

_____

_____

What spiritual markers do you use in order to measure spiritual growth? In other words, what visible signs do you use to determine if you are growing in your relationship with the Lord?

_____

_____

_____

In order to answer these questions, we will see what the Bible teaches about spiritual growth. Today and tomorrow we will focus our attention on spiritual growth by exploring *what it is not*. Let's pray.

Lord, we praise You for You are the Almighty Creator of the universe. In light of who You are, we humble ourselves before You and proclaim we are dust. As we look at the issue of spiritual growth, please clear up our misconceptions and teach us how You measure growth. O Lord, how we want to grow to be more like You! May You receive all the glory both now and forever! Amen.

What Spiritual Growth is NOT

It is easy for us to fall into the trap of using human standards to determine spiritual success or failure. In other words, we use standards imposed on ourselves or standards imposed by others. While on earth, Jesus took a stand against this type of measuring system and referred to the system as futile, cumbersome, and wrong.

The Pharisees, a group of people Jesus denounced regularly, used a human system to measure spiritual growth. These religious leaders showed more interest in the outward appearance of man than the inward reality of the heart. As we think about spiritual growth, we can learn a lot about what it is *not* as we study Jesus' interaction with the Pharisees.

Please read Matthew 23:1–36. As you read, list on the following chart each *warning* Jesus gave his followers (verses 1–12) and the *rebukes* Jesus gave the Pharisees (verses 13–36). Please note the corresponding verse for each warning and rebuke.

Warnings	Rebukes
_____	_____
_____	_____
_____	_____
_____	_____
_____	_____
_____	_____
_____	_____
_____	_____
_____	_____

In this passage of Scripture, Jesus talked with two groups of people. In verses 1–12, Jesus taught the crowds as well as His disciples and warned them about the actions of the Pharisees and teachers of the law. Jesus warned his followers about the trap of human standards of spiritual growth as seen in the religious leaders of their day. In verses 13–36, Jesus turns His attention to the Pharisees and teachers of the law as He rebukes them for their stance on human reasoning in determining spirituality. Let's examine Matthew 23 in detail and see what we can learn.

1. **Spiritual growth is NOT about power or position**. Matthew 23:2,3 states: "The teachers of the law and the Pharisees sit in Moses' seat. So you must obey them . . . But do not do what they do." According to Jewish tradition the phrase *sit in Moses' seat* refers to the fact that the Pharisees and teachers of the law were authorized to interpret the law God gave Moses.[21] Since the Pharisees and teachers of the law were authorized to interpret the law, a common Jew would naturally conclude that these people must really know their stuff. However, Jesus' warning was clear: Do what they say, but do not do what they do!

The assumption that outwardly religious behavior equals inner intimacy with God is false. If this were the case, the Pharisees and teachers of the law would have been highly regarded by Jesus as spiritual. Jesus clearly communicates the truth that just because someone has a position of power or authority does not mean the person has a right heart before God. The implication of this teaching is two-fold. First, individuals who sit in positions of power do not automatically have a growing, thriving love relationship with Jesus. Second, holding a position of power and authority does not automatically produce growth in your spiritual walk with God.

Think about your life. How often do you assume that if someone is in a position of power or authority they must have a growing, thriving love relationship with Jesus?

_____

_____

_____

_____

As a result of this assumption, have you ever fallen into the trap of seeking a position of power or authority in hopes that the position will cause your relationship with God to grow? Please describe.

_____

_____

_____

_____

If so, how does this teaching from Jesus impact your life?

_____

_____

_____

_____

2. **Spiritual growth is NOT done for men to see**. The word *see* used in verse 5 means "to look at." It appears that everything the Pharisees did was done in order for men to look at them and evaluate them. In verses 5–7 Jesus provides three examples as He states His case against the Pharisees.

- **"They make their phylacteries wide and the tassels on their garments long."**

  The phylacteries were small leather boxes containing scrolls of paper with portions of the Jewish law written on them. According to Deuteronomy 6:8, the Jews wore the phylacteries on their forehead and left arm. The Pharisees made their "phylacteries broad, that they might be thought more zealous for the law than others."[22] In addition to the phylacteries, the Jews wore tassels on their garments. The tassels reminded the Jews that they were God's chosen people and therefore set apart from the nations around them. The knots of the tassels were meaningful because they represented the Hebrew letters YHWH. YHWH represented an important name of God known in English as YAHWEH. YAHWEH means "I am that I am." By making the tassels extra long, the Pharisees tried to seem more religious than others.

- **"They love the place of honor at banquets and the most important seats in the synagogues."** Jesus took a stand against the tendency of religious leaders to desire the places of honor when they walked into a room and the places of prominence when they were seated in the synagogue. In this statement, Jesus dealt specifically with the focus of the Pharisees. By desiring a place of honor and prominence, the Pharisees misplaced their affection by taking it off of God and placing it squarely on themselves. In contrast to this focus, the apostle Paul encouraged believers to "do nothing out of selfish ambition or vain conceit, but in humility consider others better than yourselves" (Philippians 2:3).

In your opinion, what are the key concepts from Philippians 2:3? How would these concepts have changed the focus of the Pharisees?

_____

_____

_____

_____

- **"They love to be greeted in the marketplaces and to have men call them 'Rabbi.'"** Here we see Jesus' disgust towards the Pharisees as they sought attention from those in the marketplace. Jesus makes an important point about the marketplace because in New Testament times the marketplace was "the most frequented part of a city and was the chief place for commerce and discourse."[23] This fact brings extreme relevance to Jesus' rebuke. Not only were the Pharisees practicing their religion for men to see, they were practicing it in the busiest part of town!

What does this fact tell you about the focus of the Pharisees?

_____

_____

_____

In what ways do you struggle with the issue of practicing your religion for men to see?

_____

_____

_____

_____

3. **Spiritual growth is NOT reached through divided alliances**. In Matthew 23:8–10, Jesus confronted the false notion that anyone on this earth can be of equal value and importance as God. Jesus stated this in three ways—there is only one Master, one Father, and one Teacher. With these statements, Jesus clearly communicated that God is God, and the Pharisees were not.

When humans are elevated to God's level, you will find divided alliances; these lead to sin. The very essence of what the Pharisees were trying to achieve was God-like status. Make no mistake about it: God is God, and there is no one like Him. I love how David says it in Psalm 86:8, 10. David writes, "Among the gods there is none like you, O Lord . . . For you are great and do marvelous deeds; you alone are God."

As Jesus confronted the Pharisees regarding divided alliances, He taught a life-changing lesson. Read the statements below and fill in the blanks to discover this truth.
   • If God is the **Master,** then I am the _____.
   • If God is the **Father,** then I am the _____.
   • If Jesus is the **Teacher,** then I am the _____.

In what way can this lesson impact your life?

_____

_____

_____

_____

_____

4. **Spiritual growth is NOT for self-glory**. In Matthew 23:11–12 Jesus states: "The greatest among you will be the servant of all. Whoever exalts himself will be humbled, and whoever humbles himself will be exalted." With this statement, Jesus cuts to the very core of the Pharisees' problem—self-glory versus God's glory. According to this passage, the key factor in determining whose glory is at stake in a person's life is wrapped up in the word _humble_. The word _humble_ means "to lower oneself."[24] This meaning shows the active participation of intentionally moving ourselves to a lower position. Unfortunately, the Pharisees did not see this as a high priority.

Why do you think Jesus stressed the need for humility in the Pharisees' lives?

_____

_____

_____

_____

_____

Do you tend to exalt yourself instead of living a humble life? If so, please explain.

_____

_____

_____

_____

_____

Conclusion

Without a doubt, the Pharisees used a human system to determine spiritual growth. Jesus did not approve of this system and warned His followers about its traps. Tomorrow we will seek to dispel any wrong notions about spiritual growth. Please close with a time of prayer asking God to reveal any hidden sins in your life that lead to a wrong understanding of spiritual growth.

_____

_____

_____

_____

Reflecting His Glory

Week 2: " ...but be transformed..."

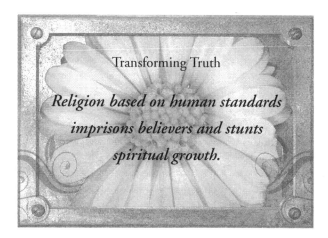

Transforming Truth

Religion based on human standards imprisons believers and stunts spiritual growth.

Day 5: Spiritual Growth—What it is NOT! (Continued)

Yesterday we introduced the topic of spiritual growth and found that Jesus had strong thoughts on the subject. Matthew 23 listed warnings and rebukes that Jesus shared with His followers as well as the Pharisees. These warnings and rebukes centered on the Pharisees' tendency to look at spiritual growth from a human perspective rather than from God's perspective. Today, we will continue this search as we discover four more warnings stating what spiritual growth is NOT. Please join me in a word of prayer.

Lord, we praise You for Your mighty power. Today as we study spiritual growth, set us free from the traps we have been taught and the traps we have created for ourselves. Lord, we want to live our lives for You and You alone. Help us to put aside anything that keeps us from loving, knowing, and serving You more. We give You this day and ask that You be honored in all things. Amen.

Please refresh your memory from yesterday's study by **reading Matthew 23:1–36.** Once you have read the passage, please list the four things we discovered that spiritual growth is NOT. (If necessary, review yesterday's study.)

1. _____

2. _____

3. _____

4. _____

Let's pick up our study by looking at the final four warnings listed in Matthew 23.

Spiritual Growth Is NOT:

5. **Spiritual growth is NOT based on tradition.** In Matthew 23:13–22, Jesus expounds on this truth. In verses 16–17 Jesus states: "Woe to you, blind guides! You say, 'If anyone swears by the temple, he is bound by his oath.' You blind fools! Which is greater: the gold, or the temple that makes the gold sacred?" With this question and others like it, Jesus draws a line in the sand by implying the things of God are never more important than God Himself. The traditions of the Pharisees found their beginning in Old Testament law. In the first five books of the Bible, God gave the Israelites instructions on how they were to live and interact with Him. These instructions dealt mainly with holy versus unclean things and actions. When Jesus came and established the New Covenant, the work of God moved from an outward to an inward focus. The Pharisees missed this vital transition and held onto the past traditions. They made the objects that were to facilitate worship of God the very focus of their worship.

   Because of the Pharisees' misplaced focus, they found it easy to get wrapped up in the notion that the sacred things of God like temples, oaths, and altars have more value than the people Christ came to save. As a result of this focus on tradition, an individual the Pharisees converted became "twice as much a son of hell" (Matthew 23:15). What a strong word!

   In your opinion, what 21st century or contemporary traditions get in the way of people knowing Jesus more?

   _____

   _____

   _____

What effect do these traditions have on new believers?

_____

_____

_____

6. **Spiritual growth is NOT a contained exercise**. In Matthew 23:23–24 Jesus explains the importance of spiritual growth touching every part of a person's life. Therefore, the notion of containing growth within one area or another is wrong.

The word *contained* means "to keep within limits and to prevent from advancing."[25] There is no doubt the Pharisees were doing just that. They were offering to God that which was easy to give and neglecting that which called for real sacrifice. We see proof of this in verse 23. The Pharisees gave a tenth of their spices but neglected the more important matters of the heart like justice, mercy, and faithfulness.

It is easy to fall into the trap of containing our relationship with God. When this occurs, we look at our lives from the perspective of compartments. We have a compartment for church, a compartment for family, a compartment for work, a compartment for friendships, and a compartment for fun. Often, we have different guidelines for each compartment. When this occurs, spiritual growth is prevented because Jesus influences only a part of our lives instead of being the focus of our entire lives.

Do you struggle with a contained walk with God? If so, what do you give to God that is easy? What are you neglecting to give that calls for real sacrifice?

_____

_____

_____

In your opinion, how will failing to give God everything affect your relationship with Him?

_____

_____

_____

7. **Spiritual growth is NOT determined by what is on the outside.** In Matthew 23:25–28 Jesus rebukes the Pharisees for being more concerned with the outward appearance of man than with the inward reality of the heart. No doubt the focus of the Pharisees was on how religious and powerful they could look before one another and the world. As a result, the Pharisees were far more interested in rules and regulations than the heart of Jesus' teachings.

Three times Jesus vividly described the Pharisees. Jesus stated: "You clean the outside of the cup and dish, but inside they are full of greed and self-indulgence." Jesus went on, "You are like whitewashed tombs, which look beautiful on the outside but on the inside are full of dead men's bones." Finally Jesus said, ". . . you appear to people as righteous but on the inside you are full of hypocrisy and wickedness."

From this passage we can know that spiritual growth is not determined by the outside appearance of man. How often do you judge a person's spiritual growth based on their outward appearance?

_____

_____

How often do you try to hold things together on the outside in hopes that others will think you are spiritual?

_____

_____

4. **Spiritual growth is NOT a solo journey.** In Matthew 23:29–36 Jesus challenged the Pharisees in regards to their acceptance of men sent by God to point the way towards Christ. In verses 29–32 Jesus reminded the Pharisees about the prophets of old and how the Pharisees' forefathers had murdered the prophets. In verses 33–36 Jesus stated that He would continue to send prophets, wise men, and teachers to point the way to salvation. However, Jesus told the Pharisees that they would not recognize these prophets, wise men, and teachers and would in fact kill them, crucify them, flog them, and run many of them out of town.

As the story of God unfolds in the New Testament, we know Jesus' prophecy came true as many New Testament leaders were killed or exiled because of their faith in Christ. Stories from the lives of Stephen, Peter, and John remind us that the Jewish religious leaders of their day never embraced the early church leaders who were appointed by God.

Why was it crucial for the Pharisees to receive the prophets?

_____

_____

How do you receive the pastors, teachers, and leaders God has placed in your life?

_____

_____

Do you think the way in which you receive these leaders evidences spiritual growth in your life?

_____

_____

Are you a Pharisee?

I will never forget the day I realized I was a Pharisee. This occurred when the Lord revealed that my approach to spiritual growth fit all eight characteristics listed in our study.

In those days, my spirituality *centered on power and position*. I thought of my spiritual walk as more like a game. I "won" by the knowledge I obtained and the spiritual contacts I made. With each win, I achieved the next rung on the spiritual ladder to success. As a result, every bit of my spiritual life was *done for men to see*. If I was around another "spiritual" person my tone, language, and demeanor quickly changed. If another "spiritual" person was not within earshot, I would do my best to save my "righteous" act for a more appropriate time. If that would not work, I quickly performed my "righteous" act and then did my best to incorporate the act into my next conversation with my "spiritual" friends.

Because my spiritual life was for everyone to see, *divided alliances* often characterized my walk with the Lord. This meant that whoever was around at the time was the most important person in the world. It did not matter if I had just had another conversation with someone else and promised him or her everything. I now focused on the new person in front of me. Because of my tendency to have divided alliances, my first allegiance to Jesus Christ was often forsaken. Unfortunately, God's glory was not at the top of my priority list. No. My goal became *self-glory*. Therefore, I worked hard to make sure I looked my very best to those around me. If you had asked me about humility, I would have said, "Oh yes, I am humble." Today I realize that it was false humility at best.

Sadly, I *based much of my life on tradition*. However, it was not tradition like you normally think. It was not the idea that "we have never done it that way before" or "my mom always told me." No, tradition for me was wrapped up in my preferences about anything and everything spiritual. As a result, I felt I knew everything from how a particular event should work, to how a Sunday School class should be formed—even to the point of knowing how my friends should live their lives. During this time, I based very few of my opinions on sound biblical principles. Instead I based my opinions on how I wanted things to work out on my behalf.

Just like the Pharisees, my approach to spiritual growth was a *contained exercise*. I gave to God areas of life that were easy and convenient. At the time, it did not matter to me if God wanted my heart to be right before Him. I was much more interested in giving God only what I wanted to give. As a result, I neglected to give God open access to every area of my life. Not only was my spiritual growth a contained exercise, it was also *determined by what was on the outside*. All of my energy and strength focused on the outside appearance of spirituality. As a result, my life was about the never-ending, always-changing list of do's and don'ts. Oh, how I prided myself on following the rules. I believed the rules, when followed, made me spiritual and without a doubt, spirituality was my goal.

Probably one of the clearest indicators that my spiritual growth was askew showed in my desire to make my spiritual walk *a solo journey*. This was a big one for me! For many years, my spiritual journey involved being the first and being the best. This left me in a position of living my life in competition with other believers. Therefore, my mind would believe the lies that "I have to do it before her" or "I have to do it better than him." This attitude left me feeling the need to stay isolated from fellow believers and keep my spiritual walk separate from those God placed around me and in authority over me. Why? Because if those around me knew what God was doing in my life, they might want God to do the same in them and thus they would grow in their relationship with God and might somehow get ahead of me.

Over the years, as these eight characteristics became the goal of my spiritual walk and the markers determining my spiritual success or failure, I took my eyes off the Lord and placed them squarely on myself. As a result, I became the center of my universe. I had my spiritual checklist made up of what I could say, what I could do, and what spiritual markers I felt like I should pass in a timely manner. All the while I was completely missing my Savior.

During these long, dry years, I had religion—a personal set of attitudes, beliefs, and practices that became a list of do's and don'ts. But, in the end, this list never really changed my life. I lived the way I lived and felt the way I felt. As a result, I became tired, defeated, and wondered what was wrong with me that I could not pull myself together or what was wrong with God that He could not do this amazing work through me. Unfortunately, during this time in my life, I did not see anything wrong with the very heart of my relationship with God. No, the eight characteristics listed in today's study were not apparent to me. In fact, if they had been, I would probably have held my ground and said, "There is nothing wrong with my relationship with God."

However, today, by God's grace, I know better. I cannot tell you how it grieves my heart to think about the many times I missed God simply because I thought I could determine my own path to spiritual growth. In the end, the Lord had to strip me of everything I knew and held onto through one of the most intense sifting seasons of my life. A sifting season occurs when the Lord allows hard times to come into your life so that your faith and trust in Him can grow. During my sifting season, I thought, "I am losing my mind!" Now I realize it was not only my mind the Lord was after but also my heart. Oh, how I praise Him for His redeeming work in my life! I still struggle with the eight Pharisaical tendencies but the Lord, by His grace, is setting me free. I thank Him for that!

Conclusion

As I sit here and feel the weight of this lesson on my shoulders and the sting of its bitterness deep in my soul, I hear the sweet sound of the Spirit whispering one of my life verses to me. Psalm 142:7 states: "Set me free from my prison, that I may praise your name. Then the righteous will gather about me because of your goodness to me." I love this verse and claim it anytime I am in a self-inflicted prison. Truly, human contrived religion is one of the scariest prisons for believers to live in. We find this especially true when we buy into the lie that religion is the path to spiritual growth. Well, dear friend, I do not know about you but I am ready to get free and stay free from this prison for life! In Matthew 23, Jesus had much to say to the Pharisees. You almost wonder if Jesus felt better by getting this off of His (holy and perfect) chest. I know the Pharisees probably did not feel better following their exchange with Jesus. During the exchange, the Pharisees were confronted with truth that went against everything they had been taught and everything they had believed. Unfortunately, the exchange did not change the

Pharisees' hearts. They continued to function out of a works-based system of belief. What a shame—to have the Savior standing in front of you, speaking truth into your life, and to reject that truth!

Today, through God's Word, we too have been confronted with truth. The question is, how are we going to respond?

Do you struggle with Pharisee-like tendencies in your life? If so, please describe your battle with human standards.

_____

_____

Of the eight characteristics listed in these studies, which ones do you struggle with and why? (Review the list below to refresh your memory.)

_____

_____

To review, we have looked at these eight factors. Spiritual growth is NOT:
1. About power and position
2. Done for men to see
3. Reached through divided alliance
4. For self-glory
5. Based on tradition
6. A contained exercise
7. Determined by what is on the outside
8. A solo journey.

Are you ready to be free from the prison of spiritual growth based on human ideas?

_____

If so, please close by journaling a prayer asking the Lord to set you free from measuring your spiritual walk based on human standards.

_____

_____

_____

_____

Reflecting His Glory

Week 3: "...but be transformed..."

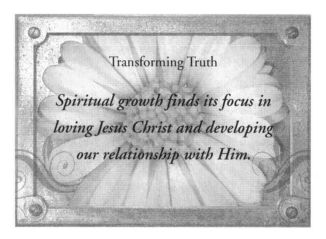

Transforming Truth

Spiritual growth finds its focus in loving Jesus Christ and developing our relationship with Him.

Day 1: Spiritual Growth—What it IS!

Welcome to Week Three! I trust God is meeting you during this study. Aren't you glad that God's Word is faithful to teach us what we need to know? In this week's study, we will continue our look at spiritual metamorphosis. Over the next two days we will study the positive side of spiritual growth as we turn our attention to what it is and how it can be part of our daily lives.

Spiritual Growth—What it IS!!

As we begin, I want to establish a biblical definition for spiritual growth. Spiritual growth IS the development of a thriving, love relationship with Jesus Christ. The apostle Paul spoke of this type of love relationship in the book of Philippians. Philippians 1:9–11 states: "And this is my prayer: that your love may abound more and more in knowledge and depth of insight, so that you may be able to discern what is best and may be pure and blameless until the day of Christ, filled with the fruit of righteousness that comes through Jesus Christ—to the glory and praise of God."

In this prayer, Paul expressed his desire for the believers in Philippi to grow spiritually. This growth took place as the believers loved the Lord more and more. As they allowed their love relationship with Jesus to grow, they were able to know the truth and make choices based on the truth. The result? Their lives displayed spiritual fruit that was rooted in a love relationship with Jesus Christ.

As we desire spiritual growth in our lives, we too must focus on a love relationship with Jesus Christ. Please take a moment and pray the words of Philippians 1:9–11 for your life. I encourage you to write the prayer in the space below. As you write, make the prayer personal by adding in your name.

_____

_____

_____

_____

_____

The Evidence of Spiritual Growth

Spiritual growth produces spiritual fruit in the believer's life. This naturally occurs as we make loving Jesus the focus of our lives. Today we will see the evidence of spiritual growth in the life of Mary, the sister of Martha and Lazarus. Please open your Bible and read two familiar stories from God's Word. Once you have read each story, please describe what took place, focusing on the actions and attitudes displayed in Mary's life.

Event 1: Luke 10:38–42

_____

_____

_____

_____

_____

_____

_____

Event 2: John 11:17–45

_____

_____

_____

_____

_____

_____

_____

_____

Spiritual growth lessons from Mary's life:

From these two events, five actions or attitudes display evidence of spiritual growth in Mary's life.

Event 1: Luke 10:38–42

In the first account from Mary's life, we see Jesus visiting the home of Martha, Mary's sister. Upon Jesus' arrival, we find Martha busy with all the preparations she felt she needed to make to host the Lord. While Martha busied herself in the kitchen, Mary found her place at the Lord's feet, taking in His every word. **From Mary's life we can learn:**

1. **Spiritual growth is evident when we sit and listen.** In Luke 10:39 Mary is introduced as "Mary, who sat at the Lord's feet listening to what he said." I get chills whenever I read this description of Mary's life. To be described as one who sits and listens is a long-term spiritual goal in my life.

   The word *sat* used in this verse is a simple active participle meaning that when Mary sat, she was carrying out an action. You will find this crucial for your understanding of spiritual growth because it teaches that sitting at the Lord's feet is not a passive activity as Martha tried to indicate. Sitting at the Lord's feet involves humbling ourselves before God, which is an active choice.

   As Mary sat at Jesus' feet, she was listening. The word *listening* means "to hear with attention, to embrace, receive, or accept what is said."[26] As Mary sat, she readied herself for the Lord's teaching and instruction. This is a noteworthy point as we realize that Mary did not sit at the Lord's feet in order to tell Him what she thought needed to be done. Mary sat at Jesus' feet in order to hear what He had to say about life. By listening, Mary had an encounter that changed not only her life but also the lives of others. We know this because Jesus used this encounter to teach Martha and the others present about the importance of letting go of the details of life and recognizing the incredible opportunity to sit at the Lord's feet and receive His words for life.

Psalm 46:10 also teaches about the importance of sitting and listening. Please read this verse and answer the questions below.

What does Psalm 46:10 encourage the believer to do? _____

As the person is still, what is she to know? _____

Psalm 46:10 encourages us to be still and know that God is God. This is exactly what Mary did in this first example from her life. As she sat at the Lord's feet, she was still and knew that He was God. For just a few minutes, I would like for you to be perfectly still. No movement. Just stillness before the Lord. During this time, I would like for you to meditate on the fact that God is God and that you are not. Allow the Holy Spirit to lead your thoughts as you think about all the ways that God is in control. Please describe your experience below.

_____

_____

_____

_____

As I take time to be still and know that He is God, I can testify that I find no better way to grow spiritually. As we recognize who God is and who we are in relationship to Him, an incredibly beneficial discipline develops in our daily walks with God. Recognizing that God is God and He is in control of every aspect of life—what a great reminder!

In what areas do you need to be reminded that God is God and that He is in control of every aspect of life?

_____

_____

_____

When you think about your opportunity to sit at the Lord's feet, how often do you sit (be still) and listen (know that He is God by embracing, receiving, and accepting His words for life)?

_____

_____

_____

How does this teaching from Mary's life impact your walk with the Lord?

_____

_____

_____

Event 2: John 11:17–45

In the second account from Mary's life, we find that Lazarus, Mary and Martha's brother, has died. As a result, Jesus comes to Bethany to comfort the sisters and to perform a miracle!

As Jesus travels to Bethany, Martha hears He is near and goes out to meet Him. While Martha goes out to meet Jesus, Mary stays at home. After Martha speaks to Jesus, Martha returns home and tells Mary that Jesus is on the way and is asking for her. Mary gets up at once and rushes to meet Jesus. Once Mary and Jesus talk, Jesus asks to go to the tomb of Lazarus. At the tomb, Jesus mourns with the family and then performs an amazing miracle. **From Mary's life we learn:**

2. **Spiritual growth is evident when we honor Christ foremost in our homes.**
   From the beginning of this account I believe we see Mary's focus is on being present in her home. John 11:20 states: "When Martha heard that Jesus was coming, she went out to meet him, but Mary *stayed at home*" (emphasis added). This may seem like an incidental point, but when it comes to the Word of God, there are no incidental points. Why would Mary stay at home if she knew Jesus was coming? Several possibilities exist.

- It could have been that Mary gave up hope since Lazarus was already dead.
- It could have been Mary was mad at Jesus and thus chose not to meet Him.
- It could have been Mary did not know Jesus was coming. This is a possibility, but I wonder if John would have mentioned the fact that Mary *stayed at home* if it had not been an active choice on her part.
- The final possibility, and the one I believe, involves Mary's sensitivity to the working of Jesus. I think Mary stayed at home because she knew Jesus is God and He would accomplish His will in whatever way He saw fit. By knowing this, Mary was able to stay at home because she trusted that Jesus had a plan and she was at peace with His plan for her life.

Let's explore this thought and see what we can learn about spiritual growth, especially in relationship to our home. I can think of nothing more vital for spiritual growth than to understand that God has a plan and to come to the point of peace with His plan. I do not know about you, but for me, oftentimes it is most difficult for me to be at peace with God's plan in relationship to those inside my home. Why? Because my home is the place where I think I know what is best.

In contrast to my struggle, we see Mary who allowed her spiritual life to be challenged right inside her home. Mary's knowledge of Christ allowed her to live a life of complete abandonment to her God—a life that was filled with peace and patience, knowing God was in control. As we examine this resolve in Mary's life, we can learn much about the concept of spiritual growth. You see, long before Mary could display outward expressions of her love to God, she first had to experience inward trust in her heart before God. This trust led Mary to willingly surrender the people inside her home. The result was her spiritual growth became evident first in her home.

Have you ever thought about the fact that spiritual growth begins inside your home?

_____

_____

_____

What challenges do you face when it comes to allowing your spiritual growth to begin in your home?

_____

_____

_____

_____

In the Old Testament, David spoke about how spiritual growth makes itself evident in our homes. Psalm 101:2–4 teaches about the importance of living a blameless life. In this passage, David lists five outward expressions of blameless living. Note the first outward expression to living a blameless life deals with how David lived in his home.

Please fill in the blanks from Psalm 101:2-3.

"I will be _____ to lead a _____ life when will you come to me? I will _____ in my _____with a _____ heart."

Psalm 101:2-3

Ultimately, to walk in our houses with a blameless heart requires coming to the point of surrender inside our homes. This means giving up our plans, dreams, ideas, and agendas and coming to a place of peace knowing God has a plan and He is in control.

Do you struggle with inner peace inside your home?

_____

_____

_____

_____

If so, how would it change your life to come to a place of rest with God's plan for your life, especially regarding your home?

_____

_____

_____

_____

_____

3. **Spiritual growth is evident when we respond to Jesus.** In John 11:28–29, we see spiritual growth in action as Mary responds to Jesus. In verse 28, Martha returned home following her visit with Jesus and drew Mary aside to let Mary know that Jesus asked for her. In this exchange between Mary and Martha, we see two important qualities displayed in the life of Mary that teach us about spiritual growth.

- **Openness to intimacy.** The first quality we see displayed involves Mary's openness to intimacy. Look at John 11:28 and see how Martha isolated Mary to give her the news about Jesus. The verse states: "And after she had said this, she went back and *called her sister Mary aside*" (emphasis added). If you will, please picture in your mind this event as it unfolds. Martha has just talked to Jesus and returned home. When she arrived at her house, Martha drew Mary aside. From this verse we sense Mary's openness to intimacy.

  The issue of openness is important as we think about our spiritual lives. Dear friend, if you want to grow spiritually, you must have a willingness to go one on one with your Savior. You need openness to the type of relationship that is easily pulled to the side.

  Does the idea of having an intimate love relationship with Jesus scare you?

  _____

  If so, why? If not, why not?

  _____

  _____

  _____

- **Quickness to respond.** Once Martha pulled Mary aside and gave her the news that Jesus asked for her, we see a second quality displayed in Mary's life. John 11:29 states that Mary got up quickly and went to Him. In this response by Mary we see wholehearted obedience as she wastes no time in following the Lord's call.

  When you receive clear instruction from the Lord, how quickly do you respond? Please describe how you typically respond to the Lord.

  _____

4. **Spiritual growth is evident when we recognize Jesus' authority.** In John 11:32, we find that Mary arrived at Jesus' location and did a very important thing.

When Mary arrived to see Jesus, what is the first thing she did? (vs. 32)

_____

Looking back at John 11:20–21, how did Martha arrive before Jesus?

_____

_____

_____

_____

Isn't it interesting that the very first thing Mary did when she saw Jesus was fall at His feet? In this act, we see complete humility as Mary recognized and established Jesus' authority over her life. Truly falling at someone or something's feet is the ultimate way to pay honor and respect to that person or thing. In John 11:32 Mary gave each of us a picture of recognizing Jesus as the ultimate King of our lives.

In contrast to Mary's encounter with Jesus, in John 11:20–21 we see Martha meeting Jesus and speaking with Him. Although we do not know the extent of Martha's conversation with Jesus, Scripture indicates that she expressed her deep sense of loss for her brother. I believe that as she expressed her loss, Martha failed to recognize Jesus' authority over the situation.

I base this belief on the fact that both women say the exact same thing to Jesus: "Lord, if you had been here, my bother would not have died." However, we see from Scripture a major difference between the encounters in how the sisters delivered this statement to their Lord. Hmmm, makes you wonder. Could it be that oftentimes in our spiritual walk with God that spiritual growth is not always measured in what we say but in how we say it? I think the answer is yes. Trust me. I have been the Martha in this passage so many times I hate to admit it! When this happened (and it still does) I had studied the Word long enough to know the right things to say; I had also been in the Lord's presence long enough to know how to phrase them. It was just that I was saying them toe to toe with my Savior instead of face to feet.

How about you? Do you struggle with knowing the right thing to say but saying it in the wrong way?

_____

When this occurs, what does it reveal about a wrong heart attitude?

_____

_____

_____

_____

Why is it important to recognize Jesus' authority in your life?

_____

_____

_____

_____

_____

Describe one or two ways you can recognize Jesus' authority in your life on a daily basis.

_____

_____

_____

_____

5. **Spiritual growth is evident when we participate in setting other captives free.** Following Jesus' interaction with Mary, He asked to be taken to the tomb of Lazarus. Once at the tomb, Jesus did an amazing thing—He asked for the stone to be rolled away. This request created a stir in the crowd because Lazarus had already been dead for four days. However, Jesus insisted on rolling this stone away. Once the stone was removed, Jesus raised Lazarus from the dead. Following this miracle Jesus gave the bystanders, including Mary, a very important instruction. This instruction teaches each of us a crucial spiritual growth principle.

What instruction did Jesus give the bystanders in John 11:44?

_____

In verse 44 Jesus states, "Take off the grave clothes and let him go." Within this verse we see that when we are growing spiritually, we have the opportunity to join Jesus in His work in another person's life. Just like Lazarus wore grave clothes, you and I may encounter people who wear spiritual grave clothes. Grave clothes in this sense represent sins from the past and failures from the present—in short, anything that keeps a believer from experiencing freedom in Jesus Christ. Oftentimes in our quest for spirituality we think our job involves pointing out people's grave clothes. However, as Christ follower's we have the privilege of joining in the process of removing grave clothes as we encourage other believers to walk in the freedom Christ provides.

Wow! What a challenging spiritual growth principle! The concept of participating in setting other captives free is in complete contrast to last week's study as Jesus rebuked the Pharisees' tendency to bind others up. From this teaching of Jesus, we can conclude that as spiritual growth takes place in our lives, it should always lead to other captives being set free.

In your opinion, what role does participating in setting other captives free play in the spiritual growth process?

_____
_____
_____
_____

How often do you play an active role in setting other captives free?

_____
_____
_____
_____
_____

Conclusion

From our time in God's Word, we learned that spiritual growth occurs as we focus on developing a growing, thriving love relationship with Jesus. As we make loving Jesus our focus, our actions and attitudes are changed. Mary provided an example of this in our study. As Mary focused on Jesus, she lived a life that produced spiritual fruit. The fruit pointed to the fact that Mary was in love with her Savior and was growing in her love relationship with Him.

As we seek to grow in our love relationship with Jesus, our actions and attitudes will change. We too will live a life that produces spiritual fruit. The evidence of spiritual growth in our lives includes *a willingness to sit and listen, a desire to be real in our homes, a heart that responds to Jesus, a resolve to recognize Jesus' authority,* and *a passion for seeing other captives set free.*

Tomorrow we will study one last event from Mary's life. For now, please write a journal entry listing any new thoughts about spiritual growth. Once you have finished your entry, please close with a word of prayer.

_____

_____

_____

_____

_____

_____

_____

_____

_____

_____

_____

_____

_____

Reflecting His Glory

Week 3: "...but be transformed..."

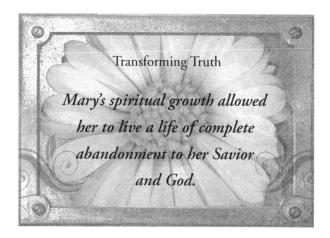

Transforming Truth

Mary's spiritual growth allowed her to live a life of complete abandonment to her Savior and God.

Day 2: Spiritual Growth—What it IS! (Continued)

As we continue to examine the spiritual metamorphosis process, the Bible has more to say on the topic of spiritual growth. Yesterday we looked at Mary, the sister of Martha and Lazarus, and found five distinct areas of spiritual growth that enabled her to reflect God's glory. We defined spiritual growth as the development of a growing, thriving love relationship with Jesus. As Mary focused on loving Jesus, her actions and attitudes were changed. Today, we will continue our look at Mary's life as we find three more evidences of her love for Jesus.

Father, we love You this day. Lord, You are holy, and we are amazed at how You work in our lives. Today, as we continue to examine the heart and life of Mary, teach us through Your Word. Teach us about loving You and giving our lives to You. Forgive us for the many times we have put other things and other people before You. Lord, we want to grow in our love relationship with You. More than anything, we desire to live lives that bless Your name and reflect Your glory. Help us this day. In Your precious name, amen.

Please open your Bible and read Matthew 26:6–13. (For additional accounts of this event, you can read Mark 14:3–9 and John 12:1–11.) Once you have read the story, please describe what took place, focusing on Mary's actions and attitudes.

- Event 3: Matthew 26:6–13 (Mark 14: 3–9 and John 12:1–11)

Event 3: Matthew 26:6–13

The woman in this account is Mary, sister of Martha and Lazarus. We know this is true because John identified the woman in his gospel account in John 12:1–8. The scene of this event tells the story. Jesus and His disciples reclined at the table in the home of Simon the Leper. Jesus and the disciples were enjoying one of their last meals together as the betrayal, crucifixion, and death of Jesus drew near. Perhaps Mary sensed that Jesus' death was a short time away, because Mary lavishly anoints Jesus with perfume and thereby prepares Jesus for burial and sets the course for how she would be remembered for centuries to come. From Mary's life we can draw these lessons.

6. **Spiritual growth is evident when we each live a life of relinquishment and complete dependency.** In Matthew 26:7, Matthew states: "…a woman came to him with an alabaster jar of very expensive perfume." When we think about Mary coming to Jesus with a bottle of expensive perfume, I wonder if we can even begin to picture what took place. We might imagine Mary placing a quick dab of perfume on Jesus' head or a quick mist of fragrance over Jesus' body.

   However, as we dig into Scripture we see a completely different event. Scripture states: "…a woman came to him with an alabaster jar of very expensive perfume, which she poured on his head as he was reclining at the table." Mary took the perfume and poured it on Jesus' head. Now this perfume was not your run-of-the-mill perfume purchased from the local market. No, this very precious perfume cost the equivalent of one year's wage.[27]

   I do not know about you, but to me, Mary's relinquishment of control over her life demonstrated an amazing act of love. Mary gave lavishly and as a result increased her dependency on her Savior. What a challenge! Daily we need to give lavishly to Jesus. As we do, we relinquish control over our very lives and place ourselves in the position of dependency on our Lord. The reality of our lives becomes, "Lord, if You do not get me through this, I will not make it."

You will find a perfect example of the call to relinquish control of your life in Luke 14:25–34. In this passage Jesus states in verse 26: "If anyone comes to me and does not hate his father and mother, his wife and children, his brothers and sisters—yes even his own life—he cannot be my disciple." As Jesus made these incredibly challenging statements, Jesus set the tone for His relationship with us. I believe He is saying, "I want you to want Me more than you want anything else. More than you want your family. More than you want your resources. More than you want to protect your own life."

What is Jesus challenging you to relinquish?

_____

_____

_____

_____

If you choose to obey, how will that lead you to a place of complete dependency?

_____

_____

_____

_____

7. **Spiritual growth is evident when we minister to Jesus.** As Mary gave so lavishly, we see a wonderful thing take place—Mary ministered to Jesus! When Mary poured the perfume on Jesus' head, the disciples rebuked her because of her extravagant gift. But Jesus rebuked His disciples!

In Matthew 26:10, what was Jesus' question to the disciples?

_____

_____

_____

In Matthew 26:10, how did Jesus describe Mary's act?

_____

In Matthew 26:12, what does Jesus say Mary did when she poured the perfume on Him?

_____

In verse 10 Jesus questions the disciples by asking, "Why are you bothering this woman?" Then Jesus goes on to state that Mary performed a beautiful act because it prepared Jesus for His burial. In essence Jesus said to the disciples: "Leave this woman alone because what she just did will prepare the way for what I am about to do." As we think about spiritual growth, this is another crucial concept. The focus of spiritual growth is not growth itself. No. The focus is always Jesus. When Jesus is the focus instead of growth, an amazing thing happens. We live our lives in such a way as to prepare for Jesus to work in and through us. Then another amazing thing takes place. We find that we grow!

Have you ever thought that the way you live your life can minister to Jesus?

_____

Please read Psalm 101:6. According to this passage, what kind of life ministers to God?

_____

8. **Spiritual growth is evident when we are known for our relationship with Jesus.** Following Jesus' rebuke of the disciples, Jesus makes a statement that teaches each of us how to have a lasting impact on the world long after we are gone.

_____

Please write Matthew 26:13 in the space below.

_____

_____

_____

In this verse, Jesus stated the act Mary performed would be remembered for as long as the gospel is preached. Jesus taught the disciples that if they wanted to be remembered long after they were gone from this earth, then they needed to live their lives so that those around them could see the difference He made in their lives. Ultimately Mary displayed this truth on that day. Jesus had made such a difference in her life that there was nothing she was not willing to give and nothing she was not willing to do. As a result, Mary will always be remembered based on her interaction with Jesus. Today we are called to the same standard: to live our lives so that the difference Jesus makes in our lives sets us apart for His glory.

When you think about the people closest to you, do you think they see the difference Jesus makes in your life?

_____

_____

_____

_____

_____

_____

As I ask you this, please know it is a question I have faced. A few years ago, I was caught in one of those moments. Life was busy—too busy. I was a wife, a mom of two active boys, and a church staff member; I was also beginning a speaking ministry for women. My days were too short to complete all the "to do's" on my list. As a result, I lived my life just trying to survive.

On one night in particular, I was frantically trying to complete a speaking outline for an upcoming women's event. My husband Jay was gone to a Bible study, and Jake and Andrew were running around the house. The dishes from dinner were still on the table, and I had so much to do that I did not know where to begin.

I told the boys, "Watch TV and do not fight." The boys obeyed, and I started working on the speaking outline. As I worked, time quickly passed. I looked up from my computer and noticed the time read 9:00 pm. This surprised me, since my boys should have been in bed by 8:30. Immediately, I went into drill sergeant mode. I told the boys, "You have to take a bath, brush your teeth, say your prayers, and go to sleep as soon as possible."

I put the boys in the bathtub and told them there was no time to play. They could talk quietly while I went and picked up their towels. I quickly walked across the house to find their towels and returned to wash the boys. As I stepped inside the door, I discovered two inches of water on the bathroom floor. I could not believe it! Immediately, I took the boys out of the tub and asked them what happened. Jake said, "Mom, we made up a game, and I won!" That did not impress me. In fact, I got very angry. I gave the boys a lecture, put them on their beds, and cleaned up the mess.

Once the floor was dry, I went into each room and told the boys how upset I was and that they needed to put on their pajamas and go to bed. That night we had no prayers, no snuggles, and no tucking into bed. I turned the lights out and told the boys to go to sleep.

After leaving the boys' rooms, I took a few minutes to shake off my anger and returned to my computer to complete the speaking outline. As I typed, the Lord spoke to my heart. "Andrea, when you act like that do you think they have any idea that I make a difference in your life?" The question took me by surprise and became a life-changing question. Do the people closest to me know that Jesus makes a real difference in my life? My heart sank because I knew the answer to that question was often no. I fell to my knees and asked the Lord to forgive me. I then returned to my boys' room and asked for their forgiveness as well.

The simple question from the Lord changed my perspective on life. The question brought an understanding that taught me that I could travel around this world telling others about Jesus, write Bible studies, and even speak at women's conferences, yet miss the real point. You see, what Jesus was teaching me was that at the end of my life what would really matter the most was that my husband and my children could say, "Jesus made a real difference in her."

Conclusion

As we wrap up our study on spiritual growth, I would like to conclude the way we began.

In your words, please define spiritual growth.

_____

_____

_____

What spiritual markers do you use in order to measure spiritual growth in your life? In other words, what are the visible signs you use to determine if you are growing in your relationship with the Lord?

_____

_____

_____

_____

_____

_____

Now look back at Day Four of last week's study and compare and contrast the definition and spiritual markers you listed on that day with your answers from today. Do you see any differences? If so, please explain below.

_____

_____

_____

_____

_____

_____

As you think about spiritual growth, please circle the most challenging areas for you.

Spiritual growth is NOT:

About power or position
Done for men to see
Reached through divided alliances
For self glory
Based on tradition
A contained exercise
Determined by what is on the outside
A solo journey.

Spiritual growth IS evident when we:

Sit and listen

Honor Christ foremost in our homes

Respond to Jesus

Recognize Jesus' authority

Participate in setting other captives free

Live a life of relinquishment and complete dependency

Minister to Jesus

Are known for our relationship with Jesus.

Please journal a prayer asking the Lord to help you apply the truths you have seen in the study of His Word on the issue of spiritual growth.

_____

_____

_____

_____

_____

_____

_____

_____

_____

_____

_____

_____

_____

Reflecting His Glory

Week 3: "...but be transformed..."

> ### Transforming Truth
>
> **Do the right thing with compassion and humility, allowing your actions to speak louder than your words.**

Day 3: Differentiation—Living Set Apart for Christ

Today we move on to the third element in the spiritual metamorphosis process—the element of *differentiation*. Over the next three days, we will focus on this topic as we seek to understand what it is and how it can help us to reflect the glory of Christ. Let's pray.

Father, we glorify and honor Your name. You are worthy of praise, and we find ourselves so inadequate to even express how great and awesome You are. Lord, help us this day as we open Your Word and study Your truth. Teach us what it means to live a life that is set apart for Your glory. In Jesus' name, amen.

Differentiation—The Call to Holiness

Webster's dictionary defines *differentiation* as "the process of becoming **distinct** or **different** in character."[28] In order to bring this definition to life, please read the similar words used for distinct or different living.

> *Distinct:* unique, unmistakable, apparent, or notable.

> *Different:* diverse, dissimilar, unusual, or separate.

Please circle the words that are most meaningful to you.

The words that are most meaningful to me are: *unique, unmistakable, dissimilar, and separate.* These words, along with the others, paint a wonderful picture of distinct or different living.

In your words, please define the term differentiation.

_____

_____

_____

_____

Please explain how you think differentiation takes place in a believer's life.

_____

_____

_____

_____

The attribute of God's *holiness* calls believers to a life of distinct living. You see, at the very heart of holiness resides the call to be *set apart.* In fact, no better phrase exists to describe God in His holiness than *set apart.* Over and over in the Bible, God calls Himself holy. In response to God's holiness, we as believers are to be holy. Please look up the passages below and explain what each passage states about God, as well as the call to holiness on our lives.

• Leviticus 20:26

_____

_____

_____

- Ephesians 1:3–5

_____

_____

_____

- Hebrews 12:14

_____

_____

_____

- 1 Peter 1:15–16

_____

_____

_____

The call to holiness resounds in the Word of God. God is holy, and therefore we as believers in Christ must be holy. The call to holiness is the call to live set apart. As this call becomes the goal of our lives, an unusual thing takes place—surrender becomes a daily reality. Why? At the very heart of the call to be holy resides the call to be more and more like Christ and less and less like the world. We are to move from conformity to spiritual transformation. In essence, we must come to the point of peace with a new reality for life—the reality of embracing a life different from what the world expects and different from what the world accepts. Oh, what a challenge we face!

The Good Samaritan: the evidence of distinct or different living

In light of the call to holiness, we will tackle the topic of differentiation by looking at the parable of the Good Samaritan. Jesus tells His followers about a Samaritan man whose character and actions really set him apart from the other people in the parable. This story shows us the reality of living a holy life that honors God and reflects the glory of Christ.

Please read Luke 10:25–37 and answer the questions below.

According to verse 25, who is involved in the conversation?

_____

What question did the expert in the law pose to Jesus in verse 25?

_____

In response, Jesus asked the expert in the law a question. What is the question?

_____

In verse 27, the expert stated two things are required to inherit eternal life. Please list the two things.

- _____
- _____

Please describe Jesus' response to the expert's answer as stated in verse 28.

_____

The expert then tries to justify himself, so he asks one more question. Please write the question below.

_____

In response to the expert's question, Jesus tells a story teaching the expert the true meaning of love. In this story four individuals are described. Please list them below.

- _____
- _____
- _____
- _____

In verse 31, a priest encounters the hurt man. How does the priest respond?

_____

_____

In verse 32, a Levite encounters the hurt man. How does the Levite respond?

_____

_____

In verse 33, a Samaritan encounters the hurt man. How does the Samaritan respond?

_____

_____

In verse 36, what was Jesus' final question to the expert?

_____

_____

What was the expert's response to the final question? _____

Please write Jesus' final words to the expert of the law. _____

As we think about this passage of Scripture and the meaning of holy living, we see an incredible example of differentiation tucked away in this very familiar parable. In Luke 10:25–37, Jesus and an expert in the law exchanged questions. The encounter ended with Jesus telling a story displaying three essential attributes of holy living. Let's examine this exchange and see what we can learn.

At the beginning of the encounter the expert in the law asked Jesus, "What must I do to inherit eternal life?" Jesus, knowing the expert thought he knew all the "right" answers, asked the question, "What is written in the Law?" The expert responded, "Love the Lord your God with all your heart and with all your soul and with all your strength and with all your mind, and love your neighbor as yourself." Jesus agreed with the expert and stated, "Do this and you will live."

The expert wanted to justify himself and asked Jesus, "And who is my neighbor?" This question lead to a powerful teaching time as Jesus told a story about a man who was on his way from Jerusalem to Jericho when he fell into the hands of robbers.

The setting for Jesus' story was a famous road that everyone in His audience was familiar with. The road wound its way down from Jerusalem to Jericho and passed through lonely, desolate, and rocky terrain[29]; it was well known as a dangerous road for travel.

In Jesus' story, a man was traveling down the dangerous road when robbers took the man's belongings and beat him until he almost died. As the man lay on the side of the road, three individuals—a priest, a Levite, and a Samaritan—passed by. Each responded to the hurt man in a telling way.

First, the priest passed by the hurt man. The Jewish priest was similar to our modern day pastor. The role of the priest involved managing the temple area, teaching the Scriptures, and leading in worship. You would expect that a religious leader like the priest would respond in the proper way by helping someone in need. However, Scripture states the priest traveled down the road and went out of his way to pass by the hurt man.

Next a Levite passed by the injured man. A Levite lived a life set apart to God through service in the temple. Just like the priest, the Levite was a religious leader. As a result, anyone in Jesus' audience might conclude that the Levite would show mercy to the hurt man and offer him help. However, Scripture states the Levite did not help the hurt man but also passed him by.

The third individual to pass by the hurt man was a Samaritan. It is important to understand that the Samaritans were an ethnically mixed race of people; the Jews looked on the Samaritans with disgust and avoided them at all cost. In Jesus' story, the Samaritan who was traveling down the road displayed compassion for the hurt man. Verse 33 states: "But a Samaritan, as he traveled, came where the man was; and when he saw him, he took pity on him."

Application

As we study the response of the Samaritan, we see a picture of holy living as the Samaritan taught each of us what it looks like to live a set-apart life. Three principles can be drawn from the Samaritan's life.

- **Principle One: The Samaritan displayed a *willingness to do the right thing.*** For just a moment, please think about the story Jesus is telling. Remember, this is a parable. It may or may not have actually happened. However, the purpose of the parable was simple. Jesus used this parable to teach His followers about the difference between right and wrong. As we look at the whole story we see one overarching theme in the Samaritan's life—he was willing to do the right thing. Without a doubt, the easy action for the Samaritan would have been to walk past the hurt man as the priest and Levite had done. But the Samaritan did not take the easy route. Instead, he made the decision to do the right thing.

At the heart of holy living resides a willingness to do the right thing based on God's standards, not the world's standards.

For just a moment, please think about how often we fall into the trap of living our lives based on the world's standards. When this occurs, we begin to see right and wrong as relative and defined by what others think, by what popular culture teaches, or by what we desire for our lives. In order to be set apart, we must move past this tendency in life and begin do the right thing in God's eyes.

How often do you fall into the trap of living your life based on what is easy instead of what is right?

_____

_____

_____

In what area(s) is God calling you to do the right thing?

_____

_____

_____

- **Principle Two: The Samaritan displayed an attitude of compassion and humility.** Luke 10:33 states: "But a Samaritan, as he traveled, came where the man was; and when he saw him, he **took pity** on him." The phrase *took pity* means "to have compassion." What a crucial aspect in the set-apart process—to live our lives with compassion and humility! Think how often people make the choice to do the right thing but once they make this choice, they become puffed up with spiritual pride. The result? They are rendered ineffective for the cause of Christ.

Have you ever experienced a situation where you or someone you know made the choice to do the right thing only to become puffed up with spiritual pride and as a result actually turned others off from the cause of Christ? If so, please explain.

_____

_____

_____

_____

_____

_____

When this occurs it breaks the heart of the Father who desires for His children to live compassionate and humble lives. Please read Colossians 3:12–14 and list the qualities Christians are to possess.

_____

_____

_____

_____

As I read Colossians 3:12–14 and think about my own tendencies, the Word of God convicts me. I can recall many times when I have fallen into the practice of taking a stand for Christ and then have become proud for doing so. Sadly, not only have I seen this take place in my life, I have seen this take place in the lives of others. When this occurs, I ask myself, "What causes someone to do the right thing and then turn from Christlike character once doing it?"

I am not sure one single answer exists to this question. There are probably many reasons. But as I have studied the Word of God, one answer surfaces time and time again. The answer involves an unwillingness or lack of understanding regarding God's desire to be the believer's shield and refuge.

Let me explain this idea to you in the context of our focus passage. Remember, the Samaritan displayed a willingness to do the right thing even though the right thing was not easy for him to accomplish. As the Samaritan did the right thing, he stopped his travel plans on a dangerous road and placed his attention on the needs of another. At the moment the Samaritan placed his attention on the needs of another, he became vulnerable to the dangers around him. The robbers who injured this man might have been still lurking, waiting for another victim. The same possibilities exist today. When you and I set out to do the right thing, we become vulnerable to those around us. We open up our lives to the possibility of ridicule, slander, and gossip by those who choose to take the easy route.

As a result, it is easy for us to feel the need to protect ourselves by putting up our guard and taking on the attitude, "You can't hurt me." When this happens, we can come across as arrogant or prideful when really we are fearful of being hurt or rejected by those around us. People who claim, "I would rather be right than be liked," may secretly long to be both. Once fear becomes the motivating factor, we lose the ability to function out of compassion and humility, and we no longer live holy lives.

So the bottom line is clear. If we are going to display a willingness to do the right thing and live our lives out of compassion and humility, we must understand two things. Ridicule, misunderstanding, slander, and gossip are a possibility for those living the set-apart life. Second, instead of fighting in order to defend our name, we must stop and allow the Lord to fight on our behalf.

Please read Psalm 91:1–4 and describe God's desire to be a shield and refuge during times of trouble.

_____

_____

_____

_____

As a result of the truth taught in Psalm 91:1–4, do you think you can come to a place of complete dependence on the Lord, knowing that He will take care of you as you make the choice to live a holy life? If so, how will this affect the way you live your life? Will it lead you to humility and compassion instead of pride and arrogance?

_____

_____

_____

_____

- **Principle Three: The Samaritan let his actions speak louder than his words.**
  Once the Samaritan displayed a willingness to do the right thing and had pity on the man, the Samaritan took care of every need the hurt man possessed. Scripture states that the Samaritan:
    - Bandaged the hurt man's wounds
    - Poured oil and wine on the man
    - Placed the hurt man on his donkey
    - Took the man to the inn and (personally) took care of him
    - Gave the innkeeper money to take care of the hurt man's needs.

From these actions we see a complete act of love on the part of the Samaritan.

I wonder just for wondering's sake, if the story Jesus told had actually happened, would the priest and the Levite have thought about the hurt man once they arrived home? At any point during the night would they have thought about the man? Would they have wondered if he was okay or if he was still lying on the road covered with blood, close to death, with little or no resources for survival?

I wonder if the priest and Levite would have asked for prayer for the man at their nightly Bible study. Or if they would have sent out a message on their prayer chain asking individuals to pray for a man they encountered along their journey home. Remember, in this parable the priest and Levite represent church people. Think how often, as church people, we give lip service to the things of God instead of putting our heart and soul into the very things of God and being a part of His solution.

Have you ever experienced a time in your life when you fell into the trap of merely talking about something that needed to be done instead of taking part in making it happen? If so, please describe the situation below.

Is God calling you to right that wrong by stepping up and doing the right thing? If so, please describe what God is calling you to do.

Conclusion

Following the parable, Jesus asks the critical question, "Which of these three do you think was a neighbor to the man who fell into the hands of robbers?" The expert's response was, "The one who had mercy on him." Jesus' final words were: "Go and do likewise."

With these words, Jesus set the standard for how we can honor and please Him by living our lives with the same qualities the Samaritan displayed. For us, as we think about living a holy life in Christ, I believe Jesus would say: **"Go and live your life by displaying a willingness to do the right thing, with an attitude of humility and compassion, always allowing your actions to speak louder than your words."** When these three qualities are present, you can know that you are living a holy life in Christ. You are also *reflecting His glory!*

As you think about your life, ask yourself the question, "Am I living a set-apart life for Christ?" The story of the Good Samaritan challenges you to examine your heart.

In your walk with the Lord, how often do you display a willingness to do the right thing?

_____

_____

_____

_____

In all honesty, have you been taking the easy road instead of the right road in life?

_____

_____

_____

_____

How about your attitude once you make the choice to do the right thing? Does your attitude honor the Lord and cause others to desire to know more about Christ?

_____

_____

_____

How about your actions? Are your actions speaking louder than your words, or is your life made up of nothing more than words with little evidence of a changed life?

_____

_____

_____

Dear friend, God desires for you to know that He loves you and wants His best for you. Without a doubt, God's best is only achieved as you surrender your heart to Him and give Him everything. Please close with a word of prayer committing to do whatever God through His Holy Spirit calls you to do.

_____

_____

_____

Reflecting His Glory

Week 3: "...but be transformed..."

Transforming Truth

Love with focus as you choose to live present and vulnerable with Jesus.

Day 4: Differentiation—The Call to Love

Yesterday we introduced the third step in the spiritual metamorphosis process—the step of differentiation. We defined *differentiation* as "the call on a believer's life to be distinct or different in character." Today we will continue our look at differentiation as we focus on the issue of **character**. This focus will challenge us to love like never before.

Before we dig in to our study, I would like to share with you what has been taking place in the preparation portion for today's study. For several weeks, I had the outline for today's study complete. The outline was on my computer waiting for me. On the outline I had the heading *Spiritual Purity*. With this heading in mind, I sat down to begin work. As I sat at my computer, I prayed, "Lord, show me what you have for us today." As I prayed, I sensed the Lord changing the direction of the study.

For some of you, this may seem incidental, but for me, this was a problem. You see, I am a planner. More than that, once I have a plan, I stick to the plan. (Yes, this makes me a control freak!) So for God to change the direction of what I had planned to write about challenged me. As I sat there, I was so unsure of what was taking place that I got up, left my house, and ran some errands. You know shopping always helps to clear the mind!

During my errands, I prayed, "Lord, what are You trying to show me? I am confused. Please help me to listen to Your direction and follow You with a whole heart." As I prayed, the Lord began to work in my heart. The work began with the Lord pouring out His **love** on me. I do not know if I have ever experienced anything like it. All of a sudden and out of nowhere, I felt the weight of God's incredible **love,** and I was overwhelmed by His presence. Then the Lord allowed me to experience the weight of my **love** for Him and others. This amount of love took me by surprise because I have not always been able to feel or express genuine God-given love. I immediately began crying out to God, praising Him and thanking Him for the life-changing work He has done. I thought about my husband and my children and how deeply I **love** them. I thought about my life and all the amazing people God has placed around me, and I thanked God all the more. During this car ride, I was reminded that everything in life is an incredible gift of His grace.

Once I had cried out to God, I turned on the radio in search of a song to sing to my King. The station I listen to was playing one of my favorite 4Him songs, *The Center of the Mark.* You are probably familiar with this song and know the chorus: "Draw back your bow, let **love** go. Shoot straight for the heart. With all of your might, set your sight. Take aim from the start. To **love** God and **love** people, that's the center of the mark."[30]

As I sang in my car, God reminded me, "Andrea, it's all about **love!"** With this reminder from the Lord, I knew the new direction for today's study. The direction had become crystal clear. Today's lesson was to focus on differentiation and see that at the very heart of the call to be distinct or different in character is the *call to **love.*** The more I thought about this new direction, the more I understood the Lord's plan, because it is our **love** that sets us apart for His glory. Let's pray.

O Father, You are amazing, and even before we begin this day we simply have to express how much we love You. You are worthy of all praise. Lord, forgive the sin of our heart and heal the wounds that are left behind. Today as we explore the subject of differentiation, challenge us to be distinct and different in our character. Teach us how to love You and love others with complete abandon. May You be glorified in all things. In Jesus' name, amen.

The Call to Love

As we talked about in yesterday's study, believers in Christ are called to be distinct or different in character. As we think about character, we must ask the question, "What is character?" According to Webster's dictionary, *character* is "one of the features that makes up or distinguishes an individual."[31] **Please read John 13:34–35** in order to discover the character quality that sets believers apart in Christ. Once you have read the passage, please answer the questions below.

Please state the new command listed in verse 34.

_____

According to verse 35, what takes place as we love?

_____

John 13:34–35 states we are to love one another as Christ loved us. As we love, an amazing thing takes place—we are known as His disciples! Do you see the correlation between love and Christ-like character? As we love like Christ, we look like Christ, act like Christ, and reflect Christ. Christ-like love ***differentiates*** or ***sets us apart*** by making us known as His disciples. This truth makes love paramount in the believer's life.

Please explain your thoughts on the importance of love in the believer's life.

_____

_____

_____

Jesus Expresses His Love

As we look through the lens of Scripture, Jesus becomes the perfect picture of love. In fact, no greater demonstration of love exists than Jesus willingly dying on the cross. Just prior to Jesus' death, He performs another act of love by washing His disciples' feet. From this event we learn a great deal about love. Please read John 13:1–17 and answer the questions below.

In verse 1, what did Jesus know?

_____

In verse 1, what did Jesus show?

_____

Verse 3 states three things that Jesus knew. Please list them below.

     1. _____

     2. _____

     3. _____

As a result of the three things, what did Jesus do in verses 4 and 5?

_____

_____

_____

Explain Jesus' interaction with Peter in verses 6–11.

_____

_____

_____

In verses 12–16, Jesus teaches the disciples by explaining what took place. Please state Jesus' teaching in your own words.

_____

_____

_____

List Jesus' encouragement to the disciples as stated in verse 17.

_____

What do you think it means for the disciples to be blessed?

_____

_____

_____

Jesus Teaches Us to Love

From John 13, **four principles** surface that illustrate the "how to's" of love. Today we will explore two of the principles and then finish our study of the other two in tomorrow's lesson. Each principle taught by Jesus challenges us to love like never before.

1. **Principle One: Know your time is at hand.**

    The first "how to" of love is to know your time is at hand. John 13:1 states: "Jesus knew that the time had come for him to leave this world and go to the Father." From this verse we can conclude that Jesus knew His physical death was near. As Jesus knew His physical death was near, He focused on the most important task—teaching His disciples. As Jesus taught, He honored His Father by living a life of integrity and obedience.

    In your own words, please describe what it means to live your life knowing your time is at hand.

    _____

    _____

    _____

    Living like you know that your time is at hand means living your life with a sense of purpose. Simply put, it means submitting to the "right now" call of God. This involves knowing that God has called you to make an impact on the world around you—right now. Not in five years when you have it all together. Or ten years from now when life slows down. Rather, right now in the midst of your busy and sometimes crazy life. Why? Because when you live your life knowing your time is at hand you understand that there are no certainties for tomorrow. Therefore, you live each day as if it is your last. Jesus modeled this attitude for each of us as He ministered with precision and focus.

    For just a moment, I would like for you to place yourself in Jesus' position. Think about it. Only a few short days remain until your death. You are with your closest friends. You have one last chance to teach and demonstrate your love to them. How would you respond? How intense, focused, and determined would you be?

    _____

    _____

    _____

Dear friend, each day you walk on this earth, you should live your life with the same focus, intensity, and determination displayed by Jesus during the days leading up to His death. You see, Jesus is God and therefore knew the number of days He would walk on this earth. As Jesus knew this, He understood the importance of focusing on the most important aspects of life.

In contrast to Jesus, you and I live in a world where we do not know the number of our days. Since this is our reality, the call to live like our time is at hand is magnified as we make it our goal to reflect the glory of Christ.

Matthew 22:36–40 states the most crucial aspect of our earthly ministry. Please read this passage and explain the call on your life.

_____

_____

_____

 If you had to use one word to summarize the teaching from Matthew 22:36–40, what word would you use?

_____

Matthew 22:36–40 states that the most important call in life involves loving God and loving others. Once again, God's Word teaches us that our time on this earth is all about love! As we think about the call to love, we must understand that loving God and loving others unlocks the door to set-apart living in Christ. Therefore, as we live our lives knowing that our time is at hand, we live it with a new focus, a new goal of each day loving God and loving others. Why? Because loving God and loving others has a way of clearing up our focus by helping us distinguish between the mundane things of this world and the magnificent things of God.

 In your life, what gets in the way of knowing your time to love God and love others is at hand?

_____

_____

_____

2. **Principle Two: Daily experience the full extent of His love.**

The second "how to" of love is to daily experience the full extent of His love. We see that as a result of Jesus knowing His time was at hand, Jesus taught the disciples an important lesson. No doubt, Jesus knew His disciples would face many tests, trials, and "forks in the road" once He departed for His heavenly home. Therefore, the lesson on the top of Jesus' list involved genuine love. John 13:1 states: "Having **loved** his own who were in the world, he now showed them the **full extent of His love**" (emphasis added).

I do not know about you, but it is hard to imagine the intensity and feeling that must have accompanied the disciples' first glimpse of "the full extent of His love." For just a moment, place yourself in the disciples' position. You are in the upper room. Jesus stands, removes his outer garment, and begins to pour water into a basin. Before long, Jesus kneels at your feet and and begins to wash them.

This act of love and service became the first glimpse the disciples received of the full extent of Jesus' love for them. Just a few days later, the disciples would see the culmination of Jesus' love as He died on the cross for their sins.

What would it have been like to experience this first glimpse into the full extent of His love?

_____

_____

_____

As the disciples experienced "the full extent of His love," I imagine they felt overwhelmed, confused, uncomfortable, and exhilarated all at the same time. I know if I had been in that room I would have felt all these emotions. No matter how the disciples felt that night, Jesus knew the lesson He had for them was much more important than their feelings. Therefore, Jesus continued to teach. What a neat thought! Even in times of discomfort, Jesus has a plan, and He works that plan for God's glory and His children's good.

Why would Jesus want to display the full extent of His love to His followers? I think the context of the passage provides this answer. Jesus knew it was essential for the disciples to begin to know and experience the full extent of His love as the cross was quickly approaching on the Kingdom calendar. I find it interesting that the way Jesus taught the disciples how to show love was by first teaching the disciples how to receive love. What a crucial lesson for all believers in Christ—the importance of receiving love in order to give it away.

For me, sometimes receiving love from my heavenly Father is a challenge. Oftentimes when He extends His love, I find myself asking questions like these. "What will I have to do in return? Will the bottom fall out of this situation? If the bottom falls out, how much will it hurt?" Allow me to share one example from my life. In February 2007 God called me to take a step of faith by transitioning out of local church work and beginning a full-time speaking ministry for women. Every feeling in my heart told me to run. I was so afraid of failure— failure on my part and failure on God's part. At the heart of my fear was one constant thought, "What if God calls me to this unknown place and then realizes how inadequate I am? Surely, He will leave me for another." You see, in my heart, I did not trust God, and I did not understand God's love for me. At the time, I did not realize that God was not calling me to a ministry but to Himself. Through the call to step out on faith and begin True Vine Ministry, God taught me how to receive His love by trusting Him no matter what.

How about you? Do you struggle with receiving love from your heavenly Father? If so, please explain.

_____

_____

_____

Today as we think about allowing the love of Christ to set us apart for His glory, we must understand that if we are going to love like Christ, then we must receive love from Christ. Dear sister, you and I cannot muster up enough love in our lives to accomplish anything for His glory. The love in our lives must flow from our relationship with Jesus Christ. For some this will require a new discipline in your walk with Christ.

 What are some ways you can ensure that you experience the full extent of His love daily?

_____

_____

As I look at this passage of Scripture and seek an answer for the question listed above, two practical steps surface. Both of these steps are displayed in the life of the disciples as they experienced the full extent of His love. The first step involved the disciples being **present** at the event. What a simple yet profound truth! The disciples made a choice to be present. More than just being physically present, the disciples were mentally present at the foot washing experience. What a difference it makes when you and I choose to be mentally present in our walks with God! When this occurs we choose to move past a relationship that just shows up for the sake of showing up and to embrace the active choice of engaging in the process of receiving the full extent of His love.

Once engaged in the process, we see the second practical step displayed in the disciples' lives. The disciples became **vulnerable** by allowing Jesus to do the work He wanted to do in their lives, even when the work was uncomfortable. What a necessary truth! In your pursuit of God, you will experience times of discomfort. This discomfort naturally occurs as the flesh and the Spirit battle for supremacy. However, as you stay vulnerable before the Lord, the Holy Spirit penetrates the core of your being, changing you into the likeness of Christ.

In your relationship with the Lord, which is more challenging for you—to be truly present or to be vulnerable? Why?

Conclusion

Please take a moment and evaluate your life based on the information presented in today's passage.

1. In your daily routine of loving God and loving others, rate your level of focus.

1	2	3	4	5	6	7	8	9	10
no focus		little focus		some focus		growing focus			very focused

2. **In your walk with God, how present do you tend to be?**

1	2	3	4	5	6	7	8	9	10
not very present			somewhat present			on and off present			daily present

3. **When you are in an uncomfortable season with the Lord, what is your typical response?**

1	2	3	4	5	6	7	8	9	10
"I am out of here!" Run and hide			Experience discomfort but display a willingness to see what God is doing				Open to uncomfortable seasons and welcome them into my life		

I pray the Lord has placed an urgent desire in your heart to love. Each day this desire can be a reality as we choose to live **present** and **vulnerable** with Him.

Tomorrow we will pick up on this idea as we continue to study the way love sets us apart or differentiates us from the world. For now, please close with a word of prayer asking the Lord to help you embrace the call to love like never before.

_____

_____

_____

_____

_____

_____

_____

_____

Reflecting His Glory

Week 3: "…but be transformed…"

Transforming Truth

Each day, love like Jesus loved with a humble and willing spirit.

Day 5: Differentiation—The Call To Love, Part 2

The call to love sets believers apart for God's glory. According to Scripture, we are known as disciples of Christ by the way we love. Therefore, in order to reflect the glory of Christ, we must embrace the call to love like never before. Let's pray.

Dear Father,

We love You and praise You. You are God. Lord, forgive us for the times we have failed to put Your love into action in our lives. We desire to move from conformity to spiritual transformation and ultimately reflect You. Today, as we study Your holy Word, teach us about love. Equip us with the ability to love the unlovable. Thank You that we do not have to do this on our own. Lord, may You receive the glory. In Jesus' name, amen.

Today we will continue to examine John 13. Yesterday we discovered two steps to loving like Christ. First, to **live like our time is at hand** by loving with focus. Second, to **daily experience the full extent of Christ's love**, as we are present and vulnerable in our walks with Him. Please reread John 13:1–17 and then join me for the third point.

3. **Principle Three: Follow the pattern of Christ.**

The third "how to" of love is to follow the pattern of Christ. John 13:3 states: "Jesus knew that the Father had put all things under his power, and that he had come from God and was returning to God." In this verse we see a clear pattern established by Christ. When we follow this pattern, we discover a God-given ability to love. The pattern involves three steps:

A. Live from a position of submission. The first thing Jesus knew was that the Father had put all things under His power. Remember, Jesus is God and so had God-given authority to be supreme. In contrast to Jesus, we are not God! Therefore, we do not have this God-given right. In light of this truth, what position are we to take in regard to living in Christ? Our position in Christ is not found in supremacy but submissiveness.

Please read Ephesians 4:15–16 and describe both Christ's position and then our position in relationship to Christ.

_____

_____

_____

How often do you usurp Christ's authority and play the role of the head in your life or in the life of others?

_____

_____

_____

Dear friend, if you and I want to love like Christ, we must recognize that Christ is supreme. Christ is the Head of the church. Ephesians 4:16 testifies to this truth. Therefore, when we surrender to the supremacy of Christ, we mature in Christ and learn how to love like Christ.

B. Accept the circumstances of the past. The second thing Jesus knew was that He had come from God. In order to love like Christ, we must accept this truth. Like Christ, we came from God. In fact, the Bible teaches that we were in the mind of God long before the world was created. In The Message (a paraphrased version of the Bible) Ephesians 1:4 states: "Long before he laid down earth's foundations, he had us in mind, had settled on us as the focus of his love, to be made whole and holy by his love." This verse gently reminds that in God's economy there are no accidents, no mistakes, and no surprises when it comes to the creation of His children.

As an adopted child, I cannot tell you the peace that this truth brings to my life. I understand that regardless of the situation and circumstances of my birth, God had me in mind. As this truth has become a part of my life, peace has taken the place of unrest and allowed me the privilege to love like Christ.

How about you? Do you struggle with the circumstances of your birth? If so, why?

_____

_____

_____

Coming to a place of peace concerning the circumstances of our birth becomes the first step in accepting the circumstances of our past experiences. The second step involves dealing with the situations of life occurring since our birth. This step is necessary as we understand that some people do not love like Christ. You see, when we were born, we were born into sin. Being born into sin and being sinners ourselves means that all of us have experienced difficulties in life. These difficulties leave each of us with memories and struggles that can only be dealt with in God's way. While it is difficult to explore these issues of life, it is critical if we desire for Christ to heal the pains of life and pave the way for forward progress in our walks with Him.

Please describe a painful memory from your past. Use this time to pour your heart out to God, either on paper or by expressing it to Him out loud.

_____

_____

_____

What steps do you need to take in order to bring a sense of closure to your painful past?

_____

_____

_____

Sweet friend, I wish I could meet you and share in your pain. Although that may never happen, I praise God that through the blood of Jesus, I feel like I know you. And since I know you, I want you to know that I will fight for you and with you until freedom from your past becomes a reality in your life.

Over the years, I have had to fight for my freedom when it came to peace with my past. My struggle involved feeling rejected as a result of my adoption. These feelings led me to embrace unhealthy attitudes and actions as I tried to force a sense of peace into my heart, but that peace did not come. Peace finally came when I stopped trying to fix my past by turning my past over to God.

The Lord used a powerful verse to help deal with the pain from my past. 1 John 3:19–20 states: "This then is how we know that we belong to the truth, and how we set our hearts at rest in his presence whenever our hearts condemn us. For God is greater than our hearts, and he knows everything." What a promise from the Word of God! Our hearts can find rest in the presence of God. Further, God knows everything, and yet He does not condemn us. Dear sister, God is greater than our condemning hearts. What a word for us to hear and embrace!

What would it mean in your life if your heart were at peace with God?

_____

_____

_____

One thing it would mean involves an incredible God-given ability to love. You see, once peace resides in your heart, you can love God and love others with complete abandon.

C. Set your sight on your future home. The third thing Jesus knew was that He was returning to God. This point offers hope and peace as it draws our attention heavenward in Christ Jesus. May we never lose sight of the fact that knowing who we are in Christ always brings us to the point of forward movement in our walks with Christ. Throughout Scripture, believers are encouraged to focus on their heavenly home.

Please read Colossians 3:1–3. In this passage believers are encouraged to set their hearts and minds on things above. What an interesting thought—to set everything within you on things that are above. As we strive to live this kind of life, we understand that an amazing thing takes place as our value system changes. What the world once said or thought was necessary quickly loses its grip, as we desire to allow God's Word to be the most important standard in our lives. As God's thoughts become first and foremost in our hearts and minds, we respond to the continual call to love like Christ.

When you think about where you are going, do you typically think in earthly terms or heavenly terms?

_____

_____

_____

If you begin to think in heavenly terms, how will that impact your ability to love?

_____

_____

_____

4. **Principle Four: Love like Jesus loved.**

The fourth "how to" of love is simply loving like Jesus loved. John 13:4–5 carefully explains how Jesus washed the disciples' feet. Jesus got up from the meal, took off His outer clothing, wrapped a towel around His waist, poured water into a basin, and washed His disciples' feet. Once they were washed, Jesus dried the disciples' feet on a towel wrapped around His waist. What a beautiful picture of the painstaking approach of loving and caring for others!

The story continues in John 13:6–11. Making His way around the table, Jesus arrived at Peter's feet. Peter stated, "You shall never wash my feet." Jesus responded, "Unless I wash you, you have no part with me." Peter, not wanting to be left out, replied, "Not just my feet but my hands and head as well!" Jesus wanted to right Peter's misconception and said, "A person who has had a bath needs only to wash his feet; his whole body is clean."

I love Peter! Oh, how I can relate to the life and ministry of Peter, especially during the days leading up to the cross. More than anything, Peter wanted to get it right. Peter wanted to step up and be the man. In this passage, I sense Peter's desire to be spiritual—saying the right things and doing the right things. But in the end, Peter got this issue all wrong. As I considered Peter's thought process, I tried to place myself in his position and ask, "What would I have done if Jesus had knelt before me and taken my foot?" I have to admit I might have displayed Peter's same response. "Lord, do not do it. Lord, let me take care of You. Lord, please. This is not right."

In your opinion, did Peter understand the principle of love Jesus taught?

_____

_____

_____

I would like to submit that Peter did not fully understand everything Jesus taught. That is okay. We do not always understand what Jesus is teaching, but we always have the chance to learn. Peter had to learn that loving God and loving others would not always be easy, comfortable, or fit into his concept of right or wrong. No. Sometimes loving people is hard. It is uncomfortable. And, from a human perspective, it does not always make sense.

John 13:12–16 records Jesus' explanation of why He had washed the disciples' feet. Once He finished, Jesus returned to His seat and asked the disciples a question. Jesus asked, "Do you understand what I have done for you?" Before the disciples had a chance to respond, Jesus spoke to the heart of the issue. He stated: "I have set you an example…do as I have done."

This truth that Jesus taught came home to the disciples when Jesus reminded them that no servant is greater than their master and no messenger is greater than the one who sent them. As a result, Jesus taught the concept that the disciples were to **follow Him!** With this concept Jesus set the bar in regards to love. Genuine God-given love will only be extended as you love like Jesus loved. Loving like Jesus loved involves living like Jesus lived with humility and a willingness to serve.

How often do you love like Jesus loved with humility and a willingness to serve?

_____

_____

_____

John 13:17 concludes the passage. Jesus stated: "Now that you know these things, you will be blessed if you do them." Blessed? Is that what Jesus said? Yes, you will be blessed. Immediately we may wonder, what kind of blessing? Listen to the meaning of the Greek word used for *blessed.* "One is pronounced *blessed* when God is present and involved in his life. The hand of God is at work directing all his affairs for a divine purpose, and thus, in a sense, such a person lives before the face of God."[32]

In this meaning for the word blessed, we find the heart of Jesus' teaching. It's as if He says, "As you love like I love and as you serve like I serve, you become different. You are set apart. You are Mine." Why? Because loving and serving Jesus allows us to be intimately involved in His plans for our lives. Therefore, as Jesus becomes our focus throughout the day, our character changes so that every part of our day accomplishes His purposes through our lives. Lord, may it be so!

Application

As you and I surrender to the truths found in John 13, we can love anyone. Yes, anyone! Please do not miss the fact that Jesus demonstrated His love to all the disciples, including the disciple that would ultimately betray Him. Christ's example challenges each of us to love not only the lovely people but also the unlovely people in our lives.

Who is God calling you to love like never before?

_____

_____

_____

Will you step out by faith and love these people no matter the cost?

_____

If you are struggling with how to get started, begin by asking the Lord to help you see the difficult people in your life from His perspective. Pray specifically for each one and ask the Lord to give you His perspective on that person. Once you have God's perspective, it will become much easier to love that person like never before

Conclusion

As I sit here today, God amazes me. I now understand why God wanted you and me to study the topic of love. Truly, this life is all about love. When thinking about love, ask yourself this question, "Do I love like Christ?" How can you know? Use the Word of God as your guide.

- Do I love like my time is at hand as seen in **focused living**?
- Do I daily experience the full extent of His love by being **present** and **vulnerable**?
- Do I follow the pattern of Christ by **living from a position of submission, accepting the circumstances of my past,** and **setting my sights on heaven**?
- Do I love like Jesus loved by **living a humble and willing life**?

The answers to these questions indicate if the character quality of love is present and active in your life. So, my friend, how are you doing with love?

_____

_____

_____

_____

_____

Reflecting His Glory

Week 4: "…but be transformed…"

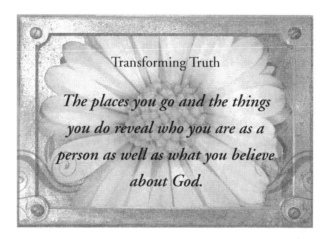

Transforming Truth

The places you go and the things you do reveal who you are as a person as well as what you believe about God.

Day 1: Changes in Habitats and Habits, Part 1

Welcome to Week Four! Dear friend, you have made it to the halfway point of the study. I am so proud of you. Let me encourage you to hold fast to the study of God's Word and particular to the study portions of these lessons. God through His Holy Spirit will teach you so many wonderful truths. Hang in there. You do not want to miss them!

This week we will continue to explore the topic of spiritual metamorphosis by examining the final step in the process—changing our habitats and habits. This part of the change process becomes the outworking of the three previous steps as it challenges each of us to examine **where we go, what we do,** and **who influences us along the way**.

As we open our study time with prayer, I would like to use the words from the classic hymn, *Revive Us Again.* As you pray this song, please allow the words to fix your heart and mind on the Lord. If possible, say or sing the words out loud in an expression of love to God.

We praise thee, O God for the Son of thy love, for Jesus who died and is now gone above. Hallelujah, thine the glory. Hallelujah, amen. Hallelujah, thine the glory. Revive us again.

We praise thee, O God, for thy Spirit of light, who hath shown us our Savior and scattered our night. Hallelujah, thine the glory. Hallelujah, amen. Hallelujah, thine the glory. Revive us again.

All glory and praise to the Lamb that was slain, who hath borne all our sins, and hath cleans'd every stain. Hallelujah, thine the glory. Hallelujah, amen. Hallelujah, thine the glory. Revive us again.

Revive us again; fill each heart with thy love; may each soul be rekindled with fire from above. Hallelujah, thine the glory. Hallelujah, amen. Hallelujah, thine the glory. Revive us again.[33]

As the words from this powerful hymn challenge each of us to position our hearts for spiritual revival, we turn our attention to the outward evidences of revival as we examine our habitats and habits. Let's dig in!

Changes in Habitats

 In your own words, please define *habitat*.

_____

_____

_____

For the purposes of this study, we will define *habitats* as "the places where something is commonly found." I love this definition because it gets straight to the point. At the heart of our individual habitats resides an inherent preference for a particular setting. As a result of these preferences, natural migrations occur that draw us to common or comfortable environments. These environments are the places where we feel at ease because our needs are met, such as our homes, a friend's home, our church, the mall, the gym, etc. In short, our habitats are the frequent, familiar, and regular places we go in order to feel comfortable, relaxed, and reassured.

Please list your top five habitats—the places where you go in order to feel comfortable, relaxed, and reassured. (Please do not feel the need to be spiritual. Be honest with yourself and the Lord!)

1. _____
2. _____
3. _____
4. _____
5. _____

Now that you have listed your top five habitats, please take a few minutes and write your thoughts about each habitat. List the positive and negative aspects for each.

_____

_____

_____

_____

_____

Changes in Habits

In your own words, please define *habit*.

_____

_____

_____

_____

_____

For this study, we will define *habit* as "a settled tendency of attitude or acquired manner of behavior that has become almost involuntary." As we look at this definition, three words jump off the page to me.

- Settled—When I think of something that is settled, I think there is no longer any resistance to that thing.
- Tendency—When I think of a tendency, I think of something that occurs regularly and without thought.
- Behavior—When I think of behavior, I think of something that always results in action. This action may be an inward attitude or an outward expression.

From these thoughts we can say that habits **occur with little or no resistance, regularly and without any thought, and always result in inward attitudes or outward actions**. For example, one of my habits is organizing when I feel like my life is out of control. Therefore, when I begin to feel like I cannot control events in my life, I regularly turn my attention to something I can control. This turning to organization occurs naturally and with little or no resistance. Unless I make a conscious choice to turn to the Lord instead of an organizing task, I will consistently organize instead of pray. This outward action is an example of a habit in my life. Isn't it amazing to think about the things we do with little or no thought?

In the space provided below, please list some of your habits—the things you do **with little or no resistance, regularly and without any thought, and that always result in inward attitudes or outward actions**. (Again, do not feel the need to be spiritual. Be honest and write down your habits as soon as they pop into your mind.)

Now that you have listed many of your habits, please take a few minutes and write your thoughts about each.

Last night I was reminded about the importance of our habits. My son Jake and I were reading a nightly devotion entitled "Changing Habits." The purpose of the devotion was to remind the child to be careful about the things that he or she does. One phrase stated, "First you make your habits; then your habits make you. So it's always a good time to ask yourself this question: 'What kind of person are my habits making me?'"[34] Jake and I talked about this statement at length. In our time of discussion, I shared with Jake that the Lord was also teaching me about the importance of my habits. I told Jake how I was learning that habits occur **with little or no resistance, regularly and without any thought,** and **always result in attitudes and actions**. I asked Jake, "What is one habit that occurs in your life that needs to change?

Jake thought about this question and then blew me away with his response. He said, "When you give me an instruction and I say, 'But, Mom…'"

I was immediately touched by Jake's response. I thought in my mind, "He is getting it!" I asked Jake, "Why is saying, 'But, Mom…' a bad habit?" Jake said, "Because I do it without even thinking." Thank You, Lord, for teaching our children!

Clear Warning from Scripture

Without a doubt, an ungodly habitat or habit undermines the process of reflecting His glory. This is true because the places we go and the things we do reveal who we are as well as what we believe about God. In light of this truth, Scripture teaches that God has set forth guidelines in the believer's life in regards to proper habitats and habits.

- **Habitats:** Please look up and read Acts 17:26–28. What truth is Paul communicating to the men of Athens regarding people's habitats?

_____

_____

_____

_____

In Acts 17:26–28 Paul communicates three truths.
- First, from one man God made every nation of men. This passage speaks of Adam and reminds God's people that God is the Creator and He has been in control from the beginning of time. In this verse, we find one reason why God made man. Verse 26 states; "…that they should *inhabit* the whole earth" (emphasis added). The word inhabit means "to dwell, to reside, settle down and live; this word suggests more than the mere presence or existence of the subject but also the establishment of a connection between him and the site."[35]

- Second, God determined the times set forth for man. From this point, we can know that we should receive each day we live on this earth as a gift from the Lord. Our lives and breath do not belong to us. Rather, the Lord grants life and breath, and we have the opportunity to honor Him in the way we live.

- Third, God set the exact places where man should live. You will find it interesting to note that the Greek word used for *exact places* means "habitation, dwelling, or abode."[36] This truth provides scriptural support to the call for examining our habitats and ensuring that our current habitats match His appointed habitats for us.

Acts 17:27 records the reason for God's actions: "God did this so that men would seek him and perhaps reach out for him and find him." God established proper habitats for His children so that as we move and breathe on His earth within the habitats that He has ordained, we are positioned to seek and find Him. What a great reason to examine our habitats!

From Scripture, do you see the call to examine the places we go? Please explain.

_____

_____

_____

- **Habits:** Please look up and read 1 Peter 4:1–3, then answer the following questions.

What do verses 1 and 2 teach regarding the benefit of suffering?

_____

_____

_____

_____

List the habits from verse 3 that we are to leave behind.

_____

_____

_____

Two important points surface in this short passage of Scripture. First, Peter provides a formula for ridding our lives of unnecessary and sinful habits. Second, Peter lists possible habits that might be a part of our lives. Let's look at each.

The formula for ridding our lives of sinful habits

1 Peter 4:1 states: "Therefore, since Christ suffered in his body, arm yourselves also with the same attitude, **because he who has suffered in his body is done with sin"** (emphasis added). In order to deal with sinful, self-gratifying habits (such as addiction, overeating, or worrying), suffering must become a part of our lives. The reason is in 1 Peter 4:2. Suffering becomes the path to freedom as it enables the believer to no longer "live the rest of his earthly life for evil human desires, but rather for the will of God."

From experience, I can share that any time I want to rid my life of a sinful habit, I find some way to apply pressure to my physical body. I do not look for ways to hurt myself, but I do look for ways to totally deny my flesh. One of the primary ways I deny my flesh is by fasting. In the fasting process, the human desire (represented by sinful habits) and the spiritual desire (represented by the moving of the Holy Spirit) go head to head in a battle for supremacy.

As you and I suffer in the flesh, we make the choice to fight the desires of the flesh by allowing the Spirit to change us. During the suffering process, everything inside wants to give in and take part in the sinful habit. However, as we stand firm against that tendency in Jesus' name, we find freedom as God's will has the power to win out over human desire.

Fasting can take many different forms. We can fast from food or by intentionally giving up any creature comfort. Fasting applies physical pressure to my body and places me in a position of surrender. As I surrender, God does a work in my heart that can only be attributed to Him. It is not uncommon for me to come out of a time of fasting over a sinful habit and not only have a lack of desire to take part in the habit but also experience a physical discomfort over the thought of taking part in the habit. In essence, the thought of taking part in the habit makes me feel sick to my stomach.

1 Peter 4:3 provides the reason for the suffering process: "For you have spent enough time in the past doing what pagans choose to do…." Do you hear the plea from Scripture? If I listen closely, I can hear Peter saying, "Enough!" Enough with all the sinful habits! How about you? Have you had enough? I hope so!

List of possible habits:

1 Peter 4:3 goes on to list possible habits that may play a role in our lives. Although we do not use many of these words in today's culture, the sinful habits are still in use. Peter lists the sinful habits of debauchery, lust, drunkenness, orgies, carousing, and detestable idolatry. For us today, we might list sinful habits like impure thoughts, excessive drinking, impure sexual actions, gossip, laziness, pride, arrogance—the list goes on and on.

Conclusion

As we close, do you see the importance of godly habitats in your life? If so, please explain.

_____

_____

_____

Do you see the importance of ridding your life of ungodly habits? If so, please explain.

_____

_____

_____

What role can suffering play in doing away with your sinful habitats and habits?

_____

_____

_____

Are you willing to do whatever it takes to reflect Christ in the places you go and the things you do? If so, please close with a prayer asking the Lord to give you a discerning heart when it comes to sinful habitats and habits.

_____

_____

_____

Reflecting His Glory

Week 4: "...but be transformed..."

> Transforming Truth
>
> *Daily you make judgment calls between two or more paths. Will you live for the things of God or the things of this world?*

Day 2: Changes In Habitats and Habits (Continued)

Today in our study we are taking the call to examine and change our habitats and habits to the next level! Join me as we pray.

Dear Lord,

We praise You, for You are God. Forgive us for the times we have placed our desires before Your desires. As we continue to examine our habitats and habits, help us to be mindful of You. Lord, may we desire to live pure lives before You. Teach us today, for Your glory! Amen.

Yesterday we defined a *habitat* as a place where something is commonly found, and we said a *habit* is a settled tendency or usual manner of behavior. Our habitats and habits are important to God because they reflect the inward condition of our hearts. Today as we seek to *reflect His glory*, we are going to go one step further regarding our habitats and habits.

One Step Further

When thinking about our habitats and habits, clear-cut issues of sin are not the only areas that keep believers from *reflecting His glory*. Sometimes the **places we go** and the **things we do** may not seem wrong by the world's standards. When we compare them, however, to God's standards, those places and things can be recognized as completely offensive to God. Leviticus 10:10 teaches this truth. Write the verse in the space provided below, then answer the following question.

Leviticus 10:10

_____

_____

_____

_____

What portion of Leviticus 10:10 communicates truth to you and why?

_____

_____

_____

_____

In Leviticus 10:1–11 we read the story of how Aaron, Israel's high priest, suffered a great loss. A high priest was a man God allowed to enter the Holy of Holies once a year on the Day of Atonement to offer sacrifice for the sins of the nation of Israel. Aaron was the first high priest, and his family line became the priestly line from which God called future high priests.

Aaron's sons Nadab and Abihu served as priests. Nadab and Abihu misused their priestly office when they offered unauthorized fire before the Lord. This meant that Nadab and Abihu did not follow the instructions the Lord had given concerning how to offer a sacrifice. As a result of their disobedience, fire came out from the presence of the Lord and consumed them, and they died. Moses instructed Nadab and Abihu's cousins to take their bodies outside the camp and then told Aaron not to mourn for his sons. The Lord spoke to Aaron and provided further direction for how the priest should offer sacrifices.

These instructions were based on the principle, "You must distinguish between the holy and the common, between the unclean and the clean."

Today, evangelical Christians believe in the doctrine of the priesthood of the believer. This doctrine teaches that we do not have to go through any other person to have a relationship with God. Rather, we have direct access to God based on the finished work of Jesus Christ on the cross, and we also have responsibility to minister to others. As a result of this truth, we too must know how to distinguish between the holy things of God and the common things of this world as taught in Leviticus 10:10. In order to study this challenge, we will examine each word of Leviticus 10:10 and gain life-changing truths from the Word of God.

• *You*—From the beginning of this verse we see an immediate and personal call. As New Testament believers, we can take the word *you* as a personal word of direction. Remember, we live on the New Testament side of the cross; as a result, we do not depend on another human being to fulfill the role of a priest in our lives. The moment Jesus died on the cross and the veil was torn in the temple, the *you* in this passage moved from a call on the priest's lives to a call on individuals' lives. Please meditate on the word *you* and record your thoughts below.

_____

_____

_____

_____

The word *you* used in this passage conveys the necessity for each individual to personally take up this call and respond in obedience.

• *Must*—When we read the word *must* it is easy to hear the imperative from this call. When you hear the word *must*, what comes to your mind?

_____

_____

_____

_____

When I hear the word *must* I am reminded that I have no choice in the matter. Either I will obey and please God, or I will ignore the call and allow sin into my life.

• *Distinguish*—The two prior words listed in the verse, *you* and *must*, lead up to the word *distinguish*. When you hear the word *distinguish*, what concept comes into your mind?

_____

_____

_____

When I hear the word *distinguish* the concept that comes into my mind involves discernment or making a judgment call.

• *Between*—The word *between* portrays the idea that the judgment call will involve at least two choices. In your daily life, how often do you make judgment calls *between* two or more paths?

_____

_____

_____

Daily I make judgment calls *between* two or more paths. These judgment calls involve issues ranging from getting out of bed or staying in bed to seeking God's direction for the day or walking through the day focused on myself. Scripture repeatedly teaches the importance of understanding the *between* concept of the Christian faith. Please look up the following verses and record your thoughts for each. Be sure to record the two choices listed in each passage. (Some of the verses use the word "choose" to convey this concept.)

Deuteronomy 30:19–20

_____

_____

_____

Joshua 24:15

_____

_____

_____

1 Kings 3:8–10

_____

_____

_____

1 Kings 18:21

_____

_____

_____

Proverbs 8:10–11

_____

_____

_____

Matthew 7:13–14

_____

_____

_____

James 4:4

_____

_____

_____

From the Scriptures listed above, we see that believers face a daily choice *between* living for the things of this world and living for the things of God. In Leviticus 10:10, two categories represent this choice. Let's look at each one.

• *Holy/Clean*

The first category involves the *holy* and the *clean*. Please read the definitions and write your thoughts below.

> **Holy:** The Hebrew word used for *holy* in this verse means holiness, holy things, or something consecrated to God. This word is different from the notion of something grand or magnificent.

_____

_____

_____

_____

> **Clean:** The Hebrew word used for *clean* means to be clean, pure, purified, or unalloyed. (The word alloyed means "to reduce the purity of by mixing with a less valuable metal."[37])

_____

_____

_____

• *Common/ Unclean*

The second category involves the *common* and *unclean*. Please read the definitions and then write your thoughts below.

> **Common**: This Hebrew word means profane or unholy and is used to denote the opposite of holy or consecrated.

_____

_____

_____

> **Unclean:** This Hebrew word is used to refer to unclean persons, animals, or things and oftentimes is used in a moral sense.

_____

_____

_____

These two categories represent two very different lifestyles. One lifestyle the believer is called to embrace. The other lifestyle the believer is called to shun.

In the *holy/clean* lifestyle, we see an individual who understands the call to live a life consecrated to God. I love two things about the *holy/clean* life. First, it does not occur on a grand or magnificent scale. What a great word from the Word! In order to be holy in God's sight, we do not have to live a life that would be attributed to a "spiritual giant." Please let this truth sink in and set you free from performance-based religion. Holiness becomes the reality of our lives not as we live a grand or magnificent life for God but rather as we live a spiritually consistent life before God. The second thing I love about the *holy/clean* life is that it occurs as we recognize that the world we live in reduces our purity by mixing in a less valuable substance. If we desire to live the holy and clean life, then the world simply cannot be added into the mix.

In the *common/unclean* lifestyle, we see an individual who chooses to live a life focused on the things of this world. This person looks to ordinary things in order to gain soul satisfaction. When this becomes our approach to life, something we may consider innocent or common becomes profane in God's sight. Our habitats and habits do not necessarily have to be identifiable sins like gossip, pride, or greed to be offensive to God. Something as common or innocent as a relationship with a person, an environment that we are drawn to, or a habit that occurs in our life becomes offensive every time we focus on it instead of on God.

Application

Today we must distinguish between the *holy/clean* and *common/unclean* in our daily walks with God.

In your daily life, do you distinguish between these two categories?

_____

_____

_____

_____

More often than not, do you live the *holy/clean* or the *common/unclean* life?

_____

_____

Conclusion

Although today's lesson has focused on the outworkings of a changed life in Christ, we simply cannot conclude this day without making a necessary point. At any point when our **habitats or habits involve repeated patterns of sin or common/unclean tendencies, the heart must become the focus for the redemptive work of Christ.**

With this thought clear in our minds, please close with a prayer asking God to continually change your heart so that the places you go and the things you do reflect His glory.

_____

_____

_____

_____

_____

_____

Reflecting His Glory

Week 4: "...but be transformed..."

> Transforming Truth
>
> *Following God's guidelines for friendships decreases our tendency to follow the crowd and increases our ability to reflect the glory of Christ.*

Day 3: Who is Influencing Your Habitats and Habits?

Over the last two days we have examined God's thoughts regarding our habitats and habits. Through Scripture we have been challenged to examine the places we go and the things we do. With this call fresh on our minds, we'll devote the next two days to the number one influencer in our habitats and habits—our friends. Let me begin by telling you a story from my life.

It was a Monday morning, but my boys had that day off school and were home. I had failed to wake up early and have my quiet time, so my day was off to bad start! Instead of spending time with the Lord, I spent my morning washing dishes and cleaning my house. Around 10:30, I knew I needed to spend some time with the Lord. I quickly called the boys and told them, "Mommy needs to have her quiet time." Once I instructed the boys to make no interruptions, I ran to my prayer closet. My prayer closet is actually my bedroom closet; that's where I go when I desire to be alone with the Lord. My boys know that when I am in my prayer closet, they are only to interrupt me for emergencies. I began my time with God by confessing my sin. I confessed that I started my day off without the Lord. God, in His grace, met me there, and we had a great time of fellowship.

Following my prayer time, I opened my Bible for a time of reading. On this particular day, I read from Exodus 23 and the second verse caught my attention. Exodus 23:2 states: **"Do not follow the crowd in doing wrong."** I read this verse a few more times and made a mental note to come back and explore this passage. I knew this verse contained a strong warning for believers, especially regarding the places we go and the things we do. I also thought, "I need to share this truth with Jake."

As I continued reading, the time simply got away from me. I was having such a good time with the Lord that I did not want it to end. After a while, I started to hear some rustling outside the door and immediately knew someone was out there. Before long, Jake stuck his head in and in his happiest, peppiest, singing voice sang, "Mom, are you almost done?" I sang back, "Jake, you're in trouble." Jake sang to me, "I know." And I could not help but laugh—Jake knew he was not allowed to interrupt my quiet time!

I then told Jake to come into my prayer closet because I had a verse that I wanted to share with him. Jake came in, and we talked about Exodus 23:2. We talked about how the crowd can lead us away from God and that it is important from an early age to walk closely with God so that we are not scared to stand alone. We discussed specific struggles that Jake faced when it comes to following the crowd and brainstormed ideas about ways he could stand firm.

We closed with a word of prayer, and then I said, "Let's talk about your consequence."

Jake was puzzled and said, "Consequence?"

"Yes," I said, "consequence. You came into the prayer closet, and it was not an emergency. You know the rules."

Jake looked at me with a straight face and said, "Mom, the Holy Spirit sent me in here because I needed to hear that verse." I had to laugh! What a kid! I thought if God granted me grace over failing to start my day with Him, then I could certainly grant Jake grace over interrupting my quiet time!

As this story from my life gives you a glimpse into my home, I pray it sets the stage for this topic—examining the crowds in our lives. The crowd represents the people who influence the places we go and the things we do. As we begin, I have one question for you: "Did the Holy Spirit send you in here to receive instruction from His Word?" I hope so! Let's pray.

Dear Lord,

You are our mighty, awesome, and powerful God. All praise belongs to You. Lord, we proclaim that there is none like You. We thank You for Your grace; we recognize that we do not deserve it, but, oh, how we need it. I thank You for the personal reminder You have given me that I daily need Your grace. May we be faithful to recognize this truth and extend Your grace to others as they have the need. Lord, as we examine the people that influence our habitats and habits, give us wisdom to discern Your will. We give You the glory, and we give You the praise. In Jesus' name, amen.

Who's in your crowd?

As we examine our habitats and habits, we also need to examine the individuals who influence our habitat and habits. I cannot overstate the importance of this process. As I have lived through my twenties and am now in my thirties, I can say without a doubt that peer pressure continues to play a role in my life. Thankfully, each year the pressure decreases, but the reality remains the same. As much as I hate to admit this truth, I would be lying to you and to myself if I did not recognize the influence others have on the places I go and the things I do.

In light of this truth, the warning from Exodus 23:2 takes on a new sense of urgency as we desire more than anything to reflect the glory of Christ. Please look up Exodus 23:2 and write the first phrase of this verse in the space below.

_____

_____

_____

Why do you think God provided this warning?

_____

_____

_____

The first phrase of Exodus 23:2 states: "Do not follow the crowd in doing wrong." God gave this clear warning to Moses on Mt. Sinai. Moses was on Mt. Sinai receiving the Ten Commandments and additional instruction the nation of Israel needed in order to properly function as the people of God. As we understand that this warning was given to teach the nation of Israel how to live as God's people, we grasp the importance of this warning for our daily lives. If we desire to *reflect His glory,* we too must live according to the standards set forth in His Word.

The *crowd* in this passage of Scripture represents the many people in each of our lives that influence us. The NIV translation *crowd* provides a wonderful word picture as each of us quickly pictures the people who come in and out of our lives. We must stand against the many people around us who take part in wrong choices. As we hear this warning from Scripture, we must examine our hearts and ask the question, "At any level in my life, am I following, participating with, or engaging with a negative crowd?"

Do you struggle with following the crowd? Please explain.

_____

_____

_____

What struggles do you have in your life as a result of following the crowd?

_____

_____

_____

Please describe your *crowd*—the people you have a tendency to follow, participate with, and engage with when you are around them. I ask you to be as specific as possible when answering this question. If you are worried about hurting someone's feelings, answer this question on another sheet of paper and then keep the sheet of paper in a safe place.

_____

_____

_____

_____

How do these individuals influence you in a negative direction when it comes to your habitats (the places you go) and habits (the things you do)? If necessary, list each individual or group of people and then answer the question in the space below.

_____

_____

_____

_____

_____

_____

_____

_____

_____

Straight Answers from the Word of God

If we are honest, we all struggle with the crowd at some level in our lives. Human nature creates tension when our hearts desire to follow those around us even when we know it is wrong. Thankfully, God in His sovereignty understood this tendency and by His grace provided straight answers from His Word. These straight answers provide tangible ways to deal with the issue of a negative crowd in our lives.

Please look up Proverbs 12:26 and write the verse in the space below.

_____

_____

Proverbs 12:26 states that one character quality of a righteous individual is *caution in friendships.* The second half of the verse gives the reason: "The way of the wicked leads them astray." God has set forth clear parameters in His Word for our friendships. As we follow these guidelines, the tendency to follow the crowd in doing wrong decreases, and our ability to reflect the glory of Christ increases.

In light of this instruction, each of us must examine our friendships. We need to ask ourselves this question, "How do the individuals in my life influence me in a godly direction?" If the answer is, "They do not," then we must set proper boundaries.

Application

Friends can be a wonderful blessing from the Lord. They can also influence us negatively. As we seek God's perspective on friendships, we must have a foundational principle firm in our mind. The following picture represents this principle.

You will note that the woman in this picture has something beautiful in her hands. It's something God created and something that brings her enjoyment. But the woman is not holding onto the object. Instead, she is allowing the object to rest in her hands.

Our friendships must follow the same guideline. We do not hold onto friendships at any cost. Rather, we allow God to bring people in and out of our lives for His glory. This newfound freedom makes a difference in our perspective as we realize that there will be people that God brings into our lives and then quickly ushers out. Once we begin to live our lives with open hands, the tendency to follow the crowd decreases as we make a choice to stop allowing friendships to influence us in the wrong direction.

Allow me to share one example from my life. When my husband and I made the transition from living as uncommitted Christians to living life totally surrendered to the Lord, an interesting thing took place in our friendships. We simply could not go out with some of our old friends. The places they went and the things they did made us uncomfortable. It was hard to let some of these friendships go, and we tried to maintain some contact. However, our life had changed. God removed those friendships from our life and replaced them with new ones. This was hard for me because I wanted to hold on to everyone. In the end, the open hand concept brought freedom as I realized that

God brings friends and He takes friends. My job is to be faithful to recognize what He is doing and cooperate.

🌼 Please share your thoughts about having open hands regarding the friendships in your life.

_____

_____

_____

_____

Do you tend to hold on to friendships even if they are not beneficial?

_____

_____

_____

_____

Does this tendency cause you to follow the crowd in doing wrong?

_____

_____

_____

_____

_____

_____

🌼 Are you open to redefining the friendships in your life?

_____

_____

_____

_____

Conclusion

We will spend tomorrow's study looking at the redefining process. For now, please close with a time of prayer committing yourself to honestly examining the friendships in your life.

_____

_____

_____

_____

_____

_____

_____

_____

_____

_____

_____

_____

_____

_____

Reflecting His Glory

Week 4: "...but be transformed..."

Transforming Truth

God allows different people to be our friends and to play different roles in our lives.

Day 4: Biblical Friendship Roles

Today we continue our look at the people who influence our habitats and habits. Yesterday we studied how the Word of God cautions each of us about friendships that lead us away from godliness. In today's lesson, we will continue to explore the topic of friendships and learn that God has allowed different people to be our friends and to play different roles in our lives. While each person is a gift from God and should be treated with love and grace, not all people should have the same level of influence in our lives. For a change of pace, I would like to invite *you* to open our time with a word of prayer. You may use the space below or speak a prayer out loud.

_____

_____

Biblical Friendship Roles

As we look to the Word of God, we can recognize three categories of friends, spotlighting the different roles individuals can play in our lives. Before we dig in, please allow me to share a brief comment about today's study. These definitions of friendship roles can never be viewed as hard and fast rules. There will always be people who blend different categories or present a unique flavor in our lives. Many of the people we know will stay in the category of acquaintances—people with whom we don't share significant experiences. Therefore, please allow the roles presented in today's lesson to set broad parameters. Ultimately, we must allow the Holy Spirit to show the personal application we should have as a result of today's lesson. With that said, let's begin.

1. **Close Friends**—We can think of these friends as the inner circle of people who encourage us to have a right heart before God. These friends hold us accountable on the tough issues of life. 1 Samuel 20 provides the biblical basis for this type of friendship. Please read 1 Samuel 20:1–42 and answer the questions below.

Please list the names of the two individuals found in this account.

_____

In 1 Samuel 20:4, what was Jonathan willing to do for David?

_____

1 Samuel 20:8 states David and Jonathan had entered into what?

_____

According to verse 8, when David and Jonathan entered into this covenant, who was it before?

_____

In 1 Samuel 20:13, what does Jonathan ask the Lord to do if he does not uphold his portion of the covenant?

_____

_____

What is Jonathan's great desire for David according to verse 13b?

_____

According to 1 Samuel 20:42, who was the central focus of David and Jonathan's friendship?

_____

As the story of David and Jonathan unfolds, we learn that David and Jonathan were more concerned with one another's relationship with God than anything else. Without a doubt, David and Jonathan held one another **accountable** on the tough issues of life. This accountability revealed the very heart of a close friendship—helping one another grow in their love relationship with Jesus Christ.

Characteristics of Close Friendships
- The Lord is the central focus of the friendship.
- There is a willingness to do anything for one another.
- Both parties recognize the authority of the Lord and as a result have a proper fear of God. This fear becomes the motivating factor for treating one another with Christ-like love.
- A high trust level exists between friends, allowing them to call on one another day or night.
- The Word of God becomes the standard by which each party lives.
- Even in times of disagreement or tension, close friends ask tough questions and seek truth. Once the truth is found, decisions are made based on God's desire, not human desire.
- Accountability plays a paramount role in this type of friendship.

Please list your close friends and record which characteristics they display in your friendship:

_____

_____

_____

_____

_____

2. **Caring Friends**—Like a close friendship, a caring friendship finds its central focus in a love relationship with Jesus Christ. Please note, close friends and caring friends are not that different. We see the primary difference in that the close friend focuses on account-ability while the caring friend focuses on loving, encouraging, and supporting. Because

of the broader focus of the caring friend, this type of friendship can occur on a much larger scale and include as many people as we like. We see this type of friendship displayed in the early church. Please read Acts 2:42-46 then record each action taken by the caring friends.

_____

_____

_____

_____

_____

The members of the early church devoted themselves to teaching, fellowship, breaking bread, and prayer. The friends had everything in common and daily praised God with one another. As we think about the category of caring friendship, the early church becomes a perfect model for us to follow.

Characteristics of a Caring Friendship

• Both people possess a passionate love for God.
• Both friends obey the Word of God and hold the Word of God as their standard for how to live.
• The friends have important things in common.
• Both parties are willing to give to one another in times of need.
• Caring friends genuinely enjoy being around one another and always feel edified after their time together.
• Both parties feel a freedom to be sincere with one anther. Caring friends do not feel the need to be superficial or be someone they are not.
• Caring friends are fun friends and available in times of need.

Please list your caring friends and record which characteristics they display in your friendship:

_____

_____

_____

_____

_____

3. **Casual Friends**—As we look at this category, we sense an immediate change in the realm of influence allowed in this type of friendship. A casual friend is someone we know and with whom we share some common interest. However, this person does not necessarily share our same beliefs, values, and moral standards. A passionate pursuit of the things of God is not seen in this person's life. Topics such as the Bible and moral standards of excellence may become dividing lines as we seek to live our lives according to the Scriptures.

Because of this critical difference in beliefs, we must set boundaries. If proper boundaries are not set, trouble looms as we may find ourselves heavily influenced in a negative direction.

Extreme caution must be used in order to honor God through casual friendships. We may enjoy being with a casual friend and find appropriate situations in order to spend time with her. However, we must be careful. We cannot disclose as much information to this person because she does not have the spiritual maturity to handle personal intimate details regarding life. Therefore, the goal of the casual friendship is for us to interact with this person so that she can see that Jesus makes a real difference in our life. Through casual friendships, God can open a door for us to minister in His name. This opportunity occurs as we **set the tone** for this type of friendship by determining the places, conversations, and activities that God deems appropriate.

Jesus shared important words of instruction regarding casual friends. In Matthew 9:35-38 we see the heart of Jesus as He looked around and saw people who needed to recognize Jesus as their Shepherd. Please read this passage and answer the questions below.

In verse 36, what did Jesus see?

_____

What feeling did Jesus have for the people he saw?

_____

Why did Jesus have compassion on them?

_____

_____

_____

What did Jesus instruct the disciples to ask the Lord?

_____

_____

_____

Why did Jesus give these instructions?

_____

_____

_____

In this passage we read an amazing teaching. Jesus looked around and saw the crowds! I find this truth incredible. Remember the instruction we read yesterday from Exodus 23:2? "Do not follow the crowd in doing wrong." As we follow this teaching from Exodus it becomes natural for us to wonder what we should do with the crowds in our lives. We find the answer to this question displayed in the heart and life of Jesus. Matthew 9:36 states: "When he saw the crowds, he had compassion on them." Why did Jesus have compassion? Verse 36 concludes, "Because they were harassed and helpless, like sheep without a shepherd." As you and I seek to have the same attitude as Jesus, we too should look at the crowds in our lives and have a heart of compassion as we look for opportunities to minister in Jesus' name.

This passage concludes with Jesus' thoughts on the topic of investing in the lives of others. Matthew 9:37 states: "The harvest is plentiful but the workers are few. Ask the Lord of the harvest, therefore, to send out workers into his harvest field." Dear friend, as you and I reach out to our casual friends in the name of Jesus, we take up God's call to be harvesters among the crowds of life.

Characteristics of a Casual Friendship
- This type of friend is placed in our lives for the purpose of investing. Therefore, as we are friends with this person, we look for spiritual opportunities to share the love and grace of Christ.
- This friendship is based primarily on mutual interests or similar life stage.
- Foundational beliefs about God, Bible, and moral excellence are not shared.
- Boundaries are imperative so that we do not lose our spiritual focus as we interact with this friend. If boundaries are not set, this person can influence us towards ungodliness.

Please list your casual friends and the way in which you set boundaries with these friends:

_____

_____

_____

_____

_____

_____

_____

Conclusion

As you examine your categories of friendships and the people in each, do you have any individuals out of place? If so, please list who they are and explain the problem.

_____

_____

_____

_____

_____

_____

_____

_____

What is God calling you to do in light of this realization?

_____

_____

_____

_____

_____

Will you do it?

_____

Please close with a word of prayer expressing your desire and willingness to follow the
Lord.

_____

_____

_____

_____

_____

_____

_____

_____

_____

Reflecting His Glory

Week 4: "…but be transformed…"

> Transforming Truth
>
> *Spiritual metamorphosis involves an inward call for change that leads to outward expressions of love and devotion to the Lord*

Day 5: Spiritual Metamorphosis Recap

Over the last three weeks, we have examined the spiritual metamorphosis process. I am amazed at the amount of lessons we can learn on this topic. Today we will recap the metamorphosis process and determine at least one final goal for each area in our lives.

Dear Lord,

We glorify and honor Your name. O Lord, You are our God, and we find everything we need wrapped up in You. May we see ourselves transformed through the power of Jesus Christ. Lord, grant each of us sensitive ears and sensitive hearts to hear and apply Your Word of truth. In Jesus' name, amen.

If you will recall, Romans 12:2 serves as the focus passage for *Reflecting His Glory*.

Do not conform any longer to the pattern of this world, but be transformed by the renewing of your mind. Then you will be able to test and approve what God's will is—his good, pleasing and perfect will. (Romans 12:2)

Over the last three weeks we examined the phrase "but be transformed." As we studied this phrase, we discovered a call to spiritual metamorphosis. By memory (if possible), please list the four areas of spiritual metamorphosis.

- _____
- _____
- _____
- _____

I hope you remembered that the spiritual metamorphosis process involves a **significant change in form, spiritual growth, differentiation, and changes in habitats and habits**. For each topic, we worked through several lessons to uncover spiritual truths about the metamorphosis process. As we studied these truths, we found an inward call for change that led to outward expressions of love and devotion to the Lord. As we wrap up this portion of our study, we are going to put the entire spiritual metamorphosis process together and see the results of a changed life in Christ.

Significant Change In Form

The first step in the spiritual metamorphosis process calls for a significant change in form. The first aspect of this process involved entering into a personal relationship with Jesus Christ through the process of salvation. As we discussed this step, we asked the question, "Do I know for sure that when I die I will spend eternity in heaven with Jesus?" If you are still not sure that Jesus is your Savior and Lord, please turn to Week 2, Lesson 2. Read the lesson again and prayerfully consider receiving Christ as your Lord. Once you have asked Jesus to be your Lord and Savior, please share your decision with a friend, a member of your Bible study, or a staff member of a Bible-believing church.

The second aspect of a significant change in form called for on-going change as we made it our goal to reflect the glory of Christ in every area of our lives. 1 Thessalonians 4:1 provided the scriptural basis for this call. Paul urged, "We instructed you how to live in order to please God, as in fact you are living. **Now we ask you and urge you in the Lord Jesus to do this *more* and *more*.**" As we discussed the concept of looking more like

Christ, acting more like Christ, and reflecting more of Christ in our daily walks, we discovered the call to put off the old self and to put on the new self created to be like Christ in true righteousness and holiness. Ephesians 4:22–24 became the formula for this approach as we resolved every day to put off our old self, be made new in the attitudes of our minds, and put on the new self created to be like Christ.

In what areas of your life do you continue to live in the old self by falling into the trap of sin?

_____

_____

_____

In the few weeks since we examined an ongoing change in form, have you made progress in these areas of your life?

_____

_____

_____

What steps are you taking to be made new in your mind?

_____

_____

_____

How determined are you to become more and more like Christ every single day? (Consider placing your answer to this question in a visible place so that you will be reminded each day to become more like Christ)

_____

_____

_____

Spiritual Growth

The second step in the spiritual metamorphosis process called for real spiritual growth. As we studied this aspect of the metamorphosis process, we saw the contrast in Scripture between *perceived* spiritual growth as seen in the lives of the Pharisees and *real* spiritual growth as seen in the life of Mary of Bethany. We learned real spiritual growth always responds to Jesus and becomes evident as others see that Jesus makes a real difference in our lives. Please read through the spiritual growth lists and refresh your memory about the real meaning of spiritual growth.

Spiritual growth is not:	Spiritual Growth is evident when we:
About power or position	Sit and listen
Done for men to see	Honor Christ foremost in our homes
Reached through divided alliances	Respond to Jesus
For self glory	Recognize Jesus' authority
Based on tradition	Participate in setting other captives free
A contained exercise	Live a life of relinquishment & dependency
Determined by what is on the outside	Minister to Jesus
A solo journey.	Are known for our relationship with Jesus.

As you read through each list, what areas do you continue to struggle with?

_____

_____

_____

What is God challenging you to do regarding spiritual growth?

_____

_____

_____

Are you committed to do whatever it takes to have real spiritual growth at work in you?

_____

_____

_____

Differentiation

The third step in the spiritual metamorphosis process called for *differentiation*, which we defined as the call to be distinct or different in character. As we studied this concept, words like unique, unmistakable, dissimilar, and separate painted a wonderful picture.

The story of the Good Samaritan served as the scriptural backdrop for the concept of differentiation. From the life of the Good Samaritan, we saw distinct or different living in action as the Good Samaritan set out to do something no one else was willing to do. From this parable, we were challenged to display:

- **A willingness to do the right thing.**
- **An attitude of compassion and humility**
- **A desire for our actions to speak louder than our words.**

We summarized these principles by stating:**"Go and live your life by displaying a willingness to do the right thing, with an attitude of humility and compassion, always allowing your actions to speak louder than your words."**

As you read through this principle, what area(s) do you need to work on?

_____

_____

_____

What areas of life do you continue to struggle with in regards to distinct living?

_____

_____

_____

With the call to distinct or different living clear in our mind, we turned our attention to the number one character quality that makes a believer distinct.
From memory do you remember this quality? If so, please list the quality. _____
Please look up and write John 13:34-35.

_____

_____

_____

The number one character quality that makes a believer distinct is **love**. In order to explore the concept of Christian love, we studied John 13:1–17 where Jesus washed the disciples' feet. From this story we learned that in order to love like Christ we must:

- Know that our time is at hand as seen in focused living
- Daily experience the full extent of His love by being present and vulnerable
- Follow the pattern of Christ as we live from a position of submission, accept the circumstances of our past, and set our sights on our future home
- Love like Jesus loved with humility and a willingness to serve.

As love became the focus of the differentiation process, we discovered that Christ-like love sets us apart by making us known as His disciples.

As you sit here today, is there someone in your life that you still need to love? Please explain.

_____

_____

_____

If so, will you commit to love that person, not out of your strength, but out of His?

_____

_____

_____

Changes in Habitats and Habits

The fourth step in the spiritual metamorphosis process called for change in our habitats and habits. This final step is the outworking of the three previous steps as it challenges each of us to examine **where we go** and **what we do**. In order to better understand habitats and habits, we defined the terms in the following ways:

• A **habitat** represents the frequent, familiar, and regular places we go to receive comfort, relaxation, and reassurance.

• A **habit** is an action or attitude that occurs with little or no resistance, regularly and without any thought, and always results in inward attitudes or outward actions.

Once we had a clear understanding of our habitats and habits, we stated that an ungodly habitat or habit always undermines the reflecting process because the places we go and the things we do reveal who we are as a person as well as what we believe about God. In light of this thought, we took our standard for habitats and habits one step further as we resolved to distinguish between the holy things of God and the common things of this world.

Please look up and record Leviticus 10:10 in the space below.

_____

_____

_____

Are you continuing to engage in a habitat or habit that does not meet the standard of God's Word? If so, please explain.

_____

_____

_____

As the desire to change our habitats and habits increased, we examined the number one influencer of each—the crowds in which we live. Exodus 23:2 was the primary Scripture for this study. This verse states: "Do not follow the crowd in doing wrong." As we thought about the crowd we understood that this word described the many people in our lives, in all the various types of relationships.

With this thought in mind, we focused on the topic of friendship. We stated God has established different people to play different roles in our lives. As we follow these God-prescribed roles, we find our tendency to follow the crowd in doing wrong decreasing and our ability to reflect His glory increasing. The picture of the open palm became the visual aid reminding each of us that we should not hold onto friendships at any cost.

Proverbs 12:26 taught each of us that "A righteous man is cautious in friendship, but the way of the wicked leads them astray." From our study regarding different roles friends should play in our lives, we learned that the Bible teaches three friendship levels should exist in a believer's life.

- **Close Friends:** Accountability partners who hold us to the standards taught in God's Word. These friends ask the tough questions and long for us to know and love Jesus more every day.

- **Caring Friends:** Supportive friends who love Jesus and want to help us love Jesus.
- **Casual Friends:** Friends who are lost or not attending church. God has placed these friendships in our lives for the purpose of investing. The goal in this friendship is for us to live in such a way that casual friends see Jesus in us.

As you read the list of friendship levels, are there any of the levels that you do not have in your life? For example, are you missing friends that fall in the close or casual levels? If so, please journal a prayer asking the Lord to bring these types of friends into your life.

_____

_____

_____

_____

Conclusion

As we review the spiritual metamorphosis process, I am amazed at the amount of material we covered. Now that the spiritual metamorphosis material has been presented, do you see the incredible call from the short phrase "…**but be transformed**…?" I hope you do.

Dear friend, if you and I desire to reflect the glory of Christ, we must commit ourselves to the transformation process no matter how long, how hard, or how uncomfortable that process may be. Looking more and more like Christ and less and less like this world provides the path to ultimate freedom in Christ and to a heart and life that reflects the glory of God.

Please close with a prayer expressing your ongoing desire to _reflect His glory._

_____

_____

_____

_____

_____

_____

Reflecting His Glory

Week 5: "…by the renewing of your mind."

> Transforming Truth
>
> *Renewing occurs as we renovate the way we think by cleaning out the ways of this world and making room for God's Word in every area of life.*

Day 1: The Renewing Process

Welcome to Week Five of *Reflecting His Glory!* I am so proud of you! You have made it to the next stage of our study—the renewing process. This week we'll focus on the next portion of Romans 12:2: **"by the renewing of your mind."** Please read Romans 12:2 and underline this week's key phrase.

Do not conform any longer to the pattern of this world, but be transformed by the renewing of your mind. Then you will be able to test and approve what God's will is—his good, pleasing and perfect will. (Romans 12:2)

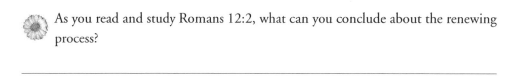 As you read and study Romans 12:2, what can you conclude about the renewing process?

_____

_____

_____

As we study Romans 12:2, we can answer three questions about the phrase "by the renewing of your mind." These questions are:

- **Where does renewing occur? The renewing process takes place in the mind.** This point is crucial as we think about the steps we must take in order to renew.
- **How does renewing relate to transformation? The renewing process provides the "how to" of transformation.** Did you catch this point? "But be transformed…(how?)…by the renewing of your mind."
- **Why should we renew? Renewing enables believers to test and approve God's will for their lives.** "Then you will be able to test and approve what God's will is—his good, pleasing and perfect will."

These truths make the renewing process paramount as we desire to reflect His glory. Let's pray.

Dear Lord,
We praise You, for You are God. Each day as we walk on Your earth and breathe Your air, we are reminded of Your greatness, Your vastness, and all Your incomparable attributes. Lord, we humble ourselves before You and proclaim, "There is none like You!" Please forgive the sin of our heart—may we get serious about You and Your ways! As we examine the renewing process this week, give each of us a desire to know You more by practicing the disciplines of the faith. May we do this with integrity of heart and openness of mind. Lord, we give You the glory. In Jesus' name, amen.

Renewing Defined

The word _renewing_ found in Romans 12:2 means "to make like new." The Greek word used is _anakainosis,_ meaning "renewal, renovation—rejuvenation."[38]

 As you read the definition for anakainosis, which term—renewal, renovation, or rejuvenation—communicated most clearly to you and why?

_____

_____

I am partial to the term *renovation* because I grew up with a great renovator. My dad has the ability to take something old and used and change it to **make it like new**—the very essence of renewal. Growing up, I watched Dad's hobby of renovating our home. Over the years, I observed several characteristics of Dad's renovating process. These characteristics, when applied to life, give us guidance as we commit ourselves to God's renewing process.

1. In renovating, the tearing down process can take just as much time and energy as the rebuilding process.

2. When renovating, it is essential to have a plan, know the plan, and consult the plan every single day.

3. Successful renovation requires us to be on the lookout for new materials and useful tools to aid in the process.

4. Renovating is hard work, and there is always work to be done.

Scriptural Basis for Renovating

Colossians 3:15-17 provides scriptural basis for each of the characteristics featured in my dad's renovating process. Please read this passage and record your initial thoughts below. Then examine each point as we integrate Colossians 3:15-17 with these concepts.

_____

_____

1. In renovating, the tearing down process can take just as much time and energy as the rebuilding process. For example, think about removing old, worn-out wallpaper from a wall. Have you ever done this? It is a tedious and frequently frustrating process. However, removing the old wallpaper is necessary in order to provide a smooth, beautiful finish.

Colossians 3:15 states: "Let the peace of Christ rule in your hearts, since as members of one body you were called to peace." Can you confirm that displaying the peace of Christ is not a natural human reaction to the difficulties and uncertainties of life? I certainly can! Natural human tendencies do not result in peace but rather strife. Therefore, it's essential in the renovation process to carefully remove the natural human tendencies that stand in the way of the Word of Christ dwelling richly and abundantly in our lives.

In the midst of difficulties and uncertainties, what are your natural **human** reactions?

_____

_____

_____

Did you list worry, anger, fear, or sadness? No matter what you listed, please describe the challenge of removing each natural human tendency in your life.

_____

_____

_____

Removing the natural human tendencies of life is a challenge, and we cannot underestimate the time and energy necessary to accomplish this task. If we are going to allow the peace of Christ to rule in our hearts, then we must rid our minds of wrong thoughts, perspectives, and motives. This does not occur quickly or naturally but only through the power of Jesus Christ as we allow His Word to change the direction and focus of our lives.

2. When renovating, it is essential to have a plan, know the plan, and consult the plan every single day. Before my dad would start a renovation project, he would sit at the kitchen table or in his brown recliner and study the blueprint. The blueprint represented the masterplan—the set of instructions that were necessary in order to successfully complete the task.

Colossians 3:16 states: "Let the word of Christ dwell in you richly." In this passage, the Greek word _logos_ is translated _word_ and means "the word of the Lord."[39]

Examine Colossians 3:16 carefully. What are we to do with the Word of Christ?

_____

Clearly, we are to allow the Word of Christ to dwell in us richly. The literal translation for _richly_ means "abundantly."[40] As we allow the Word of Christ to richly and abundantly dwell in us, it provides directions for life. Do you hear the call for the Word in your life? Please describe your daily routine for consulting the Word of God.

_____

_____

3. Successful renovation requires us to be on the lookout for new materials and useful tools to aid in the process. Shopping with my dad always reminded me of his keen eye for materials. Hardware stores served as Dad's favorite places to look for bargains that helped with current or future projects. My dad's tool shed remains full of renovating resources, and some of these renovating items have been used around my home!

Colossians 3:16b states: "… as you **teach** and **admonish** one another with all wisdom, and as you sing **psalms, hymns**, and **spiritual songs** with gratitude in your hearts to God." Each of the words listed in bold (teach, admonish, psalms, hymns, and spiritual songs) represents a different Greek word with a different meaning and application for life. This list provides a great reminder from the Word of God—expressions of faith and means of biblical intake can and should vary.

The principles taught in the Word of God do not change, but I believe our methods of intake should. By *methods* I mean the ways we take the Word of God into our lives, as well as the ways we express our praise to God. Both aspects are crucial in the renovating process. Paul instructed the Colossians to **teach** and **admonish** and to sing **psalms, hymns**, and **spiritual songs**. This clear instruction encouraged the Colossians to use a variety of methods to know, understand, praise, and serve God.

Please list the methods you use to take in the Word of God, as well as to express praise to God.

_____

_____

_____

_____

Sometimes I find it easy to fall into the trap of doing the same routine over and over again—especially in my approach to God. When I sense my approach growing stale, I look for new materials and useful tools to aid in my personal renovation process.

In your approach to God, do you tend to do the same thing over and over again?

_____

_____

_____

If so, are you open to trying new things in how you relate to God?

_____

4. Renovating is hard work, and there is always work to be done. Perhaps this is the most challenging as well as exciting aspect of the renovating process. Renovating requires hard work. Watching my dad work hard over the years provided a good example for me—I saw that true renovation continually leads to new areas to renovate. It was not uncommon for my dad to complete one renovating task and immediately begin another. Although progress was made and changes were evident, my dad never settled for mediocre change but always looked for new projects. While this openness to continual renovation was hard for me, it also proved exciting. As my dad renovated, positive changes took place. Each time my dad renovated an area of our home, we enjoyed the fruits of his hard work.

Colossians 3:17 states: "And whatever you do whether in word or deed, do it all in the name of the Lord Jesus, giving thanks to God the Father through him." I love this verse! The "whatever you do" concept challenges me at the very heart of my being. This concept reminds us that in the big and small tasks of life, one thing should remain the same— our focus. Scripture teaches we are to "do it all" for the Lord. This teaching places the final renovating concept on center stage as we understand and accept the truth that renovating is a life-long process.

As long as we are on this earth, we are to do the big and small things with our focus on Jesus Christ. This truth spotlights the never-ending aspect of renovating. Renovating is hard work and there is always work to be done, BUT the renovating work is rewarding work. God uses the renovating process to change our lives as we submit to Him, resulting in spiritual fruit. Dear friend, hear this truth. God can and will change our lives as we allow Him to renovate us. We can become more like Jesus Christ every day. What an exciting truth to embrace!

In your life, do you do the big and small things with a clear focus on Christ?

_____

_____

_____

_____

Have you accepted mediocre Christianity as the norm for your life? In other words, have you stopped the renovating process in your life?

_____

_____

_____

_____

The goal of the renovating process is Christlikeness. For the new believer, this truth teaches that the Christian walk is a long walk, a lifelong process of becoming more and more like Christ. For the believer who has followed the Lord for a few years, this truth teaches that just a little bit of renovation is not enough. For the mature believer, this truth reminds her that until she is home in heaven, the renewing work must continue.

Of the four renovating principles listed above, which challenges you and why?

_____

_____

_____

_____

_____

Conclusion

The four renovating principles listed in today's lesson provide a challenge as well as a clear call to focus on the process of renewing. The bottom line in renewing is getting a fresh start with our minds or, as Romans 12:2 states "by the renewing of your mind." This renewing occurs as we take on the challenge to change or renovate the way we think by cleaning out the ways of this world and making room for God's Word in each and every area of life. The mind plays a crucial role in the renewing process. We must not miss that Paul calls us to renew the mind. The mind and the things that take place in the mind affect the way we think, the way we act, and even the way we feel. Therefore, renewing the mind is a crucial step if we desire to reflect the glory of Jesus Christ

Over the next four days, we will focus on the **"how to's"** of renewing. This focus will provide a hands-on format with directed opportunities to renew your mind. I hope you are excited, because it is going to be great!

Please close by journaling a word of prayer expressing your excitement and openness to the renewing process.

_____

_____

_____

_____

_____

_____

_____

_____

_____

_____

_____

Reflecting His Glory

Week 5: "…by the renewing of your mind."

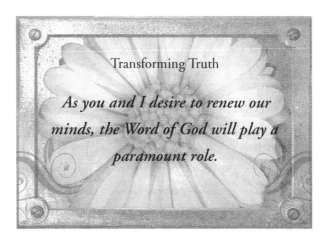

Transforming Truth

As you and I desire to renew our minds, the Word of God will play a paramount role.

Day 2: Renewing by Studying the Word of God

The format of this week's study will be very different. Each lesson will have a time of study followed by an opportunity to take part in practical ways to renew your mind. As you embark on this adventure, please know I am very excited for you! I pray you will fall in love with the disciplines of the Christian faith. A Christian discipline is a tool utilized to place ourselves before God so that He can transform us.[41] A few examples of the Christian disciplines include memorizing Scripture, fasting from an activity, or worshiping God in a quiet place. The disciplines allow us to identify sin, turn from sin, and experience renewal. The renewal occurs as we humble ourselves before the Lord and ask Him to graciously work in our lives. The result of this renewal process is the ability to reflect the glory of Jesus Christ. I can testify that the Lord has used many of the Christian disciplines to change my life! Believe it or not, there was a time when I bought into the lie that Christianity was boring and routine. Dear friend, there is nothing boring or routine about the God we serve! Let's pray.

Dear Lord,

You are our mighty God. We praise You, for You are holy, perfect, and good. Lord, forgive our sins that distract each of us from knowing, loving, and serving You. As we continue to fix our minds on the renewing process, challenge each of us to pursue You more. Lord, as we study the importance of Your Word, may we understand the role we play in constantly taking in Your truth. In Jesus' name, amen.

Studying the Word of God

Studying the Word of God is the primary way we renew our mind. Please look up and read Ephesians 6:10–17 and answer the following questions.

Verse 10 states we are to be strong in what?

_____

_____

_____

What do you think it means to be strong in the Lord and His mighty power?

_____

_____

_____

What instruction is given in verse 11?

_____

_____

Why are we to follow this instruction?

_____

_____

Verse 12 states our struggle. Please explain our struggle in your own words.

_____

_____

_____

In light of this struggle, verse 13 restates our instruction and provides the reasoning for this instruction. Please list the instruction as well as the reasoning recorded in Ephesians 6:13.

_____

_____

_____

Verses 14–17 list the armor of God. Please record each piece of armor.

_____

_____

_____

This passage of Scripture provides a call to know the armor of God and to actively partic-ipate in the equipping process. One of the primary elements of the armor is the Word of God. Ephesians 6:17 states: "Take… the **sword of the Spirit, which is the word of God**" (emphasis added). As we think about the importance of renewing via the Word of God, this passage calls us to take God's Word into our lives.

Ephesians 6:10-17 begins by stating: "Finally, be strong in the Lord and in his mighty power." Isn't it good to know that we serve a strong God? As a result we do not have to be strong in ourselves. Even though we are called to suit up with God's armor so we are equipped to do battle, we do not battle alone. We battle in the mighty power of our God.

Today do you need to hear this truth? Please list the current battles in your life.

_____

_____

_____

How do we face these battles? In Ephesians 6:11 Paul teaches us, "Put on the full armor of God." We saw the phrase _put on_ a few weeks ago and learned that it meant "to clothe oneself or wrap oneself and carries the idea of sinking into something." [42] From this definition, we can make two observations. First, the believer must take part in the process of putting on. Just like getting dressed requires thought, effort, and participation, putting on God's armor requires our involvement in the process. Second, the believer must surrender to the process. The call to sink into the armor communicates the necessity to give up control by fully trusting the armor of God to protect us in battle. Both observations call for believers to find their sufficiency and strength in the armor of God.

What are we to put on? Scripture describes the full armor of God. The benefit of this putting on process is the ability to stand against the devil's schemes. 1 Peter 5:8-9 states: "Be self-controlled and alert. Your enemy the devil prowls around like a roaring lion looking for someone to devour. Resist him, standing firm in the faith." The fact that the devil prowls around looking for someone to devour teaches that we face a very real enemy. This enemy functions as an authority or power in this dark world. In light of this enemy, the call to *put on* is restated in Ephesians 6:13. It is interesting to note that the phrase *put on* recorded in Ephesians 6:13 is different from the phrase *put on* recorded in Ephesians 6:11. *Put on* in verse 13 means "to take up, take in, and receive unto you."[43] As we think about the call to *put on* as recorded in verses 11 and 13, we see an all-encompassing approach to the full armor of God. We are to *put on* through **clothing ourselves**, which is the outward approach. And we are to *put on* through **taking in**, which is the inward approach. This comprehensive approach to the armor of God prepares us as believers to stand strong, as we are prepared on the inside as well as the outside to stand against the schemes of the devil.

Ephesians 6:14-17 records the armor of God. The armor involves the belt of truth, the breastplate of righteousness, feet fitted with the readiness of the gospel, the shield of faith, the helmet of salvation, and the sword of the Spirit, which is the Word of God.

Today as we focus our renewing process on the sword of the Spirit, we must ask why Paul used a sword to represent the Word of God. According to Albert Barnes' *Notes on the New Testament,* "The sword was an essential part of the armor of an ancient soldier. His other weapons were the bow, the spear, or the battle-axe. **But, without a sword, no soldier would have regarded himself as well armed"**[44] (emphasis added).

Today if we seek to be well armed to fight our enemy and renew our mind, the Word of God will play a paramount role in the process. This is true because the Word of God enables us to:
- Understand the difference between right and wrong
- Imitate the actions of Jesus who met temptation with the Word of God
- Be prepared when facing a decision, knowing that we do not need to rely on our reasoning or wisdom
- See the importance of encouraging others to understand the role the Word of God should play in the renewing process.

Which of these four truths challenges you and why?

_____

_____

_____

_____

Practical Ways to Renew your Mind

Now that we understand the importance of the Word of God, let's look at the disciplines required in order to take the Word of God into our lives.

Bible Study

Bible study is a consistent examination of the Word of God. The study can revolve around a topic, a passage of Scripture, or a book of the Bible. Believers must study the Word of God in order to grow in their faith.

The very fact you are taking part in this study reveals your heart's desire to study the Word of God. Let's be really honest. How hard is it for you to consistently study the Word of God?

_____

_____

_____

_____

What is your biggest challenge in Bible study?

_____

_____

_____

_____

What would help you to be more disciplined in your Bible study approach?

_____

_____

_____

Memorization

When we memorize Scripture, we place the Word of God inside our minds so that we can draw upon its truth at any moment during our day. Memorization produces many benefits. For example, when we are tempted or facing a difficult time, the Holy Spirit can bring to mind a helpful passage of Scripture to keep our eyes and heart focused on the Lord.

How hard is it for you to memorize Scripture?

_____

_____

_____

_____

If you no longer owned a Bible or had access to one, how much of the Word of God could you readily remember?

_____

_____

_____

_____

What is your biggest struggle in memorization?

_____

_____

_____

_____

What would help you to memorize more Scripture?

_____

_____

_____

_____

Often the Lord cuts through my excuses for not memorizing Scripture by asking the question, "If you no longer had access to a Bible, how much of My word could you recall?" Ouch! This question always hurts. My answer would have to be, "Not enough."

Journaling

When we record the work of God in and around our lives, we are journaling. Christian journaling can take on many forms including rewriting Scripture in our own words, expressing prayer and praise to God, noting various significant events taking place, and recording God's renewing work in our lives.

For me, journaling provides a wonderful way to express deep thoughts, hurts, feelings, and desires to the Lord. At times, I find it easier to write these feelings than to say them out loud, so I journal when I need to pour out my heart to God. When I journal, I am real with the Lord. Sometimes I cringe when my heart is revealed through the journaling process, but each time God reassures me that He can handle it. Journaling also provides a wonderful account of God's active work in my life. When I feel down or just need to refocus, I read my previous journal entries. I am always encouraged as I look back and see how God brought me through challenging circumstances.

Have you ever journaled in your walk with the Lord?

_____

_____

_____

Do you see value of journaling? If so, explain.

_____

_____

_____

_____

Are you open to journaling in your life?

_____

_____

_____

Varied Bible Translations

Using various translations of the Bible provides a wonderful renewing tool. Most people have one translation that they usually prefer to use. This is true for me. However, I try to use different translations in order to gain new perspectives on familiar passages of Scripture.

What translation do you use most of the time?

_____

What makes this translation your favorite?

_____

_____

_____

_____

Have you ever used different translations? If so, please list the translations below.

_____

_____

_____

_____

Application

Now comes the fun part! I challenge you to put the disciplines you've studied into practice. That's right—we are going to move head knowledge into heart knowledge. Listed below you will find four renewing activities that center on the discipline of taking God's Word into our lives. I want you to pick one renewing activity and implement it. If you want to try more, go for it! However, do not feel pressure to do all of them. Remember, you can always come back to this list in the future.

- **Developing a *quiet time* habit:** *Quiet time* is a term used to describe spending time alone with God in prayer and Bible Study. One of the greatest struggles women face in studying the Word of God is simply taking time to do it. I have faced this struggle in my life and asked, "Lord, when am I to study Your Word, and how am I supposed to do it?" Three practical steps helped me to become disciplined in this area of life.

First, I created a *prayer closet,* which is my actual bedroom closet. A prayer closet provides a specific **place** to go. This place can be a closet, a special chair, or even your bedroom with a note hung outside your door. I created my prayer closet out of necessity. When my children were younger, I could not find a quiet place to go to read my Bible and pray without my two little boys interrupting me. I knew I needed a prayer closet when I found myself sitting in my cold, dark car trying to study God's Word. As I sat in my car, the Lord impressed upon my heart that I needed to stop hiding from my kids in order to spend time with Him! Instead, I was to teach my children the need for a quiet time by establishing a prayer closet and going there each day. My prayer closet eliminates distractions and serves as a form of accountability. My children know that when I am in my prayer closet they can only interrupt me for emergencies. Each time I pass by my prayer closet, I am reminded about the need for God's Word in my life.

Second, I knew that in order to live out of the sufficiency of the Word of God, I had to establish early in my day that I was going to live by the teachings found in God's Word. So, I began having my quiet time before I turned on my computer or answered my telephone. I chose these two activities because once I log onto my computer or take phone calls, I find myself busy with the tasks for my day and how I will react to them. I call this my *reactive point,* since from then on I am responding to circumstances and situations. I want to make those responses with the guidance of the Holy Spirit, so I do not take phone calls, check my email, or log onto my computer, until I have had my quiet time. This principle sets up a specific **time** for when my quiet time would take place.

Third, I developed a specific **plan** for what I was going to do during my quiet time. This involved the amount of Scripture I planned to read and study each morning. After some tweaking, my plan developed into a process of reading and studying through the Bible book by book. At times, I spend more time in one book than another, but I always know where I am and where I am going next. This plan allows me to sit down and immediately dig into Scripture.

> **Once these three steps were established in my life, the struggle to have a consistent quiet time became less and less as I had a consistent place, a consistent time, and a consistent plan.**

Activity:
- Create a prayer closet in your home by selecting a designated place to have your time with God. Teach your family members the importance of your prayer closet by letting them know that when you are with the Lord, only emergencies are allowed to interrupt.

- Determine when you want to have your quiet time and make sure you have it before you reach your reactive point and get too busy with the tasks of your day.
- Talk to the Lord about the plan He wants you to do in your Bible study. This may involve another group Bible study, an individual Bible study, or a book-by-book read of the Bible.

- **Memorizing Scripture:** I use note cards to help me memorize Scripture. Each day I look for an empty two or three minutes (folding clothes, sitting in traffic, cooking dinner) that I can use to train my mind. Finding the empty minutes in your day will provide a consistent time for you to work on memorizing Scripture.

  Activity: Pick two or three verses of Scripture and write each verse on a separate note card. Post the note cards in areas that you will see each day. For me this means the refrigerator, bathroom mirror, or dashboard of my car. You can even put your note cards on a small ring and carry them with you during your day. For the next three days, look for two and three empty minutes in your day and memorize your verse or verses. If you need help selecting a verse, please refer to Appendix 1.

- **Journaling:** Purchase an inexpensive journal or notebook and begin to journal God's renewing work in your life. If you prefer, use your computer to journal your thoughts.

  Activity: Pick one or more of the following activities.
  - Take a passage out of Psalms and rewrite the passage inserting your situations and circumstances. An example is provided at the end of this lesson.
  - Take a few minutes each day and record the events going on in your life. List meaningful ways God moves in your life.
  - If you face a difficult situation, use your journal to pour out your heart to the Lord. Be real and honest as you write about the struggles going on in your life. Remember—He can handle your thoughts and feelings, and He already knows them.

- **Reading Varied Translations:** Purchase a Bible with several translations (called a parallel Bible) or log onto www.biblegateway.com to access different translations of the Word. Use different versions during your devotional reading. To see a comparison of the different translations, go to www.zondervan.com and click on the Translation Comparison link under Bible Translations.

Activity: Select a familiar passage of Scripture. Read this passage in several different translations and record any new thoughts in your journal.

Conclusion

I hope today's renewing activity or activities helped you take God's Word into your heart and life. Please close with a word of prayer expressing your love for the Word of God and your commitment to the Word in your daily life.

_____

_____

_____

_____

_____

_____

_____

_____

_____

_____

_____

_____

_____

_____

_____

_____

_____

_____

_____

_____

_____

_____

* * * * * * * * * * * * * * * * * *

Example of rewriting Scripture in your own words:

Psalm 64 from the NIV

God is our refuge and strength, an ever-present help in trouble. Therefore we will not fear, though the earth give way and the mountains fall into the heart of the sea, though its waters roar and foam and the mountains quake with their surging. There is a river whose streams make glad the city of God, the holy place where the Most High dwells. God is within her, she will not fall; God will help her at break of day. Nations are in uproar, kingdoms fall; he lifts his voice, the earth melts. The LORD Almighty is with us; the God of Jacob is our fortress. Come and see the works of the LORD, the desolations he has brought on the earth. He makes wars cease to the ends of the earth; he breaks the bow and shatters the spear, he burns the shields with fire. "Be still, and know that I am God; I will be exalted among the nations, I will be exalted in the earth." The LORD Almighty is with us; the God of Jacob is our fortress.

Andrea's version of Psalm 64

God is my safe place. He is where I go when I need strength for the day and help through the night. Because God is on my side, I will not fear. Even though the baby is sick, the budget is tight, and the future is uncertain, I will not be afraid. You see, God is inside of me. Even now He is working in my life in order to make me stronger. I cling to the fact that at the sound of His voice everything can change. Look at my life and you will see the work of the Lord. His love, His faithfulness, and His grace have no end. Because of this, I can sit at His feet and worship Him, no matter what. I trust that in His time, the Lord will restore all things to me. Praise be to God that He is with me.

Reflecting His Glory

Week 5: "...by the renewing of your mind."

Transforming Truth

Worship occurs when the inward attitude of our heart recognizes that God is God and the outward expression of our lives reflects that we know that we are not.

Day 3: Renewing—Expressing Praise to God

It was a Wednesday night, and I was driving to choir rehearsal. I was feeling overwhelmed—not sure what was going on in my life. I was so unsure that I found myself asking, "Lord, who am I?" After this question came to my mind, I felt guilty for having it. I continued talking to the Lord: "Lord, I do not want to question you. I do not want to doubt you. I just do not know who I am. Lord, please help me figure this out."

I continued driving, trying to prepare my heart for a time of worship. I parked my car, walked into the choir suite, and quietly found my seat. As always, rehearsal began with a time of praise. This is one of my favorite moments during the week—sitting with fellow worshipers and singing to our King. My heart was stirred by God's presence, and I began to ask the Lord to speak to me. At the same time, I continued to sense confusion in my spirit, so I prayed all the more. The time went by quickly, and before I knew it, practice was complete.

Our worship pastor thanked everyone for coming and then closed with a word of prayer. During the prayer, he made an amazing statement: "Lord, we are never more who You call us to be than when we worship You." Immediately, I began processing this statement. My mind thought back to my question during the car ride. "Lord, who am I?" The answer was evident: "A worshiper of the Living God."

Each day this statement should set the tone for the way we live our lives. Each morning we can wake up and proclaim, "Today, Lord, I worship You!" This cry revolutionizes our walks and provides an avenue for renewing. Today we are going to explore this avenue as we discipline ourselves to worship God. Join me in a word of prayer.

Dear Lord,
You are worthy of all praise. Scripture teaches that the rocks, the trees—all of creation cries out to You. Lord, for the times we have failed to cry out, forgive us. We thank You for the constant reminder that we were created to worship. I pray we will experience a fresh outpouring of Your Spirit this day as we humble ourselves and recognize that our identity is wrapped up in worshiping You. Lord, we proclaim, "We are worshipers of the Living God." We love You. In Jesus' name, amen.

God is God and We are Not

Expressing praise to God often occurs through the form of worship. Worship occurs when the inward attitude of our hearts recognizes that God is God and the outward expression of our life (meaning the way we actually live) reflects that we know that we are not. Scripture repeatedly teaches this truth—God is God and we are not. Daily incorporating this truth into life renews our minds and positions us to reflect the glory of Christ.

Please look up each Scripture passage below. Read the passage and discover truths about who God is as well as who you are. After you read each passage, fill in the chart with the information you discover. The first column lists the passage. The second column asks you to list who God is based on the passage. The third column asks you to list who you are. The final column asks you to take the information from the second and third columns and draw conclusions based on your knowledge of the word pictures used. I have completed the first one as an example.

Passage of Scripture:	God/Jesus is:	I am:	Lessons learned from this truth:
Genesis 2:7 and Psalm 103:13-14	Creator	Creation	God formed me. I was made from dust. Therefore, I need someone bigger, stronger, and more powerful directing the daily operations of my life.
Isaiah 64:8			
John 15:5			
John 10:11–18			

Matthew 26:18-19			
1 John 3:1			
Psalm 38:22 and Mark 2:17			

I hope your chart looks something like this.

Column Two

God/Jesus is:

- Creator
- Potter
- Vine
- Shepherd
- Teacher
- Father
- Savior

Column Three

I am:

- Creation
- Clay

- Branch
- Sheep
- Student
- Child
- Sinner

Column Four

Lessons learned might include: (There are no right or wrong answers.)

- **Creator/Creation:** God formed me. I was made from dust. Therefore, I need someone bigger, stronger, and more powerful directing the daily operations of my life.
- **Potter/Clay:** God is sculpting me into the vessel He desires. He is in charge! My job is to be moldable, changeable, and agreeable to His plan.
- **Vine/Branch:** I must be rooted and grounded in Christ. My sufficiency must come from Him. I bear His fruit, not my own.
- **Shepherd/Sheep:** God watches over me and cares for me. As a sheep, I am clueless. In order to be safe, cared for, and useful, I must follow my Shepherd.
- **Teacher/Student:** As the Teacher, God has all the information. He knows the answer because He is the answer. As the student, I am lost without Him. I should focus on remaining teachable. More often than not, the appropriate response involves listening to His instructions for life.
- **Father/Child:** God is our father. He is our daddy. His love is unconditional and unending. As the child, we are to stay close. We are to obey. We are to respect. We are to love not because we have to but because His great love allows us to. (For those who do not or did not have a godly father figure on this earth, this truth may be difficult to comprehend. Even today the Lord brought to my mind individuals who have experienced abuse by their earthly fathers. If this is you, dear friend, please know your heavenly Father stands in holiness and purity and holds His arms out wide. Go to Him and ask Him to help you see Him as the daddy you never had.)
- **Savior/Sinner:** Jesus lived a perfect life and died so that I can spend eternity in heaven. Both the Old and New Testaments spotlight Jesus' sacrificial death as the atoning work for sin. (I love how the Old Testament describes God as our Savior. How often we miss this point! From the beginning, God's plan was a plan of redemption. This truth makes God our saving God. The fact that we are sinners reminds each of us that we need a savior. Recognizing this truth places us in positions of dependence on God.)

As we look for practical ways to use this list, we turn our attention to today's renewing work. Worship is the avenue by which we remember that God is God and we are not. Why? Because at the heart of worship resides each perspective listed above.

God is the Creator. We are His creation.
God is the Potter. We are the clay.
Jesus is the Vine. We are the branches.
Jesus is our Shepherd. We are His sheep.
God is our Teacher. We are His students.
God is our Father. We are His children.
God is our Savior. We are the sinners.

Please take a moment and describe how these truths stir your heart to worship God.

_____

_____

_____

_____

Each morning as I get out of bed, these words are on my lips: "Today, Lord, you are the Creator and I am the creation, You are the Potter and I am the clay, You are the Vine and I am the branch, You are the Shepherd and I am Your sheep, You are the Teacher and I choose to be the student. Lord, You are the Father, and I thank You that I am Your child. May I know that You are my Savior and confess that I am a sinner." Each day God does not need to be reminded of these truths because He is God. However, I do because I am not.

Application: Expressing Praise to God

Today's application focuses on two aspects of worship. These aspects are on opposite ends of the worship spectrum. One calls for inward meditation. The other calls for outward expression of praise. While very different, both aspects provide meaningful times of renewal. I want to encourage you to pick one of the following renewing activities and incorporate it into your day.

Inward Meditation

The first aspect involves meditation or sitting before the Lord. 2 Samuel 7:18 states: "Then King David went in and sat before the Lord." As David sat, he thought about the Lord.

Meditation Activity: Sit before the Lord. Take a few minutes and go to a secluded place. Take your Bible and journal with you. Sit before the Lord and focus on Him. Worship Him. Praise Him. Adore Him. Clear your mind of worldly thoughts and upcoming "to do's." Simply worship your King. As David physically went in to worship, you must mentally go in and worship. In order to do this, see yourself sitting before the Lord. Ask the Lord to surround you with His holy presence. Focus your mind on all the reasons to praise Him. Write down the reasons as they come to mind. Read Scripture and pray the Scripture back to God. Conclude your time in prayer.

Outward Expression of Praise

The second aspect of worship involves expressing praise to God through personal worship. Personal worship involves praising God in a personal, intimate, one-on-one way. The book of Psalms instructs the believer to *sing, declare, make known, worship, ascribe, rejoice, give thanks, praise, exalt* the Lord. Each of these words calls believers to action as they take part in worship. I can testify that personal worship is a crucial step in the renewing process. When I experience anxiety, moodiness, or spiritual apathy, I begin to sing to my King. Worshiping always provides a way to take the focus off of myself and place it back on God.

Personal Worship Activities: Praise Him (Choose one of the following activities; if you can, try two or more!)

- **Goodnight walk with God:** Before you go to bed, slip out of your home for a quick walk around the block. Listen to music and allow the Lord to remind you that He is God and you are not. Look at the vast array of stars and know that God created the heavens and the earth and yet He knows your name. Use this time to praise the Lord and allow Him to evaluate your day.
- **Praise and worship during morning routine**: First thing in the morning, slip on an iPod or compact CD Player. Listen to praise and worship music as you do your morning routine. If you exercise in the morning, use praise in worship during this time as well.
- **Sing to your King:** When you are driving, turn off your cell phone and turn on Christian music. Use this time to sing to your King. My car is my personal sanctuary where I regularly meet God. Any time I am in my car alone, I worship and talk to the Lord. Give this discipline a try—I promise this is a time you will grow to love.
- **Worship through hymns:** Hymns of the faith play a role in my renewing process. I have a copy of the hymnal used at my church. I use this hymnal

regularly in my morning praise and worship. Often I find a familiar hymn and sing to the Lord. As I sing I study the words of the hymn and reflect on the truths being taught about God. I challenge you to study and sing the great hymns of the faith. Of course, ask to borrow the hymnal for this time of renewing.

Conclusion

I hope you can see from today's study that expressing praise to God provides a wonderful avenue for renewal. I simply do not know how to state this strongly enough. Personal worship should play a paramount role in the believer's life. I hope you have enjoyed this day and trust the Lord has met you as you have sought His face.

Please close with a word of prayer expressing your desire to daily know that God is God and you are not.

_____

_____

_____

_____

_____

Reflecting His Glory

Week 5: "…by the renewing of your mind."

> Transforming Truth
>
> *The purpose of spiritual disciplines is to seek God until our will surrenders to His will. Through surrender, renewal takes place as the Father's character becomes our own.*

Day 4: Renewing—Practicing the Spiritual Disciplines

Day Four, and the renewing continues!! I hope you are enjoying this week's practical look at the topic "by the renewing of your mind." Today we are going to focus on renewing as we study three spiritual disciplines of the faith—giving, praying, and fasting. Let's pray.

Dear Lord,

We praise You, for You are good. We stop and humble ourselves before You and remember that You are loving, merciful, and sovereign over all things. Lord, forgive each of us for the times we fail to recognize these truths. Please teach us about the disciplines of the Christian faith; help us to focus on the call to pray, fast, and give. May our renewing time be so much more than routine—may it be an expression of

love and praise to You. As we surrender to Your call on our lives, may we experience Your freedom. We praise You in Jesus' name, amen.

The Call to Give, Pray, and Fast

Spiritual disciplines encompass an array of activities and attitudes within the believer's heart. Remember we defined a discipline as a tool utilized to place ourselves before God so that He can transform us. **One of the great benefits of practicing the spiritual disciplines is that they often provide an avenue for our will to surrender to God's will.** Through that surrendering process, renewal takes place as the Father's character becomes our own. Today we will zero in on three disciplines that play a key role in the renewing process. Please read Matthew 6:1–18; then answer the questions below.

Verses 1 and 2 provide a strong warning. Please explain the warning.

_____

_____

_____

Verses 2 through 4 provide specific instruction about which discipline?

_____

Please explain how we are to give.

_____

_____

_____

Why do you think Jesus provided these instructions?

_____

_____

_____

Verses 5 through 15 provide instruction about what discipline?

_____

Who should we not imitate in our prayers? _____

How do these people pray?

_____

_____

_____

What reward comes from praying like the hypocrites?

_____

Please list the specific instructions regarding prayer listed in verses 6 through 8.

_____

_____

_____

Why should we avoid babbling in our prayer life?

_____

_____

_____

What well-known prayer is recorded in verses 9 through 13?

_____

Why do you think Jesus provided this prayer for the disciples?

_____

_____

_____

Verses 16 through 18 teach about what discipline?

_____

When fasting, what are we **not** to do?

_____

_____

_____

When fasting, what are we **to do**?

_____

_____

_____

What is the reason we should fast in this way?

_____

Why should we fast?

_____

Matthew 6:1–18 provides a wealth of instruction regarding the call to **give, pray,** and **fast**. Let's examine the passage and see what we can learn.

Matthew 6:1–2 provides a strong warning regarding performing righteous acts for men to see. The warning speaks straight to the heart of why we practice the spiritual disciplines. Verse 1 states: "Be careful not to do your 'acts of righteousness' before men, to be seen by them." I will be very honest—this is a warning that I need to hear. It is easy to fall into the trap of giving, praying, or fasting simply because someone else is watching.

Why should we avoid practicing 'righteous acts' before men? Verse 2 states: "If you do, you will have no reward from your Father in heaven." From this verse we can draw two conclusions. First, there is a reward for practicing the disciplines. Second, the reward is reserved for those who practice those disciplines as God has directed through His holy Word. Please tuck these thoughts in the back of your mind as we explore the specifics of how to give, pray, and fast.

Giving

Matthew 6:2–4 deals with the discipline of giving. From these verses we learn that we should give to the needy. Our giving should occur in such a way that our right hand does not know what our left hand is doing. Now let's stop right here. If you are like me, you have heard the phrase, "Do not let you right hand know what your left hand is doing." I have just one question, "What does this phrase mean?" I wonder if this phrase involves understanding that the resources in our possession actually do not belong to us but rather are entrusted to us by God. I have no doubt that this concept plays a role in the giving process. If I am going to come to the point where my right hand does not know what my left hand is doing, then I am going to have to release ownership of "my" possessions. Why? Because in my humanness the only way I can counteract the need to track, monitor, and delegate resources is to recognize that God has placed the resources in my possession for His purposes. Therefore, I am to distribute them as He sees fit.

What difference would it make in your giving if you embraced the concept that the resources in your possession are not really yours but rather placed in your control for God's purposes?

_____

_____

_____

Praying

Matthew 6:5-15 deals with the discipline of **praying**. When praying we are to make sure we do not pray like the hypocrites. The passage states that a hypocrite prays in the synagogue and on the street corner so that men can see. A person who takes this approach in their prayer life will receive the reward of recognition from other people but little else.

Instead of praying like the hypocrite, we are to go into our room, close the door, and pray to the Father. The focus of this type of prayer life becomes one-on-one intimate time with the Lord. A proper prayer life always finds its foundation in private prayer time.

Does your prayer life find its focus in one-on-one time with the Lord, or do you pray only in public? Please explain your answer.

_____

_____

_____

Scripture instructs that we should avoid babbling when we pray. The word for _babbling_ in the Greek means, "stammer, word, utterance, to jabber, utter nonsense or gibberish. It refers to the rote and meaningless repetition of prayer formularies. By constant repetition pagans believed that God would be inclined to hear their prayers or recognize their devotion to Him."[45] In reality, this type of prayer life boils down to works-based religion. Why? Babbling prayers focus on proving how good I am, how long I can pray, or how devoted I might be. Jesus clearly taught that we are to avoid babbling. After all, God already knows what we need even before we can express the need to Him.

Have you fallen into the trap of trying to force God to work on your timetable by frequent and fervent prayer? This may occur when you think that you have to ask for something a certain number of times before God will answer you. If so, how does this teaching change your approach?

_____

_____

_____

_____

This teaching reminds me that I am to pray fervently but ultimately trust God to work and move when and how He sees fit. To help counterbalance the tendency to babble, Jesus provided a model prayer in Matthew 6:9-13. This prayer is often called the Lord's Prayer. From studying the context of this passage, we can see that Jesus did not intend for believers to simply recite the prayer. Jesus provided this prayer as a model to ensure that each of us would have a balanced prayer life more focused on Him than focused on us.

In your prayer life, where is your focus—on God or on yourself?

_____

_____

_____

_____

Fasting

Matthew 6:16-18 deals with the discipline of **fasting**. These verses provide instructions for fasting that are similar to the instructions about praying. When fasting we are to avoid hypocritical behavior, including looking somber and disfiguring our faces to show others we are fasting. Instead, we are to look normal on the outside. Scripture teaches we are to put oil on our heads and wash our faces, thus hiding all evidence of a fast. Why? The reason we fast is to place our focus and attention on the Lord, not on ourselves. Therefore, it is only natural that we minimize ourselves in order to maximize our God.

Application

Remember a few minutes ago I asked you to tuck a small amount of information in the back of your mind so we could explore the "how to's" of giving, praying, and fasting? Well, it is time to bring that information back to the front of our mind as we ask the question, "Why should we want to practice the spiritual disciplines?"

In Matthew 6:1-18 the word reward is used seven times. Please read the passage carefully and record each occurrence, listing the verse number and the context of the teaching with in the verse.

1. Verse: _____
Context:

_____

_____

2. Verse: _____
Context:

_____

_____

3. Verse: _____
Context:

_____

_____

4. Verse: _____
Context:

_____

_____

5. Verse: _____
Context:

_____

_____

6. Verse: _____
Context:

_____

_____

7. Verse: _____
Context:

_____

_____

The word *reward* is used in Matthew 6 verses 1, 2, 4, 5, 6, 16, and 18. In verses 1, 2, 5, and 16, Jesus used *reward* to describe a benefit that is given to those who practice their acts of righteousness for men to see; He called this group of people the hypocrites. In verses 4, 6, and 18, Jesus used *reward* to describe what God will bestow on those who practice the disciplines in a godly manner with their focus solely on God and not on themselves.

As we think about renewing our minds through the disciplines of giving, praying, and fasting, we need to understand that the English word *reward* used in the two settings represents two different Greek words. I hope this fact grabs your attention because I do not think you want to miss this! Take a look at the chart below and discover the difference between the *reward* for the hypocrite and the *reward* for the righteous. Take a look at the chart on the next page.

Reward for the Hypocrite used in verses 1, 2, 5, and 16	Reward for the Righteous used in verses 4, 6, and 18
Greek Word: *misthos*[46] **Greek Meaning:** dues paid for work, used of the fruit naturally resulting from toils and endeavors. **Related Words:** Other words used to describe this word include hire, hired, and wages. **Implication:** This type of reward points to a works-based system. "God, I will do this for You, and in turn You will do that for me." No real change in our hearts is ever evidenced in this type of relationship. The bottom line is showing God and others how spiritual we think we have become as the focus of practicing the discipline remains on us.	**Greek Word:** *apodidomi*[47] **Greek Meaning:** to deliver, to pay off, to give back, restore. **Related Words:** Other words used to describe this word include deliverance, give, pay, render, recompense, and repay. **Implication:** This type of reward involves deliverance—deliverance from our sinful ways to God's holy ways. When we surrender to God's plan and seek Him in a way that honors Him, we are changed into His likeness. Our sinful ways are confronted by God's truth as we seek Him. We are delivered from our sin. As we **give, pray,** and **fast** with our focus solely on Christ we are delivered from sinful self and find the greatest reward in life—a changed heart that reflects the glory of Christ. Oh may it be!

As you and I desire to *reflect His glory*, we must take on the challenge of practicing the spiritual disciplines. In essence, this means putting the Word of God into action as we surrender our will to His will. This week, let's give, pray, or fast with all of our heart. Why? Because we want to experience deliverance from our sinful ways as we surrender to Christ's work in our lives.

Application

I want to ask you to take the disciplines we have studied today and put them into practice. Listed below you will find three challenges. I encourage you to pick one of the three challenges and practice it this week. As you practice this spiritual discipline, remember to keep your focus on Christ.

Challenge 1: Give sacrificially

This week I challenge you to give sacrificially. Giving usually refers to money but can also include time and resources. The gift you give should be above and beyond your normal routine. First, start by determining what you would like to give. This gift may involve money, time, or resources. Sometimes the gift God calls you to give will be obvious. Other times, it will not be as easy to give. God may call you to give financially at a time when you are strapped for money. Answering this call will require faith as you give sacrificially. Remember, once God calls, obedience requires a quick response.

If God is calling you to give financially, one way is to take the amount of money you believe God would have you give and tuck it into your wallet. Then prayerfully watch for opportunities to give. (If you are married, be sure and discuss this challenge with your husband. He needs to be in agreement with you doing this before you proceed.) Remember the giving should be done in secret and with complete focus on the Lord. You are a steward of the money that you possess. Whether it is a large or small amount, the money belongs to the Lord. For me, giving always provides an opportunity to stretch my faith as I seek to live dependent on the Lord.

If God is calling you to give a resource, look for items around your home that are rarely used. This renewing discipline challenges you to give sacrificially by donating items instead of selling them for additional income. Often when I am feeling a financial pinch, I will clean out our closets with the thought of organizing a garage sale or making a trip to the consignment store. While I am in the process of cleaning, the Lord often lays on my heart to look for people who really need those clothes and then to give these items away. This giving process becomes another way to sacrificially give as the Lord brings me to a place of dependence and trust on His ability and desire to provide for our family.

If God is calling you to give of your time, be open to opportunities to volunteer at your church, at your children's school, or in the community where you live. Giving of your time shows your priorities as you make your time on this earth about the things that really matter.

Activity: If God is calling you to take part in the challenge to give sacrificially, then determine what type of giving you are to practice. Prayerfully ask the Lord to show you how and when you are to give. When God opens a door for you to give, give with all your heart and with your focus clearly on Him.

Challenge 2: Pray thoroughly

Jesus gave us one model prayer listed in today's passage. Believers can and should use various types of prayer in order to remain focused in their prayer lives. I like to keep things simple, so I use the ACTS prayer model. Give it a try and see what you think.

Activity: Over the next three days, use the ACTS prayer model and write or voice your prayers. This model helps you practice a balanced prayer life that focuses first on God and then focuses on others and yourself.

Explanation of ACTS Prayer Model

Spend a portion of your prayer time focusing on these four aspects of prayer.
A: **Adoration**—Praise and worship God.
C: **Confession**—Confess sins that you have committed.
T: **Thanksgiving**—Be grateful to God for His blessings.
S: **Supplication**—Intercede for yourself and others.

Challenge 3: Fast diligently

There are many forms of fasting. The most obvious fasting involves giving up food for a specific time. However, fasting can cover a much broader scope and can include giving up any creature comfort like television, computer activity, dating, shopping, or offering your opinion. Make sure that the item you select for your fast is meaningful to you. (For example, if you do not watch television, do not "fast" from television!) The purpose of the fast is to create a void in your life so that your mind is continually drawn back to Jesus.

Activity: I challenge you to fast from food, television, or any other creature comfort. Before you begin, pray and ask God to show you what He would have you fast from. If you have never fasted from food before, please start small and check with your doctor regarding health risks. Additional information regarding fasting can be found in Appendix 2 of this book.

Conclusion

Practical application is a big step for many people, so I hope and pray you found this day's study beneficial. I am proud of you for your efforts and love you in the Lord. I hope today began a love affair in your life with the spiritual disciplines of the Christian faith. I pray the Spirit of God revealed the great importance of giving, praying, and fasting. Please take a few minutes and close with a word of prayer.

_____

_____

_____

_____

_____

_____

_____

_____

_____

_____

_____

Reflecting His Glory

Week 5: "...by the renewing of your mind."

> Transforming Truth
>
> *The primary goal of the renewing process is to move beyond a life based on emotions and feelings to a life based on the Word of God.*

Day 5: Renewing Applied to Life

The last three days we examined practical ways to renew our minds. Today, we will bring the renewing work together and see how the spiritual disciplines we've learned can change the direction of our lives. Please know that much of today's study is my personal story. God has called me to share my renewing journey with you. Without a doubt, I am only at the beginning, but what I have learned I gladly share. Truly, I am overwhelmed by God's grace and find myself in a position of complete humility as I give you a glimpse into my heart. Let's pray.

Dear Lord,

I have to stop and praise You. I am overwhelmed by Your grace. O Father, how I love You. To You be all the glory. Lord, I pray for each person who is reading this prayer, that You would speak to each heart about Your renewing power. Teach us about the

importance of the mind in the renewing process. You know how I missed this one for so many years—how my walk with You was more about rules and regulations and less about a passionate pursuit of Your righteousness and holiness. Lord, may we be passionate about You, and in that passion may we know Your truth and may Your truth set us free! In Jesus' name we pray, amen.

The Goal of Renewing

The primary goal of the renewing process is to move from a life based on emotions and feelings to a life based on the Word of God. Day One's study taught that renewing focuses primarily on the mind. Remember, the mind and the things that take place in the mind affect the way we think, the way we act, and even the way we feel. Therefore, renewing the mind is a crucial step if we desire to reflect the glory of Jesus Christ.

Renewing Example From My Life

Setting the Stage

Over the course of my life, I have struggled with wrong feelings and wrong perspectives. God uncovered these wrong feelings and perspectives and revealed to me how often they influenced the course of my life. They determined if I was okay, if it was a good day or a bad day, and which way I should go. Because these feelings and perspectives were not based on the Word of God, they led me straight to defeat as I chose to give into them.

I could spend the rest of today's study sharing experience after experience. Many times I found myself in difficult situations, and instead of going to the Lord and His Word, I went straight to my feelings in order to try to find my way out. But sharing those experiences would not benefit you. Instead, I want to share two specific struggles I face and how God's grace and His Word provide strength to take every thought captive to Christ. I will also share how victory comes when we are at our lowest, weakest, and most teachable points.

The Struggles

The two major struggles I have dealt with are my feelings about being adopted and my battle with food addiction.

Adoption. Over the course of my life, I have struggled with being adopted. Even as I type these words, I shake my head. I do not have a sad adoption story. On the contrary, wonderful Christian parents adopted me and raised me in a loving Christian home. For some reason, I could never get my mind around the truth that God had intentionally placed me in the home of a loving Christian family. All I could focus on was my perceived rejection by my biological parents. That rejection led to years of questioning as I wondered, "What was wrong with me?"

It was not until I recently revisited these feelings that I began to understand that as a child, I experienced feelings of abandonment. These feelings led me to make many wrong assumptions as well as wrong choices. People who feel abandoned frequently have intense desires to fit in and feel a sense of belonging. This is such a strong need that they will go to extreme lengths to gain that feeling of belonging. This was true for me. When I think back over my life and look at some of the decisions I made, I wonder what I was thinking. What was I trying to prove? This need negatively affected my relationships. I often kept the majority of my friends and family at arm's length, not being willing to share my feelings or my life with them. Then I would focus on one person and try to get that person to love me. If I could get that person to love me, then I would feel okay. If that person chose not to love me, then I would assume that they also were rejecting me. This vicious cycle left me looking to people to fill my emotional needs in an unhealthy way.

Food addiction. I love food! I am smiling as I type this, but my love for food has not always been a healthy love. During my life, I have repeatedly turned to food in order to gain comfort, reassurance, and security.

Just to give you an idea of the role food played in my life, there were times when food was the only thing that would get me out of bed in the morning. I would wake up thinking about food. I would go to bed thinking about food. I would spend many hours wondering what I should eat next.

This love of food began at a very early age. One day when I was young, I saw a commercial for Kentucky Fried Chicken. Following the commercial, I knew I had to have that chicken. I begged so hard my mom finally gave in and took me to KFC, and I can remember sitting on the front porch eating a bucket of chicken! Now that is one sad chicken story!

The Battle

The battles of adoption and food addiction played an ever-present role in my life. I felt empty because of my adoption so I turned to food in order to fill up the void. This vicious cycle went on for years. Slowly, I began to recognize the cycle. As my walk with the Lord deepened, I knew I wanted and needed freedom from this destructive cycle—but I was afraid that freedom would never come. To me, this battle was a part of my life, and I did not know if I could ever break free. If freedom could come in these two intertwined areas, then it could come in every area of my life.

Finally, it came to a point in my walk with the Lord that God through His grace drew a line in the sand. He said, "Andrea, you can be free!" I wanted to believe God, but I did not know how. "Lord, what do I do? Lord, how can I be free?" I asked.

I did not know where to begin, but I knew the Word of God would play a key role in the freedom process. I began to pray and ask God for one verse to claim over my struggles. I prayed frequently and fervently, "Lord, send me hope through Your Word."

The Weapon

As I prayed, I read His Word. I read the Bible in the morning, in the evening, and during the day. I poured His Word into my heart. One day I read the most amazing verse—Psalm 142:7.

Please look up Psalm 142:7 and write it in the space provided below.

_____

_____

_____

The Fight

I knew this was the verse for me. I started to claim the verse. I walked around the house saying the verse. I put the verse on my refrigerator and my bathroom mirror. I knew the fight was on, and I was ready for battle. I had my weapon! I did not know what I was getting into, but I knew I was ready to fight with all of my might.

The first week of fighting my battle went by quickly and easily. I did not eat too much food, and I felt good about myself. My resolve to walk in freedom from my sin was strong. The second week came, and it was a different story. The second week was trouble. The realities of life started to intrude, and my family experienced a week full of difficulties. From finances to job related issues to child rearing difficulties, we felt like we were under major attack. If something could have gone wrong, it went wrong. At one point, I sat on my living room floor and cried with all my might. I fought the urge to eat everything in my pantry. I did not want to run to my old way of handling problems, so I thought about going shopping. I remember thinking, "If I can just get out of my house and get my mind on something else, I will be okay." But I sensed the Lord telling me to stay at home and fight.

Not sure how to fight, I lay on my living room floor and spoke Psalm 142:7 over and over again, "Lord, set me free from this prison. Lord, set me free from this prison. Lord, set me free from my prison. Lord, I want to praise Your name, more than anything. I want to praise Your name. Lord, I want You to bring the righteous around me and, oh, how I want to tell them about Your goodness and Your grace. Lord, please set me free." Over and over again, I claimed this verse.

All I can tell you is that I fought like never before. Everything inside of me wanted to quit, but more than anything, I wanted God to get the glory. Not knowing what else to do, I went to my prayer journal and began to write. Out of my journal came an amazing realization—a life changing experience, to say the least. Please read the journal entry.

"Lord, be lifted high in my life. Lord, I praise You and thank You. I magnify Your name. Lord, Your servant is here and she needs You. Minister to my downcast heart. Lord, please pick me up. Lord, help me. My heart is broken. Father, You know the situations we face. Lord, I feel crushed. Lord, I feel like the walls of life are caving in on me."

As soon as I wrote the sentence, "Lord, I feel crushed," the Spirit of God spoke to me, not in an audible voice but in my soul. The Spirit said, "But we are not crushed." It took me by surprise. It was so clear, so crisp, as if God were in the room with me. I picked up my pen and wrote in my journal, "We are not crushed." I knew it was a New Testament verse, but I could not remember the context, so I looked up the passage and began to read.

2 Corinthians 4:7-9

"But we have this treasure in jars of clay to show that this all-surpassing power is from God and not from us. We are hard pressed on every side, but not crushed; perplexed, but not in despair; persecuted, but not abandoned; struck down, but not destroyed."

Right there in the Word of God—"WE ARE NOT CRUSHED." I knew God was up to something big. I continued to read the passage over and over again. Slowly, the Spirit of God began to show me that this verse was confronting the wrong perspectives and feelings that I had believed for so many years. I realized that this passage was teaching me about the difference between reality according to the Word of God and perceived reality based on my own emotions and feelings.

Further Application

I could not get 2 Corinthians 4:7-9 off my mind! God challenged me to dig into this passage and gain new perspectives based on the authority of the Word. What I found revolutionized my thinking process. Read the passage carefully and complete the chart below.

WE ARE:	BUT WE ARE NOT:
_____	_____
_____	_____
_____	_____
_____	_____

Your chart should read **WE ARE** hard pressed, perplexed, persecuted, and struck down. **BUT WE ARE NOT** crushed, in despair, abandoned, or destroyed.

How often do you fall into the trap of believing that you are crushed, in despair, abandoned, or destroyed?

_____

_____

_____

Look at the meaning of each of these words and make notes in the margin. (Remember this is what we are **NOT**.)
- Crushed: to be sorely strained in spirit, to be in a narrow place[48]
- In despair: to be utterly at loss, to renounce all hope[49]
- Abandoned: totally abandoned, forsaken, left in straits, helpless[50]
- Destroyed: rendered useless, to put out of the way entirely, put an end to.[51]

Now look at the meaning for what we **ARE**.
- Hard pressed: to suffer tribulation, afflict, to press as grapes[52]
- Perplexed: to be without resource, not to know which way to turn, to be at a loss with oneself[53]
- Persecuted: driven away, to be mistreated[54]
- Struck down: to throw to the ground, to put in lower place, to cast down.[55]

This passage taught me that believers in Christ suffer tribulation, confusion, mistreatment, and even times of lower position. However, believers are never totally strained in spirit, without hope, forsaken, or useless! What a powerful, life-changing word from the Word of God!

This passage became a lifeline as I confronted all the wrong feelings and perspectives I had based my life on. I, like many people, had grown up attending church, reading my Bible, and even taking part in ministry, yet I had based my life on a perspective that was contrary to the teachings of God's Holy Word. I lived as one crushed in spirit and abandoned in my heart. Realizing that God's Word clearly taught otherwise became a motivating factor in my life that caused me to dig deeper into the Word of God as I wanted to base my life on His truth.

How about you? Do you understand that 2 Corinthians 4:7-9 teaches that although we will experience hard times in our life, we will never face a time when we are completely without hope? What difference does it make to know that during the difficult times in your life you may be feeling hard pressed, perplexed, persecuted, and struck down but you are **NOT** crushed, in despair, abandoned, or destroyed?

_____

_____

The Outcome

The truths taught in 2 Corinthians 4:7-9 changed my life. God confronted my wrong perspectives and feelings and challenged me to embrace His truth. Today, I continue to fight. I wish I could tell you that I am completely past my old feelings, but I am not. There are days when these wrong attitudes show themselves, but I can tell you that by the grace of God, I am making progress. My wrong perspective about my adoption is being made right through God's Word. I was not rejected by my biological parents. I was placed by my sovereign Creator into the family that He had selected for me. As I understand this truth, my need to fill my life with manmade things like food and unhealthy relationships ceases to control me.

You may be wondering why I am sharing this with you. As my sister in the Lord, I want you to know that Christ can change your life. He is real, and He is able to move in your heart and in every challenging difficulty that you face. My friend, given the invitation, He will meet you, and He will change you.

Applying Renewal to Your Life

The renewing of the mind is a fight. It will always be a fight. It will never be easy or automatic. However, by God's grace and through the application of His Word, freedom comes. Praise His holy name!

Now it is your turn to delve into the deep recesses of your soul. Please complete today's study by filling in your struggles and the renewing processes that you plan to use in order to renew your mind. I love you, my friend!

Setting the stage: Take a few minutes and write about your life. Set the stage for the work the Lord is currently doing in your life.

_____

_____

_____

_____

_____

The Struggles: List the top two or three sins and issues that you struggle with on an ongoing basis.

_____

_____

_____

The Battle: Initiate the battle by declaring your desire to be free from the sins listed above. Pour out your heart to the Lord and cry out for freedom.

_____

_____

_____

The Weapon: Scripture teaches that the Word of God is our sword. Begin to find verses that speak directly to the sins you face. You can use a concordance to find verses that help you in your areas of struggle. For example, if you struggle with worry, look up the word *worry* and find all the passage that speak to that issue. As you discover these passages, list the Scriptures in the space below. Then, memorize and meditate on these verses.

_____

_____

_____

The Fight: Begin to fight. Fight like never before. Incorporate the renewing principles we discussed during Days Two, Three, and Four of this week's study. These principles include:

- **Consistent quiet time**
- **Scripture memory**
- **Journaling**
- **Using varied translations**
- **Personal worship**
- **Meditation**
- **Balanced prayer life**
- **Fasting**
- **Giving**

Further Application: Please record your thoughts and list any underlying issue of sin the Lord uncovers during your fighting process.

_____

_____

_____

Two Possible Outcomes

First, you can experience an immediate release from the bondage of sin. I have experienced this type of release from sin. I sought the Lord, and the Lord answered in an immediate renewing of my mind. The sin I once felt energized by quickly became a source of disgust as I had God's perspective on the actions.

The second outcome, and the one I experience more often than not, is gradual, daily freedom as I daily fight with the Word of God. While this outcome proves to be more work, it provides just as much freedom as the first.

Conclusion

Please read and record Galatians 5:1.

_____

_____

_____

What does freedom mean in your life?

_____

_____

_____

Close with a word of prayer expressing your love to the Lord and your thankfulness for the opportunity to stand free in Christ.

_____

_____

_____

Reflecting His Glory

Week 6: "…Then you will be able to test and approve what God's will is—his good, pleasing and perfect will."

> Transforming Truth
>
> *Performance-based religion perpetuates a self-centered, finite focus on an infinite God, devoid of genuine love, devotion, and surrender to Jesus, who has given everything.*

Day 1: The Trap Of Seeking God's Will from the Wrong Perspective

Week Six! This week and next we will study the last phrase from Romans 12:2. Please read the verse and underline the final phrase.

Do not conform any longer to the pattern of this world, but be transformed by the renewing of your mind. Then you will be able to test and approve what God's will is—his good, pleasing and perfect will. (Romans 12:2)

The final phrase states: "…Then you will be able to test and approve what God's will is—his good, pleasing and perfect will." The ***will of God* is the very heart of this phrase**. The Greek word used for *will* means "desire, inclination, choice, or determination."[56]

In Romans 12:2, the word *will* conveys God's good pleasure to be carried out by believers. God's will is what He wants done; it is the set of actions and attitudes that bring Him glory and advance His kingdom. We accomplish God's will by obeying His revealed commands, recognizing His work in our lives, and fulfilling the things He calls us to do. When we obey God's will, our hearts long to please Him and reflect His glory.

 Do you struggle with knowing and fulfilling the will of God? If so, please explain.

_____

_____

_____

If we are honest, each of us struggles with understanding God's will for our lives. *The will of God* is a concept bigger than our minds can comprehend. That is okay. The very fact that we cannot understand God should make us worship Him all the more. I rest in the fact that I will never fully understand the greatness of God. Not only that, I surrender to the truth that as long as I am on this earth, I will fight the ever present reality of my sinful nature getting in the way of fully comprehending His will for my life. Where do these truths leave us in regards to the topic of God's will? I believe they leave us completely dependent on His sufficiency and strength to work and move on our behalf. Join me now as we go to the Lord in a word of prayer.

Dear Lord,

We praise You because of who You are. Your greatness, Your holiness, and Your incredible power cause us to tremble before You. Lord, forgive each of us for the times we fail to recognize Your power and Your might. As we come to this week of study, teach us about Your will. May we see this topic from Your holy perspective. We surrender to the truth that we will never fully understand You, but, Lord, in spite of our limited abilities, we are here, and we are waiting to hear from You. Thank You for Your holy Word. We pray that You will be glorified and honored during our time of study. How we love You! In Jesus' name we pray, amen.

The Trap Exposed

At different points in my life, the process of seeking God's will became a trap. Please let me explain. For years, I viewed God's will from a human perspective. This meant that I viewed God's will with me as the central focus instead of God. During this time, life was more about what God could do for me or what I had to do to get God to work on my behalf than about me living for God. This perspective was wrong because the focus was on me, not God. Two misconceptions surfaced as I sought to understand and fulfill the will of God.

The bulk of today's lesson will explain how these misconceptions affected me and caused me to constantly struggle in my efforts to know and do God's will. As I share, I want to encourage you to examine your life. There is a good chance that you have bought into one of these two traps. As humans, we naturally view life from our perspective. We just need to be aware of this tendency and ask God to broaden our perspective when it comes to knowing His will for our lives.

Misconception One
My first misconception was thinking that God the Creator was dependent upon me the creation to accomplish His work on this earth. I cannot tell you how deeply this idea affected my life. As a result of this misconception, I viewed my walk with God as an equal partnership. He performed 50% of the work in my life, and I performed the other 50%. As a result, the human trap became, "Lord, have I done my part? Have I read enough, prayed enough, fasted enough, and studied enough?" Each time I attempted to know His will for my life, I would go into the process wondering, "Lord, what will be enough?" I perceived the answer to this question in the following ways. If I sensed God moving in my life (meaning that I had a good feeling in my heart or the situations seemed to work out), my actions had been sufficient. If I did not sense God moving in my life (meaning I had a sinking feeling in my heart or the situations appeared to be failures), I drew the conclusion that I had not performed up to my 50% standard. Therefore, the next time I attempted to seek God's will, I read more, prayed more, fasted more, and studied more in hopes that my acts of obedience would meet the required 50% of the load, thus compelling God to work on my behalf.

Finally, by God's grace, I came to the point where I threw my hands in the air and said, "Lord, I cannot do this! I cannot read enough, pray enough, fast enough, and study enough. Lord, help me!" His response was, "Child, I know. I have been allowing you to figure that out."

Through this challenging process, I realized that God's will is not something that I accomplish on my own or even in a 50/50 partnership. Rather, God's will is accomplished as God works and moves in and through my life and I display those actions and attitudes that bring Him glory and advance His kingdom. This truth brought amazing freedom as I came to the point of letting go of my desire "to do my part," understanding that I cannot meet a 50%—or any other percent—requirement.

Do you struggle with the concept of viewing your relationship with God as a 50/50 partnership?

_____

As a result, do you feel the pressure to ask, "Lord, have I done my part?" Please explain.

_____

_____

If you struggle with this issue, know that the Word of God addresses your struggle. Please look up and read Philippians 2:12-13, then answer the questions below.

Please list the believer's responsibility as stated in verse 12.

According to verse 13, who does the work? _____

Where does God do the work? _____

Why does God do the work? _____

This passage cuts to the very heart of the 50/50 partnership struggle. Our responsibility is to obey God. Philippians 2:12 states: "Therefore, my dear friends, as you have always **obeyed**—not only in my presence, but now much more in my absence—continue to work out your salvation with fear and trembling" (emphasis added). You and I work out our salvation with fear and trembling as we demonstrate obedient hearts and listen for our Father's voice. This obedience does not come as a result of taking part in a list of rituals or routines that somehow force God to work on our behalf. Rather, this obedience occurs as we recognize the truth taught in Philippians 2:13. Verse 13 states: "for it is God who **works** in you to will and to act according to his good pleasure" (emphasis added). This phrase should bring you to your feet with a shout of praise. It is God's work in your life and mine that leads to the accomplishment of His good will—an accomplishment that is not dependent on human ability to make things happen. Rather, this accomplishment depends on a merciful Father graciously choosing to move on behalf of His children for His good pleasure. Thank you, Lord!

Misconception Two
The second misconception involved buying into the notion that if obedience equals blessing, I choose obedience.

My life is full of stories regarding this struggle. I set God's blessing as the end goal of every decision I made. This struggle left me with the exhausting task of figuring out just the right steps to take to obtain God's blessing. Why? Because I believed that only the right steps led to God's blessing in my life. This focus (more like obsession) trapped me as I sought to find God's perfect will for life. As I sought God's perfect will, I lost focus on God and became focused entirely on myself. This was a problem!

Thinking back to the height of this struggle, I can remember attending church, attending Bible study, reading my Bible, sharing my faith, honoring those around me, and seeking to make the right decisions all for the sake of locking in a desired blessing from God. This pursuit became very tiring and empty as God withdrew the sense of His presence from my life because I was more focused on myself than Him.

Today as I think back on my experience, I wrestle with this notion. The Bible clearly teaches that believers should strive to take the right steps in their walk with God. Passages like Genesis 17:1, Psalm 26:3, and 2 Chronicles 7:16–18 testify to this truth. Additionally, seeking God's blessing should be a motivation in the believer's life. Deuteronomy 4:1-2 affirms this truth. Therefore, what is the answer to discovering God's will and obtaining God's blessing in our lives?

The answer comes in realizing that any time you and I seek God's will for the primary purpose of securing a blessing, we miss the point. Seeking and accomplishing God's will is not about God blessing us but rather about His righteousness. Deuteronomy 6:25 provides the biblical basis for this point. Moses states: "If we are careful to obey all this law before the Lord our God, as he has commanded us, that will be our righteousness." Why should we seek God's will? Seeking His will positions us as believers in Christ to continually have a right heart before the Lord.

 Do you struggle with choosing obedience in hopes that your choice will secure a blessing from God?

Conclusion

I believe millions of Christians struggle with thinking that God is somehow dependent upon them to accomplish His work on this earth; they may also desire to fulfill God's will for the primary purpose of receiving a blessing. As I interact with believers in Christ,

I see many of the characteristics I described from my walk displayed in their lives. My eyes are continually opened to the approaches believers take in order to know and fulfill God's will for their lives. From trying to earn or buy a blessing to trying to carry their end of the load, many women struggle with knowing and doing God's will for their lives.

Each time, my heart breaks as I encounter women caught in the trap of performance-based religion as evidenced in the two misconceptions described in today's study. *Performance-based religion perpetuates a human-based focus on an infinite God.* This focus is devoid of genuine love, devotion, and surrender to Jesus, who has given everything.

Please take a moment and react to the highlighted statement.

_____

_____

_____

This statement sums up why we should want to view God's will from a clear perspective and a pure heart. Performance-based religion puts God in a box and tries to confine Him to a formula. Dear friend, our God does not fit into a formula! God will never be A+B=C! Not only that, when we only seek God for the primary purpose of a blessing we may become devoid of genuine love, devotion, and surrender to the One who has already given us everything we need for life and godliness.

Today, I hope God has challenged your outlook on His will. Specifically, I hope this study is testing your heart to see *why* you desire to accomplish the will of God in your life. Please close with a prayer. If you feel the need to confess the sin of seeking His will for the wrong reasons, please take this opportunity to confess.

_____

_____

_____

Dear friend, I want you to know that I love you! I know there is a good chance that this lesson created a sense of tension in your heart and life. Pleases let me encourage you to embrace that tension. Tension is not always a bad thing. It can help us clarify our heart's desires. At the same time, allow me to encourage you. The fact that you are at this point in our study demonstrates your desire to know God and to seek His will for the *right* reason. Tomorrow, we will refocus on God alone as we seek to know His will for our lives.

Reflecting His Glory

Week 6: "…Then you will be able to test and approve what God's will is—his good, pleasing, and perfect will."

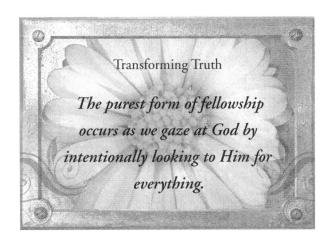

Transforming Truth

The purest form of fellowship occurs as we gaze at God by intentionally looking to Him for everything.

Day 2: Refocusing on God Alone

Yesterday we introduced the human trap of seeking God's will. Today, we will take a deep breath as we refocus our attention on God, and God alone. This time of refocus will prepare our hearts to examine God's good, pleasing, and perfect will from His perspective, not our own. Please join me in a word of prayer.

Dear Lord,

We praise You, for You are worthy to be praised! Today, we come to sit at Your feet and focus on You alone. May we see You for who You are—our King, high and lifted up and worthy of all praise. Lord, teach us this day. In Jesus' name we pray, amen.

Refocusing on God Alone

Psalm 25:15 serves as our focus passage of Scripture for today's time in the Word. Please look up Psalm 25:15 and write it in the space below.

_____

_____

_____

What a powerful word! David proclaimed, **"My eyes are ever on the LORD for only He will release my feet from the snare."** Each word or phrase is crucial as we seek to refocus on God alone.

- **My:** The first word in Psalm 25:15 is *my*; it shows us the important role our personal desires play in the refocusing process. In our walk with the Lord, we have two choices. We can **glance at Him** or we **can gaze at Him**. A *glance* involves taking a quick look or referring to the Lord briefly or indirectly. We *glance* when we only turn to the Lord when we need help or find ourselves in trouble. A gaze, on the other hand, involves fixing our eyes in a steady intent, looking often with eagerness and studious attention. We *gaze* when we seek the Lord each and every day.

  Daily we are called to make a choice. Will we glance or will we gaze? On some days it is easy to gaze; on other days, it is not. As we daily make the choice to gaze, we establish a godly habit of fixing our eyes on the Lord.

Today, do you find yourself glancing at Him or gazing at Him?

_____

The use of the word *my* indicates David's resolve to actively participate in the process of gazing. David took on the challenge to gaze and, as a result, developed a love relationship with the Lord that moved his walk forward, allowing the will of God to be accomplished in his life. Other passages of Scripture support David's resolve as well as sensitivity to gaze. Please look up the following verses and fill in the blanks.

- Psalm 9:1-2: "___ will praise you, O Lord, with all ___ heart; ___ will tell of all your wonders. ___ will be glad and rejoice in you; ___ will sing praise to your name, O Most High."
- Psalm 62:1: "___ soul finds rest in God alone; ___ salvation comes from Him. He alone is ___ rock and ___ salvation; he is ___ fortress, ___ will never be shaken."

- Psalm 91:2: "____ will say of the Lord, He is ____ refuge and ____ fortress, ____ God, in whom ____ trust."

These passages indicate that David's focus was on the Lord. With each proclamation, David resolved to take personal responsibility to gaze. As David gazed, his soul found rest and fellowship with God. This fellowship became the central focus of David's walk, allowing him to know and understand the will of God in his life.

 Why do you think it is important to take on the personal responsibility to gaze?

_____

_____

- **Eyes:** The second word is *eyes*. This word challenges us to examine what our eyes are looking to and looking for. If we gaze at the Lord, then our eyes will obviously be focused on Him. By clearly focusing on the Lord, we begin to know and experience His truth. This knowledge enables us to test the will of God from a new perspective. The apostle John writes about this concept in 1 John 1:1-3. This passage comes to life in the Amplified Bible.

"[We are writing] about the Word of Life [in] Him Who existed from the beginning, Whom we have heard, Whom we have seen with our [own] eyes, Whom we have gazed upon [for ourselves] and have touched with our [own] hands. And the Life [an aspect of His being] was revealed (made manifest, demonstrated), and we saw [as eyewitnesses] and are testifying to and declare to you the Life, the eternal Life [in Him] Who already existed with the Father and Who [actually] was made visible (was revealed) to us [His followers]. What we have seen and [ourselves] heard, we are also telling you, so that you too may realize and enjoy fellowship as partners and partakers with us. And [this] fellowship that we have [which is a distinguishing mark of Christians] is with the Father and with His Son Jesus Christ (the Messiah)."

This passage of Scripture challenges me. To paraphrase John, "what we have seen, what we have heard, what we have experienced, we pass on to you so that you too may know truth and experience truth." How did John and his fellow disciples know and experience truth? Very simply, truth became apparent through the process of fellowshipping with God the Father and Jesus Christ the Son. **The purest form of fellowship occurs as we gaze at God by intentionally looking to Him for everything.** The result of the gaze occurs when our eyes see what the Father sees, when our ears hear what the Father speaks, and when our experiences continually point us back to the Father's heart. When this occurs, we too can say, "what we have seen, what we have heard, what we have experienced, we pass on to you."

Please describe the role continual fellowship plays in knowing and fulfilling the will of God in your life.

_____

_____

• **Are ever on:** The third phrase is *are ever on*. The word *ever* in the Hebrew means "continually, perpetually, daily, morning and evening, without interruption, and regularly." From this definition we can sense David's desire to focus on the Lord. In essence David states, "My eyes are continually, perpetually, daily, morning and evening, without interruption, and regularly on the Lord."

Does this resolve by David challenge you? Please explain.

_____

_____

David's desire to focus on the Lord left little room for wondering how serious he was about fellowship with the Lord. From this definition I believe we can know that when David was confused, sad, glad, or apathetic, his desire was the same—"My eyes are ever on."

Is your life characterized by a continual, perpetual, daily, morning and evening, without interruption, and regular looking at God?

_____

_____

How do you think this kind of commitment to gazing would enable you to know and fulfill the will of God in your life?

_____

_____

• **The LORD**: Where were David's eyes? The fourth phrase answers this question by stating *on the LORD*. This phrase teaches the focus of our love, devotion, and affection; it is the most important phrase in this verse and communicates the recipient of David's continual love and attention. Let me explain. Please fill in the blanks using Psalm 25:15.

___ ___ ___ ___ ___ the LORD ___ ___ ___ ___ ___ ___ ___ ___ ___ ___.

I hope you noted that everything in this verse points to the phrase, "the LORD." Think about it. The first phrase is "My eyes are ever on…." The final phrase is "… for only he will release my feet from the snare." Both phrases point to *the LORD*.

Today as you and I seek to gaze at God in order to refocus on Him alone, our lives should reflect the same concept. Everything about our lives should point to the LORD.

How often can you say that everything in your life points to the Lord as your focus?

_____

_____

The word *LORD* (spelled with all capitals) in Psalm 25:15 represents Yahweh, the covenant name for God. This name was held in such high esteem that the Jews would not speak the name but rather substituted another name for God in its place. Today as we think about refocusing our lives on the Lord, we can praise God that we have the opportunity to speak His name and to know Him in a personal way. As this truth brings us to a place of intimacy with our Father, we must be careful that we do not miss an important truth. We daily need to recognize our Father as the *LORD*. As a result, we need a sense of reverence, respect, and godly fear in our thoughts of Him. Each day we need to recognize who He is and who we are in response to Him.

In your walk with God, do you reverence, respect, and fear the LORD?

_____

_____

• **For only he:** How do we reverence and respect God? By submitting to the truth of the fifth phrase—*for only he*. Every day we need to be reminded of this thought—*for only He*. Take a moment and say this phrase out loud. "For only He. For only He." The *for only He* aspect teaches that God is unique and the only one who can truly provide deliverance in our lives. Dear friend, we serve the one true God! In Psalm 35:10 David says, **"My whole being will exclaim, who is like you, O Lord? You rescue the poor from those too strong for them, the poor and needy from those who rob you."** Without a doubt, David knew the *for only He* aspect of God.

The apostle Paul echoed the *for only He* concept in the New Testament. Paul states that Christ "is the image of the invisible God the first born over all creation. For by him all things were created: things in heaven and on earth, visible and invisible, whether thrones or powers or rulers or authorities; all things were created by him and for him. He is before all things, and in him all things hold together" (Colossians 1:15-16).

Do you hear the proclamation of the Old and New Testament? For only He. Please take a moment and rewrite each verse in your own words. As you write, be mindful of the *for only He* implications in each.

Psalm 35:10

_____

_____

Colossians 1:15-16

_____

_____

- **Will release my feet:** This sixth phrase of this verse is *will release my feet*. In this phrase we begin to see the deliverance that comes from gazing at God. Two words in this phrase prove critical to our understanding.

- First, the word *release*. The word *release* means, "to come forth, go out, to proceed, or go forth." The word carries the idea of **movement**. When we are released from a snare, God desires for us to move forward in our lives. What does this truth mean to you?

_____

_____

_____

- Second, the word *feet*. The word *feet* literally means "foot." What is the primary use of your feet? The answer is simple. Feet were made for walking.

What I love about Psalm 25:15 is that we see the words *release* and *feet* used together within this verse. When we think about the words *release* (to come forth, go out, to proceed, or go forth) and *feet* (signifying walk), we discover that the Lord desires to move or release us forward in our walks with Him.

For just a moment let's think about the concept of our walk with God. In the NIV Bible, the word *walk* is used 244 times. The word is often used to encourage believers to live or walk a faithful life before the Lord. Please look up a few examples and fill in the blanks:

Genesis 17:1: "When Abram was ninety-nine years old, the LORD appeared to him and said, "I am God almighty; _____ before me and be blameless."

2 John 1:6. "And this is love: that we _____ in obedience to His commands. As you have heard from the beginning, his command is that you _____ in love."

These passages encourage us to walk before the Lord with a heart that pleases Him by focusing on Him. As we walk before the Lord with a right heart, our lives are impacted.

- **From the snare:** In the final phrase, we discover the benefit of walking before God with a right heart that is focused on God alone. The final phrase teaches that we are released *from the snare*. The word *snare* used in this passage means "net" and describes an object used for catching. You can probably visualize a fishing net or something similar. Have you ever been there? Have you been caught in the snare? The snare may represent a sin in your life or a set of troubling life circumstances that overwhelm you.

Please describe one or two of your current snares.

_____

_____

_____

Recap

Deliverance comes as we take God at His Word. The principles found in today's passage provide a good set of instructions as we make the choice to refocus on God alone. Take a look at the recap below.

- *My:* A personal commitment to the process of **gazing** at God. Gazing involves fixing your eyes in a steady intent, looking eagerly and often with studious attention.
- *Eyes:* Making **fellowship** with the Lord the number one priority of your day and moving past a habit of glancing that merely looks to God when you are in need or in trouble.

- *Are ever on:* Allowing the fellowship to occur **continually, perpetually, daily, morning and evening, without interruption,** and **regularly.**
- *The LORD:* Reflecting the concept of this passage by finding your focus in life on the LORD as **reverence, respect, and godly fear** become priorities in life.
- *For only He:* Why? For only He! There is none **like Him.**
- *Will release my feet:* **Forward movement** in your walk becomes a reality in your life.
- *From the snare:* **Freedom** results as you are freed from sin to continually focus on the Lord.

Conclusion

How does Psalm 25:15 tie into this week's study on the will of God? This verse provides encouragement to refocus our thoughts and attention solely on the Lord. This refocusing process combats the tendency to focus on the will of God from a self-centered perspective as described in yesterday's study.

As we close, please read Romans 12:2 and underline the noun and pronoun used to describe whose will is being accomplished in our lives.
Do not conform any longer to the pattern of this world, but be transformed by the renewing of your mind. Then you will be able to test and approve what God's will is—his good, pleasing and perfect will. (Romans 12:2)

Clearly God's will is being accomplished. Have you ever noticed this truth? So often we believers seek God's will from a perspective of "me." As we take this approach, we fail to recognize that it is God's will at stake, not our own. Therefore, as we spend the remainder of our Bible study looking at the good, pleasing, and perfect will of God, we will examine this topic from His holy perspective, not our own. Why? Because it is His will that is being accomplished in our lives. As we follow His will, we *reflect His glory.*

Please close with a word of prayer expressing your desire to know God's will for your life.

_____

_____

_____

_____

_____

_____

Reflecting His Glory

Week 6: "…Then you will be able to test and approve what God's will is—his good, pleasing and perfect will."

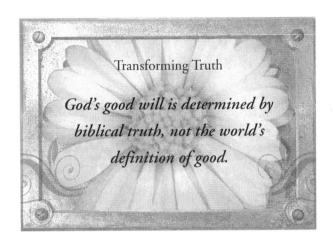

Transforming Truth

God's good will is determined by biblical truth, not the world's definition of good.

Day 3: God's Good Will

In Romans 12:2, the apostle Paul used three words to describe God's will. The first word he used is *good*. Over the next two days, we will study God's **good** will for our lives. I trust your heart is prepared to embark on this adventure. Hold on—it's going to be fun! Let's pray.

Dear Lord,

We praise You because You are worthy to be praised. As we seek to know and understand Your good will for life, teach us to view this topic from Your perspective. Lord, forgive the narrow vision from our past and challenge each of us through Your amazing Word. We give You all the glory. In Jesus' name we pray, amen.

Defining God's Good Will for Life

Defining the *good will of God* becomes a challenge as we choose to view God's good will from His perspective, not our own. In Day One, we defined God's will as His good pleasure carried out by believers. God's will is what He wants done; it is the set of actions and attitudes that bring Him glory and advance His kingdom. We accomplish God's will by obeying His revealed commands, recognizing His work in our lives, and fulfilling the things He calls us to do. When we obey God's will, our hearts long to please Him.

For the purpose of this study, we are going to also look at God's will from the vantage point of God's work in our lives. This is necessary because before we have the ability to carry out God's good pleasure on this earth, we first must understand the nature of His work in our lives.

The Greek word used for *good* in Romans 12:2 "represents something as being advantageous to another, promoting welfare. It often signifies inherent goodness, and describes something as virtuous."[57]

Today, as we think about the *good* will of God, God's Word will challenge us to broaden our understanding of the word *good*. God's Word will teach us that *good* involves anything that is advantageous and promotes spiritual welfare in our lives. The beauty of understanding God's good will becomes a realization that *good* encompasses difficult as well as easy times in our lives.

It is important to note that God's definition of *good* is not the same as the world's definition. The world's definition of *good* involves things going well as prescribed by a worldly measurement system. God's measurement system is different from the world's system. God uses both easy and difficult times to produce His virtuous character in us. Understanding this truth allows us to recognize God's good will in our lives and to see how His good will is displayed in the Word of God.

What difference does it make to know that God uses both difficult and easy things in your life to produce His good will?

_____

_____

_____

Are you currently going through a difficult situation or circumstance in your life? If so, please describe.

_____

_____

_____

Are you open to the idea that God may be allowing this situation or circumstance to occur in order to draw you closer to Him?

_____

Do others try to tell you God's good will only comes in the form of easy times as demonstrated in the world's definition of *good*?   YES   NO

If yes, please describe the difficulty this presents.

_____

_____

Three Principles for Seeking God's Good Will

Now that we have set the stage for the good will of God, let's open the Word of God and discover three foundational principles that allow us to recognize and experience God's good will in our lives.

Please open your Bible to Deuteronomy 13:1-5. Before you read, allow me to share some background information. In this passage, Moses provided instruction to the children of Israel as they prepared to enter and possess the Promised Land. Within these instructions, Moses cautioned the children about accepting false prophets' teachings that focused on outward signs and wonders instead of following truth as revealed by God and His authentic spokesmen. Moses' instructions are relevant to us as we seek to understand God's good will in our lives. We will be challenged to look past *good* as seen in the world's definition and embrace biblical truth as taught in God's holy Word.

Please read Deuteronomy 13:1–5.

We can draw three foundational principles from this passage. Each principle teaches the necessity of a discerning heart that understands that God's good will is based on God's Word, not the world's definition of *good*.

- **Principle 1**: Seeking to obey God's good will always reveals to God the individual's heart. Please reread Deuteronomy 13:1–3 and answer the questions below.

Please describe the main theme of Moses' warning found in Deuteronomy 13: 1–3a.

_____

_____

_____

According to Deuteronomy 13:3b, why would God allow the false prophets to arise?

_____

_____

_____

The theme of Moses' warning centered on the rise of false prophets and the tendency the Israelites would face in following the "good" predictions, instructions, and directions the false prophets supplied. Moses knew that once the Israelites entered the Promised Land, they would be tempted to embrace worldly views. Additionally, Moses knew that when times got tough, the Israelites would be easy prey for anyone providing a "good" word that boosted morale and delivered information that was pleasant to hear.

As the Old Testament unfolds, Moses' warning proved to be valid as the Israelites' desire for peace and prosperity during times of difficulty and pain caused the nation to embrace false hope by turning from God. Time and time again, the Israelites experienced difficult events, and false prophets arose with a "good" word of encouragement that promised easier times in the future. The people often accepted these words and bought into the lies the false prophets provided. As this occurred, the Israelites failed to recognize the reality that God allowed times of difficulty and pain in order to get their attention and lead them to repentance. When the Israelites chose to turn from God's discipline and embrace the false prophets' words, the people fell deeper and deeper into sin. Lamentations 2:14 reflects the sad reality the nation of Israel eventually faced: **"The visions of your prophets were false and worthless; they did not expose your sin to ward off your captivity. The oracles they gave you were false and misleading."**

Each time the Israelites turned from God in order to create a "good" reality, the result was further captivity. Today we face the same tendency as we seek advice, counsel, or direction from any well-meaning person who willingly tells us what our ears desire to hear instead of what our hearts need to know.

List the people in your life who tend to tell you what your ears want to hear instead of what your heart needs to know.

_____

_____

_____

The false prophets played a God-prescribed role in the Israelites' history. Deuteronomy 13:3 states: "You must not listen to the words of that prophet or dreamer. The Lord your God is testing you to find out whether you love him with all your heart and with all your soul."

God allowed the false prophets to arise within the nation of Israel in order to reveal the hearts of His people. As the false prophets arose, the people had a clear choice to make—would they hold fast to God's instructions or would they embrace the teachings and practices the false prophets provided?

Why do you think God allows people with false messages into our lives?

_____

_____

_____

One great test in the Christian walk occurs as we ask ourselves the question, "Do I really desire to know God's thoughts on the situations and circumstances of my life?" The answer reveals our heart and reflects our true motive in seeking the will of God. If the Israelites had truly desired God's answers to the problems they faced, false prophecy would never have been an issue. Why? Because the hearts of the Israelites would have been focused on the Lord.

As you think about this principle, please respond to the concept that seeking God's good will always reveals what is in the believer's heart.

_____

_____

_____

What is in your heart? Do you really desire God's thoughts on your situations and circumstance, or do you tend to desire "good" predictions because they are more pleasant?

_____

_____

_____

• **Principle 2: Seeking to obey God's good will requires that we keep His commands and follow His ways**. Deuteronomy 13:4 states: "It is the Lord your God you must follow, and him you must revere. Keep his commands and obey him; serve him and hold fast to him." The Hebrew word *keep* used in this passage "expresses the careful attention paid to the obligations of a covenant, to laws, or to statutes."[58] Keeping God's commands and following His ways does not occur as a one-time event in our lives. Rather, the Word of God instructs believers to follow, revere, keep, obey, serve, and hold fast to the Lord. This process occurs daily and provides a safety net for believers who must fight the temptation to follow the "good" predictions of others as well as the confusing desires in our hearts.

Do you strive to keep the commands of God on a daily basis?

_____

_____

Explain how following, revering, keeping, obeying, serving, and holding fast enables you to know the good will of God.

_____

_____

The above actions of following, revering, keeping, obeying, serving, and holding fast to God's Word ensure that we seek and find God's thoughts on the situations and circumstances going on in our lives. The Bible provides the starting point in this process and becomes the plumb-line by which everything is measured. Once you and I have God's thought firm in our hearts, we can know that God will enable us to discern His good will for our lives.

• **Principle 3: Seeking to obey God's good will separate us from the outside influencers of this world.** Moses in Deuteronomy 13:5 states: "That prophet or dreamer must be put to death, because he preached rebellion against the Lord your

God, who brought you out of Egypt and redeemed you from the land of slavery." The clear instruction to "put to death" the false prophet who tried to turn the hearts of the people away from God was real. God was and is serious about His holiness.

As you and I are serious about the holiness of God, we also find the need to deal with outside influencers in our lives. These are people who try to turn us away from seeking God's good will as revealed in His Word. Of course, we are not to put these people to physical death but rather deal with them in a spiritual manner. We can discipline ourselves to intentionally limit the amount of influence we give to people who have not demonstrated a commitment to obey God's will.

Who are the people in your life that you need to redefine your relationship with so that you are separated from their influence?

_____

_____

_____

I find it interesting that in the process of teaching the people about the danger of false prophets, Moses stated who God is and what God had done. Please reread Deuteronomy 13:5 and answer the following questions.

List the title Moses used to remind the people of who God is.

_____

What did Moses remind the people that God had done?

_____

Today, as you and I seek the good will of God, the same reminder applies. We serve the Lord our God; He has delivered us from the land of slavery and will continue to deliver us from the land of slavery. The deliverance occurs as we know who He is and what He has done.

Conclusion

Moses clearly warned the Israelites to be on their guard against people who enticed them with outside signs and wonders. Although these signs and wonders seemed "good," they were actually a test revealing the inner quality of the people's hearts. If the Israelites had passed the test, they would have discerned the good will of God and embraced biblical truth—the truth that was God's word as communicated through His prophets. Thus, the people would have experienced the very meaning of God's good will. They would have recognized God's good pleasure to be carried out in their actions and attitudes. As a result, the people would have experienced a development in virtuous character and spiritual welfare that resulted from knowing and fulfilling the good will of God.

Today as you and I seek God's good will, we also must avoid the world's definition of good as evidenced in outward signs of material blessing and a life that is free from pain and stress. Instead, we must embrace biblical truth, which focuses on the heart and always falls in line with God's Word. We must surrender to the fact that God's good will encompasses difficult as well as easy times with the designed purpose of producing virtuous character and promoting spiritual welfare in us.

From the three principles listed in today's study, please describe the most challenging principle for you and tell why.

_____

_____

_____

_____

What steps do you need to take in order to implement this principle in your life?

_____

_____

_____

Tomorrow we will examine three more principles as we continue to seek God's good will from His perspective, not our own. Please close today's lesson with a word of prayer asking the Lord to help you know His good will for your life.

_____

_____

_____

Reflecting His Glory

Week 6: "…Then you will be able to test and approve what God's will is—his good, pleasing and perfect will."

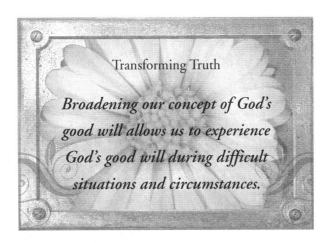

Transforming Truth

Broadening our concept of God's good will allows us to experience God's good will during difficult situations and circumstances.

Day 4: God's Good Will (Continued)

Today we continue our look at the good will of God. Remember we defined God's will as His good pleasure carried out by believers. We further defined God's will as what He wants done; it is the set of actions and attitudes that bring Him glory and advance His kingdom. We accomplish God's will by obeying His revealed commands, recognizing His work in our lives, and fulfilling the things He calls us to do. When we obey God's will, our hearts long to please Him and reflect His glory.

As we look at God's good will, we must remember to examine it from His perspective, not our own. Yesterday, we broadened our view of God's *good* will by examining the word *good*. In Romans 12:2 *good* represents something as being advantageous to another, or promoting welfare. Good in this context often signifies inherent goodness and describes something as virtuous. The beauty of understanding God's good will becomes a realization that good encompasses the difficult as well as easy times in our lives. The principles from yesterday's study reflect the truth that God's good will is often different than the world's definition of good. Let's refresh our memory.

- **Principle 1:** Seeking to obey God's good will always reveals the individual's heart to God.
- **Principle 2:** Seeking to obey God's good will requires that we keep His commands and follow His ways.
- **Principle 3:** Seeking to obey God's good will separates us from the outside influencers of this world.

Today we will discover three more principles that can help us understand God's good will in our lives. These principles teach that we can be following God's good will—giving Him pleasure and reflecting His glory—even when our circumstances are very difficult. Join me as we pray.

Dear Lord,

We praise You for Your awesome power! Today we are reminded that You are alive and that no amount of uncertainty, evil, or apathy can stop Your plans. As we open Your holy Word, teach us about Your good will. May we desire You and Your thoughts more than anything else. To You be all the glory! Amen.

Three More Principles For Seeking God's Good Will

Please turn in your Bible to Acts 27. Verses 1-26 serve as our focus passage for the final three principles in seeking God's good will for life. Before we dig in, allow me to set the context. In Acts 26, Paul, imprisoned for his faith, eloquently states his case before King Agrippa. As a Roman citizen, Paul appeals to Caesar and therefore is sent by King Agrippa to Rome. Acts 27 and 28 record the events of Paul's journey from Caesarea to Rome. During this journey, we see God's good will in action as God continually provides for Paul's every need. We also discover three more principles for seeking God's good will for life.

- **Principle 4: God's good will is worked out in both difficult and easy life situations.** Please read Acts 27:1-20. As you read, list the "negative" situations or circumstances Paul faced.

_____

_____

_____

_____

_____

_____

_____

As I read Acts 27:1-20, I noted the following "negative" situations or circumstances:

- Paul was a prisoner (verse 1)
- Paul was forced to sail to Rome (verse 2)
- The winds were against Paul and the other travelers (verse 4)
- Paul had no control over his life (verse 6)
- Paul and his companions made slow progress as they traveled, and their journey took longer than expected (verses 7–8)
- The sailing was dangerous (verse 9)
- None of the authorities would listen to Paul's warning (verses 10–11)
- A terrible storm occurred (verses 13–20)
- Paul and the others gave up hope of being saved (verse 20).

As you read this list, can you feel the helplessness of Paul's situation? I can. Paul had no control over his life and his circumstances were deteriorating. I wonder what it must have been like for Paul and his fellow travelers to experience the day after day beating of the storm. Did you notice the intensity of Acts 27:20? "When neither the sun nor stars appeared for many days and the storm continued raging, we finally gave up all hope of being saved." Without a doubt, the situations and circumstances of Paul's life were negative. Yet God's good will was still at work.

How about you? Can you relate to the situations and circumstances Paul faced? Are you experiencing a major storm or two in your life? If so, please make a list of the negative situations and circumstances currently affecting your life.

-
-
-
-
-
-
-
-

Were you able to list several negative situations in your life? It seems like life is always producing challenges. As we examine the good will of God, I hope you are encouraged by the fact that God's good will can be worked out in difficult as well as easy situations. There will be times when your "negative" list is long. However, you can rest in God's Word that His good will can be in effect during these times.

- **Principle 5: God's good will often produces reassurances in the form of a specific word or promise.** Please read Acts 27:21–24 and answer the following questions.

Who appeared to Paul the night before? _____

What did the angel say? _____

What do you think this message meant to Paul?

_____

_____

_____

I love the fact that the Word records that the *angel stood near*. In the face of the most trying situations and circumstances of life, God is near. As the angel stood near, he provided a reassuring message. The angel said, "Do not be afraid, Paul. You must stand trial before Caesar, and God has graciously given you the lives of all who sail with you" (Acts 27:24).

What a gift of grace Paul received that night! He received assurance that the situations and circumstances of his life were neither out of God's sight nor out of God's control. This word teaches us a vital lesson. **As we seek the good will of God, God's Word often gives us reassurances in the form of a specific word or promise. These specific words or promises bring peace into our hearts as we face unknown situations and circumstances in our lives.**

Today as we think about the good will of God, we need to understand that the good will of God does not always come in the form of a tidy solution to every problem we face. Sometimes the good will of God comes as He walks us through the messy situations of life by graciously providing help, comfort, and direction. We make ourselves available to this help, comfort, and direction as we read His word, fellowship with other believers, and spend time listening to His voice.

Perhaps you can relate to Paul's experience that night on the ship. You too have received a specific word of encouragement from the Lord during a trying situation or circumstance of life. I just wonder if you have recognized that word as God's good will at work in your life?

Please describe a time when you faced a difficult situation or circumstance and the Lord reassured you through a word of encouragement.

_____

_____

_____

• **Principle 6: God's good will always brings us into a closer, deeper relationship with Christ Jesus our Lord.** Paul states in Acts 27:25: "So keep up your courage, men, for I have faith in God that it will happen just as he told me." The words *have faith* come from the single word *pisteuo* in the Greek. This word means "to be persuaded in the truthfulness of."[59] Paul was persuaded of the truthfulness of his God. The result? Paul's love and devotion for the Lord grew. Although Paul's situation and circumstance did not change and were negative from the world's viewpoint, Paul's faith in the Lord grew as a result of his encounter with the Lord on the ship that night. Thus the good will of God was at work in the heart and life of Paul.

Today we are challenged with the same principle. Independent of the situations and circumstances of life, can we say, "I have faith in God that it will happen just as He told me?" We will only make this type of statement when we embrace the notion that the focus of God's good will must be on bringing us into a closer, deeper relationship with Christ Jesus our Lord.

How did today's time in the Word challenge your perspective on the good will of God?

_____

_____

_____

_____

_____

Our time in the Word challenges me to view God's good will from His perspective, not my own. Everything in me desires for the situations and circumstances of my life to be neat and tidy. I want Jay's and my marriage to be perfect, our children to behave, our finances to be stable, no sickness in our immediate or extended family, Jay's job to be secure, our vehicles to run, our home to be just right, our pantry to be full—the list goes on and on. However, God's Word cautions me about my narrow vision. Just as Paul faced trying situations and circumstances in his life, I too will face times when the goodness of God cannot be based on our evaluation of visible circumstances. Embracing this truth brings freedom as I begin to trust the good will of God in difficult as well as easy times of life. The truth of the matter is this. The good will of God does not rest on any of the indicators that I listed above but solely on the truth that God is with me. No matter what situation or circumstance I face, He is enough. I praise God for this truth and know that as He graciously provides words of encouragement via His Word and His people, I can make it through anything.

Conclusion

As you and I seek to define God's good will for our lives, we must move past the tendency of thinking that the good things strictly come in the form of the world's definition of good. Instead we must embrace the concept that God deeply desires for believers in Christ to be conformed to the image of His Son. This truth leads each of us to know and embrace God's good will for our lives. Accepting this concept focuses our eyes on God's good will from His perspective and results in the situations and circumstances of life leading each of us to a closer, deeper relationship with Christ. As our lesson on God's good will comes to a close, I pray that you have a better understanding of God's good will for your life. Let's take one final look at all six principles for God's Word that taught us how to seek and understand the good will of God.

- Principle 1: Seeking to obey God's good will always reveals the individual's heart.
- Principle 2: Seeking to obey God's good will requires that we keep His commands and follow His ways.
- Principle 3: Seeking to obey God's will separates us from the outside influencers of this world.
- Principle 4: God's good will is worked out in both difficult and easy life situations.
- Principle 5: God's good will often produces reassurances in the form of a specific word or promise.
- Principle 6: God's good will always brings us into a closer, deeper relationship with Jesus Christ our Lord.

Record your thoughts about God's good will as you think about all six of these principles.

_____

_____

_____

Please close by journaling a prayer to God.

_____

_____

_____

_____

_____

_____

_____

_____

_____

_____

_____

_____

_____

_____

_____

_____

_____

_____

_____

_____

Reflecting His Glory

Week 6: "…Then you will be able to test and approve what God's will is—his good, pleasing and perfect will."

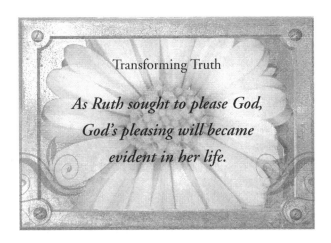

Transforming Truth

As Ruth sought to please God, God's pleasing will became evident in her life.

Day 5: God's Pleasing Will

Today we continue our study on the will of God by focusing on the *pleasing* aspect of God's will. As we have in previous days, we will look at this topic from God's perspective, not our own. Please join me in prayer.

Dear Lord,

We praise You, for You are God. This day I am reminded of Your faithfulness—not just to my family and me but to the generations that have gone before. Your Word is true, and You are true. You are worthy of our praise. Lord, we choose to rest in You; no matter what challenges we face, we find our home with You. Please forgive the sins of our hearts and the sins of our flesh. Lord, teach us this day about Your

pleasing will and may we desire that will above the things of this world. In Jesus' name, amen.

Romans 12:2 states: **"Do not conform any longer to the pattern of this world, but be transformed by the renewing of your mind. Then you will be able to test and approve what God's will is—his good, *pleasing* and perfect will"** (emphasis added).

The word *pleasing* used in this passage means "well-pleasing, acceptable, that which God recognizes."[60] As we think about the pleasing will of God, we immediately see the focus is on pleasing Him not ourselves. This occurs as we follow His plans. Remember, we defined the will of God as His good pleasure being carried out by believers. God's will is what He wants done; it is the set of actions and attitudes that bring Him glory and advance His kingdom. We accomplish God's will by obeying His revealed commands, recognizing His work in our lives, and fulfilling the things He calls us to do. When we obey God's will, our hearts long to please Him and reflect His glory.

Today, as we seek to know God's pleasing will for our lives, we will focus on our actions and attitudes and make sure they are pleasing in God's sight.

The Life Of Ruth

The Bible records the account of a special woman whose life displayed the pleasing will of God. Ruth lived her life with a clear focus and sought to please God. Through Ruth's life, we learn that our actions and attitudes play a role in us fulfilling the pleasing will of God by positioning us to live the life God has called us to live. In no way does this make God dependent upon us; rather, it increases our dependency upon Him.

As we study the first two chapters of the Old Testament book of Ruth, we will see how Ruth's actions and attitudes positioned her to experience the pleasing will of God. As we seek to do the same, we can note several principles from Ruth's life that show the importance of our actions and attitudes in the identification of God's pleasing will.

In order to understand Ruth's life, we must familiarize ourselves with the book of Ruth. Much more than that, we must imagine ourselves in Ruth's situations and circumstances and ask the questions, "How would I feel? What would I do?"

Please read Ruth chapters 1 and 2 and answer the following questions. As you read, allow your heart to became completely involved in the story. Remember, these were real people facing real obstacles and serving the same God we serve today.

Chapter 1

• According to verse 2, please list the names of the family members who left Bethlehem to escape a famine and settled in the land of Moab.

_____

_____

• In verse 3, what happened to Elimelech?

_____

• In verse 4, what did the sons do? What were the women's names?

_____

• In verse 5, what happened to the sons?

_____

• List the decision Naomi makes in verses 6–7.

_____

• Verses 8–19 record Naomi's desire for Ruth and Orpah to return to their homeland. Please describe the decision each daughter-in-law makes.

_____

_____

• Please describe Naomi's perspective on life as listed in verses 20–22.

_____

_____

Explanation of Chapter 1

Chapter 1 of the book of Ruth sets the stage for this amazing story. It describes how a family of four—Elimelech, his wife Naomi, and their sons Mahlon and Kilion—departed from Bethlehem to go to the land of Moab in search of food. Once in Moab, Elimelech died, leaving Naomi with her two sons. The sons married Moabite women named Ruth and Orpah. Following ten years of marriage, both Mahlon and Kilion died.

Upon hearing that the Lord had come to the aid of His people in Bethlehem, Naomi set out to return to her homeland, accompanied by Ruth and Orpah. On the way, Naomi pleaded with her daughters-in-law to return to their families in Moab. Orpah struggled with this decision but finally decided to return to her home in Moab.

In contrast, Ruth clung to Naomi and refused to return to Moab. Ruth's feelings are summed up in Ruth 1:16-18: "Don't urge me to leave you or to turn back from you. Where you go I will go, and where you stay I will stay. Your people will be my people and your God my God. Where you die I will die, and there I will be buried. May the Lord deal with me, be it ever so severely, if anything but death separates you and me." With Ruth's firm resolve, Naomi and Ruth continued their journey to Bethlehem.

In Bethlehem, Naomi's return created a great deal of excitement. (I imagine the presence of a young, beautiful Moabite woman helped to stir up the talk in town—funny how things never really change!) Although the people of Bethlehem were excited to see Naomi, Naomi's heart was broken over the events of her life. When Naomi left Bethlehem her life was full—she had a husband and two sons. Naomi's outlook on life becomes clear in Ruth 1:12. Naomi expressed that she had no hope—life seemed empty. Can you relate to Naomi? Do you know what it is like to feel like there is no hope in your life? If so, please take a few minutes and express your thoughts below.

_____

_____

_____

_____

_____

Chapter 1: Pleasing Character Qualities

From chapter 1, we discover a character quality that demonstrates Ruth's desire to please God in her life.

- **Ruth clung to the right things in life:** Ruth 1:14 states: "Orpah kissed her mother-in-law goodbye, but Ruth clung to her." Orpah chose to return to her family, friends, and gods in Moab. With this choice, Orpah displayed the priorities of her life. Although Orpah loved Naomi and was broken over leaving her, Orpah's love for Naomi never really changed her life, and Orpah turned back to her nation and her gods. Although Orpah struggled with the decision, her actions displayed the true desires of her heart. Orpah made the choice to turn back and in the process she clung to her familiar culture.

On the other hand, Ruth clung to Naomi. This resolve, displayed by Ruth, provides a glimpse into her heart. When Ruth became the wife of Naomi's son, her life was forever changed. Her allegiance moved from one culture to another. Did you hear the words of Ruth in Ruth 1:16-18? Ruth stated, "Don't urge me to leave you or turn back from you. Where you go I will go, and where you stay I will stay. Your people will be my people and your God my God." From this passage, I believe that Ruth's allegiance moved from the Moabite nation to the Jewish nation because her words and actions prove it. I think this happened because God was working in Ruth's life. He was positioning Ruth to play an important role in the hearts and lives of His people.

Today as we seek the pleasing will of God, we must examine our allegiances. In our daily walks, do we display the same resolve as Ruth? You see, we are the bride of Christ. The Bible uses the imagery of marriage to describe the relationship between Christ and the church. Jesus is the groom. The church is His bride. The church is made up of every believer in Jesus Christ. According to 2 Corinthians 11:2, the role of the bride is to keep herself clean while she waits on the groom to return for her. One day, Jesus will return for the church. In the meantime, we are to remain pure or clean before Him. This truth should bring the topic of our allegiances to the forefront of our minds. When we entered into a relationship with Jesus our hearts were forever changed and our citizenship transferred from one country (this earth) to the next (heaven). Just like we saw in Ruth's life, this fact changes the way we live our lives here on this earth. Our actions and attitudes should display the fact that heaven is our home even while we live on this earth. So the question is, "Who or what do you cling to?" Are you like Orpah, who was a bride with a divided heart? Or is your life evidenced by a clinging relationship to Christ? Please take a few moments and respond to this thought.

_____

_____

_____

• **Ruth lived a determined life:** Ruth 1:18 states: "When Naomi realized that Ruth was determined to go with her, she stopped urging her." Although Naomi tried to change Ruth's mind, there was no way anyone could change Ruth's mind. Ruth was determined to go with Naomi. She had reached her decision, and she was resolved. As we seek God's pleasing will in our lives, we also must display determination. We must know what God has called us to do, and we must do it with all our might.

Do you know God's specific will for your life? If so, what has God called you to do? What level of commitment are you displaying?

_____

_____

_____

Chapter 2:

- Ruth 2:1 introduces a man. What is the man's name? _____
- What does Ruth desire to do in verse 2? _____
- What is Naomi's response to Ruth? _____
- Where does Ruth glean? _____
- Did Boaz notice Ruth? (circle your answer)   YES or NO
- Did Boaz treat Ruth with respect? If so, please list the specific ways.

_____

_____

_____

- When Ruth returned to Naomi, what was Naomi's reaction?

_____

_____

_____

Explanation of Chapter 2

Chapter two tells of Ruth's entrance into the heart and lives of God's chosen people. In verse 1, Boaz, a man of good standing who is also related to Naomi, enters the story. Verse two relates Ruth's desire to go into the fields and glean food for herself and Naomi. Naomi granted Ruth permission to go to glean. Ruth set out to find a field and gleaned in the field of Boaz. As Ruth gleaned, Boaz arrived and immediately asked about Ruth. The foreman related that Ruth, a Moabite woman who returned to Bethlehem with Naomi, had asked permission to glean in the field and worked steadily throughout the day. Boaz showed great respect for Ruth when he took the following actions on her behalf:

- Invited Ruth to continually glean in his field (vss. 8–9)
- Offered protection from the dangers of the field (vs. 9)
- Provided for Ruth's physical needs (vs. 9)
- Invited Ruth to eat at his table (vs. 14)
- Cared for Ruth's emotional needs (vs. 15).

Following Ruth's day in the field, she returned home excited to share the events with Naomi. I can only imagine how excited Ruth must have been as she ran home with her grain! Anytime God works in a mighty way in my life, I am always anxious to share the news with my close family and friends. Ruth must have been beside herself just thinking about the events of the day—the way Boaz allowed her to glean in his field and his acts of kindness. When Naomi saw the bounty Ruth provided, Naomi asked, "Where did you glean?" Ruth shared all the details with Naomi, and together they rejoiced.

Chapter 2: Pleasing Character Qualities

- **Ruth displayed initiative:** In Ruth 2:2, Ruth displayed initiative when she asked permission to glean in the fields. Ruth stated: "Let me go to the fields and pick up the leftover grain behind anyone in whose eyes I find favor."

Please note that as Ruth displayed initiative, she respected the authority God had placed in her life. Ruth said, "Let me go." Ruth did not demand. Ruth asked permission. Dear friend, if we want to experience the pleasing will of God, then we must embrace the authority that goes along with His call on our lives. For many people, this idea is difficult to accept, especially for Type A personalities like myself. We enjoy our independence! This independence becomes a problem when we step outside of God's line of authority by ignoring the people God has placed in positions of authority in our lives. Often we do this by making the choice to take matters into our own hands.

Your line of authority begins with God. Then, depending on your situation in life, your authority might involve a husband, a boss, or a ministry leader. No matter who you are, you have a line of authority in your life, and it becomes crucial that you treat that line of authority with respect.

Once Ruth received permission to glean, Ruth took the initiative to provide food for Naomi and herself. We must realize that God's will is not achieved as we fold our arms or sit on our hands. Oftentimes God's pleasing will is demonstrated as we jump in and begin to work in order to accomplish His will for our lives.

How can you display initiative in your walk with God?

_____

_____

_____

Are you sensitive to your line of authority? _____

Please describe a situation in your life where you had to jump in and begin working in order to accomplish God's pleasing will.

_____

_____

_____

Ruth worked hard: When Ruth worked, she worked in a specific way. Ruth 2:7 verifies that Ruth worked *steadily*. The word *steadily* portrays a picture of Ruth's commitment to the task God called her to perform. Ruth worked hard, ensuring that she completed each portion of her task. Ruth did not experience merely an emotional commitment to the job, as seen in making a quick commitment and then allowing her enthusiasm to dwindle over a period of time. Ruth worked *steadily*. As Ruth worked, her actions displayed the attitude of her heart. Today we need to understand the same truth. The way we work shows others the attitude of our hearts and, in a real sense, what we believe about God. Why? Our work proves to be an overflow of our relationship with God.

Think about the work God has called you to perform, whether that is being a wife, a mom, a professional, or a mixture of all three. Would you describe yourself as a hard worker? If so, what advantage does that give you in Kingdom work?

_____

_____

_____

Do you fall into the trap of making an emotional commitment to a task and then allowing your commitment to complete it to dwindle over a period of time? If so, how could this hinder you from accomplishing God's pleasing will?

_____

_____

- **Ruth practiced humility:** In response to Boaz's provision for her needs, Ruth bowed with her face to the ground (Ruth 2:10). Ruth displayed a sense of humility as she recognized that Boaz did not have to provide for her needs but chose to anyway. This reminds us that we are not entitled to anything but that everything in life is a gift from God. The proper way to receive the gift is always with humility and thankfulness.

How often do you receive the gifts God provides with a humble heart?

_____

_____

_____

- **Ruth sought proper refuge:** In Ruth 2:12, Boaz commended Ruth for seeking proper refuge. Boaz said, "May the Lord repay you for what you have done. May you be richly rewarded by the Lord, the God of Israel, under whose wings you have come to take refuge." In this passage the word *refuge* means, "to trust in, confide in, or hope in."[61] Please note that in order for Ruth to experience the pleasing will of God, she had to come to the point of placing her complete trust, confidence, and hope in the Lord. She had to move to the place of no longer defending herself and put her complete trust in God.

Today, you and I face the same choice. We too must put our trust, confidence, and hope in the Lord. Often, without even realizing it, we say, "Lord, do this," or "Lord, do that," and ask God to prove Himself to us. But in reality, God has already proven Himself to us, and now we face the opportunity to respond by faith.

As you think about your heart and your life, do you seek proper refuge? Where is your trust, confidence, and hope?

_____

_____

_____

- **Ruth was a life giver:** In Ruth 2:14-18, we discover another amazing quality displayed in Ruth's life. Ruth was a life giver. After a morning of gleaning in the fields, Boaz invited Ruth to sit at his table and eat. Following the meal, Ruth continued to glean. That evening Ruth returned home and gave Naomi a portion of her meal. As Ruth shared her resources, Ruth allowed the life-giving measure of food to flow through her life.

How do we become a life giver? We allow the measure of Christ to flow through our lives. You see, before Ruth could help Naomi with her needs, Ruth first had to encounter the life source. She had to sit at the table with Boaz. Today, as we desire to allow the full measure of Christ to flow through our lives, we too must ensure that we are encountering Him on a daily basis. We too must make it a priority to sit with the Lord by studying His Word, spending time in prayer, and focusing our hearts on Him through worship.

Do you consider yourself to be a life giver?

_____

How often do you sit with the Lord?

_____

Conclusion

Next week we will conclude our study of Ruth. For now, please close with a word of prayer, asking the Lord to help you examine your actions and attitudes so that you can know and accomplish His *pleasing* will for your life.

_____

_____

_____

_____

_____

_____

_____

_____

Reflecting His Glory

Week 7: "…Then you will be able to test and approve what God's will is—his good, pleasing, and perfect will."

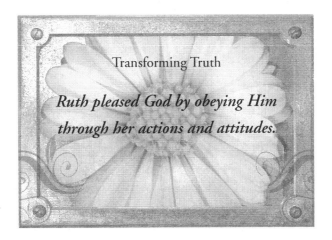

Transforming Truth

Ruth pleased God by obeying Him through her actions and attitudes.

Day 1: God's Pleasing Will (Continued)

Week Seven! You have made it to the final week of our study. Can you believe how quickly the time has passed? I am so proud of you. Beginning a Bible study is easy, but actually completing such a study proves more difficult. May God bless you, my dear friend, for being disciplined and faithful. I pray God has blessed your time of obedience in His amazing Word.

This week we will continue our study of God's good, pleasing, and perfect will. Again, our desire will be to see this topic from God's perspective, not our own. Please join me in a word of prayer.

Dear Lord,

We praise You, for You are the sovereign creator of the universe. You made the heaven and the earth. You spoke, and everything came into being. You know everything, and You are worthy of all our praise. Lord, forgive each of us for the times we have failed to recognize that You are sovereign over all things. This week as we complete our study, continue to teach us. Place within our hearts a passion for Your perspective on life. In the name of Jesus, amen.

The Life of Ruth (Continued)

Today we will complete our examination of Ruth's life. Last week we introduced Ruth as a person who sought to please God through her actions and attitudes. As Ruth sought to please God, the pleasing will of God became evident in her life. Remember, God's will is His good pleasure to be carried out by believers. God's will is what He wants done; it is the set of actions and attitudes that bring Him glory and advance His kingdom. We accomplish God's will by obeying His revealed commands, recognizing His work in our lives, and fulfilling the things He calls us to do. When we obey God's will, our hearts long to please Him and reflect His glory.

In Ruth 1 and 2, we discovered seven pleasing character qualities that Ruth displayed. Today we will explore chapters 3 and 4. During this process, we will find additional character qualities. **Please read Ruth 3-4.** (Feel free to review chapters 1 and 2.) When you have finished, answer the questions below.

Chapter 3

- In verse 1, what is Naomi's desire for Ruth?

_____

_____

_____

According to verse 2, what was Boaz's relation to Naomi's family?

_____

- What instructions did Naomi give Ruth in verses 3–4?

_____

_____

- What was Ruth's response in verse 5?

_____

- After Ruth obeys Naomi's instructions, how does Boaz respond (v. 7–15)? (please circle one)   Positively   or   Negatively

- In verses 16–18, Ruth relates the events of her evening to Naomi. What instruction did Naomi give Ruth in verse 18?

_____

_____

Explanation of Chapter 3

Ruth 3 is the heart of Ruth's story. The chapter opens with Naomi's desire for Ruth. In Ruth 3:1, Naomi stated: "My daughter, should I not try to find a home for you, where you will be well provided for?" I love Naomi's heart at this point in the story. Naomi centered her concern on Ruth. Naomi wanted Ruth to have a home—a place where she was taken care of and perhaps even loved. Not only did Naomi desire this for Ruth, Naomi put her desire into action and formulated a plan.

In Ruth 3:2, we are reminded that Boaz, who had already taken good care of Ruth, was a kinsman of Elimelech, Naomi's late husband. According to Jewish law, "when a man dies childless his brother was bound to raise an heir to him by the widow."[62] Naomi sought to find a home for Ruth by acting to see this law put into practice. Naomi instructed Ruth to wash and perfume herself, put on her best clothes, and go down to the threshing floor. Once there, Ruth was to conceal her identity until Boaz had eaten and was in good spirits. Ruth responded with wholehearted obedience to her mother-in-law's instructions.

Ruth approached Boaz and lay down at his feet. During the night, Boaz was startled and noticed a woman lying at his feet. Boaz asked, "Who are you?" When Ruth revealed her identity, Boaz responded out of love. He commended Ruth for not chasing younger, more attractive men. This exchange between Boaz and Ruth revealed the genuineness of their developing relationship and also set in motion the kinsman-redeemer process. A kinsman-redeemer was a person who was a near relative and had the right and responsibility to marry a widow in order to provide an heir for the deceased family member as well as status for the widow.

Boaz, a man of honor, told Ruth that he was not the closest kinsman-redeemer. A closer relative existed, and that relative had to be given the opportunity to marry Ruth. However, Boaz did not allow this fact to stand in the way of ministering to Ruth by providing her with reassurance. Ruth spent the night at Boaz's feet and returned home the next morning. When Naomi asked about what happened, Ruth shared each detail. In response, Naomi instructed Ruth to wait and see what would occur.

Chapter 3: Pleasing Character Qualities

• **Ruth listened and obeyed.** Naomi had a plan, and the plan involved Ruth. In order for the plan to work, Ruth had to follow clear instructions. In Ruth 3:5, Ruth responded, "I will do whatever you say." This reply displayed Ruth's teachable spirit. Ruth did not have her life so planned out that she could not yield to the instructions of another. Ruth displayed an attitude of obedience.

Today as you and I seek the pleasing will of God, we too must *listen* and *obey*. We must not over-plan, over-prepare, and over-organize our lives to the point where God is no longer in the mix. When this occurs, we become our own final authority as we determine the course of our lives. If you are like me, you know how easy it is to plan out your life and in the process forget God's call to listen and obey. I remember a time when I had a ministry opportunity at a local church, and I really wanted to take the job. To me, working in the local church was the next step on my professional "to do" list. I took the position without really praying about it. Don't get me wrong, I prayed about the position—I prayed that God would bless my plan! However, I never stopped to listen for His plan, and in the end, the ministry situation did not work out. My heart was broken, but I knew God was teaching me the importance of listening and obeying.

Listening and obeying are great ways to combat the self-sufficiency of over-planning, over-preparing, and over-organizing. Why? Because listening and obeying places us in a position of response to the Lord.

Do you struggle with over-planning, over-preparing, and over-organizing to the point where it becomes difficult for you to listen and obey?

_____

_____

- **Ruth knew the value of waiting.** In the final verse of chapter three, Naomi gave Ruth an important task—one that was easier said than done. Ruth 3:18 states: "Then Naomi said, 'Wait, my daughter, until you find out what happens.'" In this verse, Naomi told Ruth to *wait*.

The process of waiting plays a vital role in the pleasing will of God. I believe waiting is essential because waiting reveals the true motives in our hearts. Do we really want to please God? If so, are we willing to wait on His time and His way? Without a doubt, waiting is often difficult, especially if we feel like God has forgotten us.

Have you ever struggled with waiting? You felt you had done everything God had called you to do. You kept your eyes focused clearly on the Lord, and the answer was "wait a little longer." If so, take heart! While waiting is difficult, in the end waiting is rewarding to those who obey through the entire waiting process.

List one area from your life where you have sought the Lord and the call has been "wait a little more."

_____

_____

Please describe the difficulty of the waiting process.

_____

_____

_____

Do you see the value of the waiting process? If so, please explain.

_____

_____

_____

Chapter 4
- What actions did Boaz take in verses 1–2?

_____

_____

- What information did Boaz share with the man in verses 3–4?

_____

- What additional information did Boaz share in verse 5?

_____

- What was the man's response to this information as recorded in verse 6?

_____

- The decision was finalized through what process? (vs. 7–8)

_____

_____

- Verse 13 relates two events. Please list them.

_____

_____

- As a result, what do the women say in verses 14–15?

_____

_____

_____

- Who cared for the child?

_____

- According to the genealogy listed in verses 16–22, what position does this child play in the line of David?

_____

Explanation of Chapter 4

Chapter 4 completes the story of Ruth. Ruth 4:1–4 provides a glimpse into Boaz's commitment to Ruth. Boaz went to the city gate in order to wait for the kinsman-redeemer. When Boaz saw the kinsman-redeemer, Boaz invited him to sit down and talk with ten elders from the town to witness the conversation. Boaz shared that Naomi was selling a piece of property, and as the closest relative, the kinsman had the first opportunity to buy the land. The kinsman quickly agreed to buy the land. Boaz said that once the land is purchased, the owner would also acquire Ruth in order to produce an heir for her late husband. After learning this information, the kinsman told Boaz he was no longer interested in buying the land. I believe this was good news to Boaz, as he quickly purchased the land and took Ruth as his wife. After the marriage, the Lord enabled Ruth to conceive a child; Boaz and Ruth had a son named Obed.

When the women of the town heard the news about Obed, they rejoiced in God's provision for Naomi, as well as Ruth's commitment to her mother-in-law. Then, Naomi took Obed and laid him on her lap and cared for him. According to the genealogy listed in Ruth 4:16-22, Obed is the great-grandfather of David, the future King of Israel and man after God's own heart.

Chapter 4: Pleasing Character Quality

Ruth recognized and met the needs of others. Realizing that Naomi had lost two sons, Ruth displayed a lack of selfishness by allowing Naomi to take and care for Obed. I am amazed by this act of love on Ruth's part. I can tell you when I had my first son, I did not want anyone else to hold him, change him, feed him, rock him, or care for him. He was mine. As Ruth watched Naomi care for Obed she becomes a picture of genuine love and a great desire to meet the needs of others. For many years, Naomi's arms had been empty. It must have been incredible for Naomi to hold Obed. I believe this baby not only filled the heart of Ruth and Boaz but also the heart of Naomi. Today, as you and I seek the pleasing will of God, meeting the needs of others will play a role in the process.

How often do you respond to the needs of others?

_____

_____

Please describe one area where the Lord is challenging you to respond to the needs of others.

_____

_____

_____

How can responding to the needs of this person help you to know God's pleasing will in your life?

_____

_____

_____

Conclusion

As we read and understand the story of Ruth, we see God using Ruth to accomplish His pleasing will in many different ways. First, Ruth experienced a life she probably never dreamed possible as she pleased God with her actions and attitudes. Second, Naomi benefited from Ruth's actions and attitudes as she discovered that God would fill her life once again with good things. Third, the nation of Israel profited from the actions and attitudes of Ruth as God used Ruth to bear a child who would provide the line for King David and ultimately King Jesus.

Without a doubt, Ruth pleased God by obeying Him through her actions and attitudes. As we stated last week, this did not make God dependent upon Ruth but did increase Ruth's dependency upon God. We have the opportunity to live the same kind of life— a life dependent on Christ. The result of this life is the pleasing will of God working in and through our lives for His glory.

Of the ten actions and attitudes discovered in the story of Ruth, circle the one(s) that mean the most to you. Then explain why each characteristic provides meaning in your walk with God.
- Ruth clung to the right things in life.
- Ruth lived a determined life.
- Ruth displayed initiative.
- Ruth worked hard.
- Ruth practiced humility.
- Ruth sought proper refuge.
- Ruth was a life giver.
- Ruth listened and obeyed.
- Ruth knew the value of waiting.
- Ruth recognized and met the needs of others.

_____

_____

_____

_____

_____

_____

_____

_____

_____

_____

_____

_____

_____

Please close today's study with a word of prayer expressing your desire to bring your actions and attitudes into alignment with God's pleasing will for your life.

_____

_____

_____

_____

_____

_____

_____

_____

_____

_____

_____

_____

_____

Reflecting His Glory

Week 7: "…Then you will be able to test and approve what God's will is—his good, pleasing and perfect will."

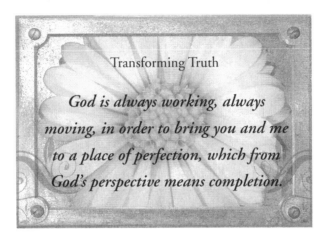

Transforming Truth

God is always working, always moving, in order to bring you and me to a place of perfection, which from God's perspective means completion.

Day 2: God's Perfect Will

Today we focus on God's *perfect* will. As we think about this topic, I want to challenge you again to examine the perfect will of God from His biblical perspective, not your own.

According to your thoughts, please define the word *perfect*.

_____

_____

_____

_____

I wonder if your definition matches Webster's definition? Webster defines *perfect* as "being entirely without fault or defect; corresponding to an ideal standard or abstract concept."[63] Clearly the word *perfect* is used to describe something being ideal, just right, or great—free from problems or perceived errors.

As we think about the *perfect* will of God, we must make sure that we view this concept through the lens of Holy Scripture. In order to do this, we must understand the meaning of the word *perfect* as used in the context of Romans 12:2 which states: **"Do not conform any longer to the pattern of this world, but be transformed by the renewing of your mind. Then you will be able to test and approve what God's will is—his good, pleasing and *perfect* will"** (emphasis added).

The word *perfect* used in this passage means "that which has achieved or reached its goal, objective, or purpose. Complete, perfected, or proficient. Referring to the final stage of glory."[64]

Please describe the differences between the two definitions of *perfect*.

_____

_____

_____

Why is it important to note the differences in these definitions?

_____

_____

_____

Webster's dictionary definition of *perfect* clearly focuses on something being free from problems or errors. In contrast, the definition of *perfect* from our Bible passage portrays the idea of completion. This difference is important in understanding and accepting the perfect will of God. Why? The difference between the two definitions forces each of us to move past a worldly perspective of perfection that desires a life free from problem or errors and to embrace a godly perspective that desires a life that is complete or whole in Him. **God is always working, always moving, in order to bring us to a place of perfection, which from God's perspective means completion.**

Today in our study we will see a real life example of the perfect will of God. I am going to ask you to trust me as you work through this lesson, even if you don't initially understand why we're looking at these particular Scriptures. When you reach the conclusion of today's lesson, you will discover the significance of the material.

For a change, I would like to ask you to lead us in our time of prayer. Please take a few minutes and express your heart to our Heavenly Father.

_____

_____

_____

_____

_____

_____

_____

_____

_____

_____

_____

_____

_____

God's Perfect Will—In Peter's Life

Today we will study two events from Peter's life which, when viewed together, provide an example of how God works and moves in the hearts and lives of His children. Before Peter enters this story, let's learn about a man named Cornelius. Please read Acts 10:1-8 and answer the following questions.

Please list the details provided in Acts 10:1–2.

_____

_____

Please describe Cornelius's vision (vss. 3–6).

_____

_____

_____

Please describe Cornelius's response to the vision (vss. 7–8).

_____

_____

_____

In this brief passage of Scripture, God sets the stage for an amazing event that involves Peter. Acts 10:1–2 provides the following details about a man from Caesarea.

- His name was Cornelius.
- Cornelius served in the military.
- Cornelius and his family were devout and feared God.
- Cornelius practiced his faith by praying fervently and giving generously to those in need.

The most important fact about Cornelius and his family is that they were Gentiles. The significance of Cornelius's Gentile origin will become clear as we continue our study.

In Acts 10:3–6 an angel of the Lord came to Cornelius and told him God had noticed his prayers and gifts to the poor. The angel further told Cornelius to send men to Joppa in order to bring back a man named Simon, who was called Peter; the angel even provided Peter's location. Immediately Cornelius moved into action, instructing his servants and a soldier to go to Joppa and bring Peter to Caesarea.

Peter now enters the story as we pick up the account in Acts 10:9-23. Please read this passage and answer the following questions.

Please list the element of time recorded in verse 9.

_____

_____

According to verse 9, what was Peter doing?

_____

Please describe what happened to Peter in verses 10–13.

_____

_____

Record Peter's response and his reasoning as listed in verse 14.

_____

_____

Please write the clear instruction the Lord gave Peter in verse 15.

_____

How many times did this conversation between the Lord and Peter take place?

_____

Who arrived at Peter's location following the vision?

_____

Please describe the Spirit's instruction to Peter in verses 19–20.

_____

_____

Please describe Peter's response as seen in verse 21.

_____

Once the men explained who they were and why they were there, how did Peter respond in verse 23?

_____

As Cornelius's men were on their way to find Peter, Peter goes to the roof to pray. It was around noon, and Peter was hungry. While he was waiting for food to be prepared, he fell into a trance and saw a vision. This vision proved to be very significant in Peter's life and even impacted the future direction of the early church.

Acts 10:9–23 provides the details of Peter's vision. Peter saw a large sheet descending from heaven containing various animals, reptiles, and birds. As the sheet came down,

God instructed Peter to get up, kill, and eat. Peter's clear response is recorded in Acts 10:14. "Surely not, Lord!" Why would Peter respond in this manner? Scripture answers this question for us.

The Old Testament book of Leviticus records clear dietary instructions for God's chosen people, the Jews. Leviticus 11:2–3 states: "Of all the animals that live on land, these are the ones you may eat: You may eat any animal that has a slit hoof completely divided and that chews the cud." Animals that did not fit into this category were considered unclean and therefore unfit for the Jewish people to eat. When the sheet descended and every kind of animal was offered, Peter immediately knew that many of the animals were considered unclean based on the Old Testament laws. As a result Peter said no to God's instruction to eat.

In response to Peter's refusal to eat, the Lord said, "Do not call anything impure that God has made clean" (Acts 10:15). This conversation between Peter and the Lord took place three times, and then the sheet was taken back into heaven. Scripture states that as Peter was wondering about the vision, the men sent by Cornelius arrived at Peter's location. The Spirit prepared Peter for their arrival by telling him exactly what would take place. Acts 10:19 states: "Simon, three men are looking for you. So get up and go downstairs. Do not hesitate to go with them, for I have sent them." Peter responded in obedience and went downstairs. The men explained that they were there on behalf of a God-fearing man named Cornelius and also explained that an angel appeared to Cornelius instructing him to send for Peter. Peter welcomed the men inside and invited them to be his guests.

Read the rest of the story in Acts 10:24–48 and answer the following questions.

According to verse 24, when did Peter start out and who did he take with him?

_____

_____

_____

_____

How did Cornelius receive Peter in verse 25?

_____

What truth did Peter communicate to Cornelius and family in verse 28?

Peter spoke words of truth in verses 34 and following. According to verse 44, what took place?

_____

_____

_____

Why do you think this event is significant?

_____

_____

_____

The day after Peter's vision and subsequent arrival of Cornelius's men, Peter and his friends set out to visit Cornelius in Caesarea. Cornelius had anxiously awaited their arrival and even assembled his family. When Peter arrived, Cornelius fell at Peter's feet. Peter quickly instructed Cornelius to get up; Peter clearly desired to accurately portray himself as a man, not a spiritual super saint. I love the honesty and humility of Peter. Peter was not in Cornelius's home in order to be a seen as a god. Peter was there to represent the one true God. May we never forget that our job is not to supercede our God but rather to represent Him and reflect His glory.

Peter entered the home of Cornelius and found a large group of people waiting. He addressed the group by stating: "You are well aware that it is against our law for a Jew to associate with a Gentile or visit him. But God has shown me that I should not call any man impure or unclean." Peter then asked Cornelius why he sent for him. Cornelius recounted how the angel appeared and instructed him to send for Peter. Acts 10:34-48 provides insight into Peter's thoughts as this event took place. From these verses we can conclude that God was teaching Peter the following truths:
- God does not show favoritism.
- God accepts men from every nation who fear Him and do what is right.
- Everyone who believes in Jesus Christ receives forgiveness through His name.

While Peter preached and expressed the lessons God had taught him, an amazing thing took place. The Holy Spirit descended on **everyone** present—the Jews and the Gentiles. Peter and his friends were astonished as they saw the Gentiles clearly receive the message of Jesus Christ. This conversion might have made more sense to Peter and his friends if Cornelius and his family had first converted to Judaism and then to Christianity. But to see the Gentiles receive the message of Jesus Christ without first accepting the laws and traditions of the Jewish nation amazed Peter and led him to state, "Can anyone keep these people from being baptized with water? They have received the Holy Spirit just as we have" (Acts 10:47).

The Importance of Acts 10 in the Early Church

The significance of this event was not fully understood until the message of Jesus Christ penetrated more and more hearts. This account of the spread of the gospel message is recorded in Acts 11-14. As the message spread, questions regarding the traditions of the Jewish faith and the portion of the Jewish faith the Gentiles should keep surfaced. One subject that came up time and time again involved the issue of circumcision. Circumcision was a sign of the covenant between God and Abraham (then named Abram); this story is in Genesis 15. The covenant was simple. God was the one true God, and Abraham and his future descendents were God's chosen people. Because Abraham and his future descendents would live among ungodly people, God instructed Abraham to enter into a covenant with a specific sign—every male was to be circumcised. The purpose of circumcision was to show the uniqueness of Abraham's people. Throughout the Old Testament, circumcision was not a choice. The Jews were to be circumcised in obedience to the covenant God made with Abraham.

Once God began drawing Gentiles to Himself, the question arose, "Should the Gentiles be circumcised too?" This question was difficult for the apostles and early church leaders to answer. There were many opinions on the subject, and disputes developed. Therefore, the early church leaders convened a meeting in order to deal with this issue. The account of meeting, called the Council of Jerusalem, is in Acts 15. Please read Acts 15:5–11 and answer the following questions.

What question did the elders meet to consider?

_____

After much discussion, who took the lead and addressed the crowd?

_____

What event from his own life did Peter draw on to help process the current situation in his life?

_____

_____

_____

Please summarize Peter's conclusion on this question as seen in verses 10–11.

_____

_____

_____

As the elders met to determine the way the Gentiles should confirm their faith in Jesus Christ, Peter stands up to take the lead. As Peter tackles this crucial question, he draws on the experiences of his past—specifically the experience recorded in Acts 10. Peter, under the leading of the Holy Spirit, draws a significant conclusion to the question the early church faced. The Gentiles should be allowed to become believers in Jesus Christ just as the Jews were. This statement by Peter was huge for the early church and ultimately charted the course for how Gentiles, like you and me, would enter into a saving faith with Jesus Christ—just as we are.

Application

Today, as we think about the perfect will of God, the example from Peter's life teaches us so much. The accounts in Acts 10 and 15 show us a perfect example of God's perfect will in action. As we view these chapters together, we see the significance of God working in Peter's heart and life. For just a moment, please view all the events that took place as one continuous event in God's Kingdom calendar.

- An angel of the Lord appeared to Cornelius and instructed him to send for Peter.
- As Cornelius's men were on their way to find Peter, Peter received a vision from the Lord instructing him to eat items that had long been deemed unclean.
- Peter refused to eat, but God taught Peter that everything He made is clean.
- As the vision ended, Cornelius's men arrived at the door and asked for Peter.
- The Lord told Peter that men were asking for him and he should go with them.
- Peter invited the men into the home and the next day left for Cornelius's home in Caesarea.
- Peter preached the message of Jesus Christ to Cornelius and his family.
- The Gentiles received the message of Christ as the Holy Spirit descended upon them in power.
- The message of Jesus Christ continued to spread to the Jews and Gentiles as recorded in Acts 11–14.
- Questions arose regarding the traditions and practices the Gentiles should follow as they entered into saving faith in Jesus Christ. The questions specifically dealt with the practice of circumcision.
- The Jerusalem Council was convened in Acts 15, and Peter shared all that God taught him from his experience with Cornelius and his family.

From this study I just have one thing to say: "What a mighty God we serve!" You see, way back in Acts 10, God worked in the heart of Peter and prepared him for such a time as Acts 15. As Peter surrendered to the moving of the Holy Spirit, Peter was prepared to address one of the most crucial questions facing the early church. In the end, God's perfect will was demonstrated in Peter's life.

Conclusion

Without a doubt, God's will is *perfect.* God is always working, always moving, in order to bring us to a place of perfection, which from God's perspective means completion. In today's text, we saw God at work in the heart of Peter as He challenged Peter's idea of clean and unclean. As God revealed Himself to Peter, Peter was perfected; he became more and more like Jesus as he understood God's plan to redeem both Jews and Gentiles. In the end, God's perfect will was accomplished in Peter's life as he reflected God's glory and moved one step closer to completion in God's eyes.

Just like God prepared Peter for the task of graciously receiving the Gentiles into the Christian faith, God prepares us in order to accomplish His perfect will in our lives. Daily God teaches and equips each of us so that we are able to glorify and reflect Him. This process is not always easy, and it is not always obvious. Often it is not until we reflect on an event that we see the significance of that event in our lives. Tomorrow we will look at this concept more closely. For now, I pray you have a new perspective on God's perfect will for your life. Please record your thoughts in the space below.

_____

_____

_____

_____

_____

Please close with a word of prayer asking the Lord to give you the ability to see His perfect will in your life.

_____

_____

_____

_____

_____

Reflecting His Glory

Week 7: "…Then you will be able to test and approve what God's will is—his good, pleasing and perfect will."

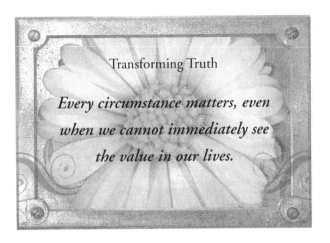

Transforming Truth

Every circumstance matters, even when we cannot immediately see the value in our lives.

Day 3: God's Perfect Will (Continued)

Today we are going to take the concept that we introduced yesterday regarding the perfect will of God and view it in our own lives. This hands-on approach will help each of us to train our minds to view life from God's biblical perspective, not our own. Let's quickly refresh our memory regarding the perfect will of God. Please circle the word/words that describe the perfect will of God from His perspective.

Complete   Free from problems   Whole   Focused on final glory

Three of these phrases describe the perfect will of God from His perspective. The only phrase that does not describe God's perspective is "free from problems." If you will recall this phrase was listed in Webster's definition of *perfect* and reflects a human perspective on the word.

As we desire to reflect the glory of Christ, we must have the ability to view the situations and circumstances of our lives from a big picture perspective. In yesterday's study we saw how Peter had the opportunity to do this. As God worked in Peter's heart and life, Peter was challenged in his faith. This challenge allowed Peter to grow spiritually as he conformed to the desired goal, objective, or purpose God had for him. Hence, God, by His grace, worked in Peter's life in order to propel Peter to a point where he looked like Christ, acted like Christ, and ultimately reflected Christ. Today we have the opportunity to view our lives from the same vantage point as Peter as we take a step back and see life from God's big picture perspective. Let's pray.

Dear Lord,

We praise You, for You are God. As we seek Your holy and perfect face, may we see how You have graciously worked in our past in order to prepare us for the present as well as the future. May the goal of our lives be completion before You. In the mighty name of Jesus, amen.

The Goal—Completion in Christ

Throughout the New Testament, the concept of perfection, which means completion, resounds. As the New Testament saints encountered situations that included times of joy as well as times of pain, we see how God used different kinds of experiences to bring about His perfect will in their lives. Today we are going to examine two passages of Scripture that set the bar for God's perfect will in our lives. Please read each passage of Scripture and describe the key relating to the perfect or complete will of God.

Philippians 1:3–8:

_____

_____

_____

James 1:2–4:

_____

_____

_____

Both of the passages listed above mention two things.

1. **The value of being complete or whole in Christ**. Did you catch how each passage continually found its theme in the value of being complete in Christ?

   - In Philippians 1:6 Paul states: "being confident of this, that he who began a good work in you **will carry it on to completion** until the day of Christ Jesus" (emphasis added).

   - In James 1:4 James states: "Perseverance must finish its work so that you may be **mature and complete, not lacking anything**" (emphasis added).

Each of these reminders from Scripture reflects God's value system when it comes to the perfect will of God. God desires for us to be complete or whole in Him. How do these verses change your perspective on God's perfect will?

_____

_____

_____

2. **The use of hardships in order to reach completion in Christ**. God often uses times of pain and difficulty to propel us to the point where we reflect Christ by our actions in our daily situations. Interestingly enough, each passage of Scripture links the point of completion in Christ and the value of hardships in reaching the point of completion in Christ.

   - In Philippians 1:7 Paul states: "For whether I am **in chains** or defending and confirming the gospel, all of you share in God's grace with me" (emphasis added).

   - In James 1:2 James states: "Consider it pure joy, my brothers, whenever you face **trials of many kinds**…" (emphasis added).

Please list some of the hardships you have experienced in your life or that you are currently experiencing.

_____

_____

_____

As we desire the perfect will of God, we must shift our focus from a human perspective of perfection that desires a problem-free life to a godly perspective of completion that longs to be conformed to the image of Jesus Christ. When this occurs, the big picture perspective of God working and moving in each and every situation and circumstance rings true in our hearts. Once this perspective becomes a part of our daily walks with God, we begin to realize that every circumstance matters, even if we cannot immediately see the value in what God is doing in our lives.

God's Perfect Will—An Example from My Life

I want to share a personal example of the perfect will of God in my life. This is one of those events that in the beginning seemed insignificant but in the end was life changing. I share this story to encourage you to look at your life and observe ways God has worked in your situations and circumstances to accomplish His perfect will.

I have previously shared some of the difficulties I faced growing up. I was adopted, and as a result of my adoption, I experienced feelings of rejection and abandonment. Words cannot express how I struggled in my childhood and teenage years. I felt empty and continually sought people, places, and things in the hope that the void in my life would be filled. As you might guess, this constant search for love and acceptance left me with a very needy spirit and a heart that questioned God about everything. Deep in my heart, I wondered if the pain would ever go away.

I want to share a series of events that led to one of the special ways the Lord taught me that I have never been abandoned or rejected. In 1989 I attended the Billy Graham Crusade at War Memorial Stadium in Little Rock, Arkansas. Although I was only 13 years old, the fact that my mother took me to the crusade was a blessing to me and a wonderful memory.

The night we attended the crusade, Sandi Patty (my favorite singer) was scheduled to perform. My excitement level for the evening was pretty high. For whatever reason, we got off to a late start that day. The traffic, the parking, and the walk to the stadium all took longer than we expected. As a result we were late arriving at the crusade, and once we finally made our way into the stadium, we could not find seats. I remember walking up, up, up in hopes of finding an empty bleacher.

Mom and I finally found seats high in the stadium and enjoyed the evening. I have never forgotten the incredible memory of attending that crusade. I was literally transfixed as Billy Graham preached, and I loved hearing Sandi Patty sing. Just being in the environment with thousands of believers and singing and praising God was a thrilling experience.

Now, fast forward 13 years to August 2001. The place was the Arkansas Baptist State Convention building in Little Rock, Arkansas. The event was my first day of attending seminary at Southwestern Baptist Theological Seminary. (SWBTS utilizes the classrooms of the Arkansas Baptist State Convention as one of their extension campuses.) As you might guess for me as a control freak, my first day of seminary was stressful. Even as I type this, the butterflies flutter in my stomach. I was uncomfortable, unsure, and completely nervous. Everything about attending seminary was outside my comfort zone. In fact, I used every argument I could to gently tell God what a bad idea this was. However, God's direction was clear—I was to go.

I cannot even begin to describe to you the questions and feelings that were going on inside of me on that first day—questions like, "Lord, what am I doing here? Lord, why me? Lord, are You sure?" Looking back I now have the ability to better analyze my feelings; what I was really trying to say was "Lord, not me. Lord, I am not ready. Lord, I am such a mess." And the amazing God-size truth is that every bit of that was correct. I was not ready, and I was a mess. But that was okay, because God, whom I served that day and still serve this day, does not depend on me having things all together.

I remember walking around the campus on that first day, thinking about my life and trying to make sense of the path God had chosen for me. The entire day I was overcome with emotion, thinking about all the questions I had in my life, all the doubts. As I walked, I prayed, "Lord, please help me." This simple request was all that I knew to voice. Then an amazing thing happened. The Lord led me over to a picture that was hanging on the wall next to the classroom where my seminary class was to meet. I was very drawn to the picture and when I looked at it, I realized it was a picture of the Billy Graham crusade held in Little Rock many years before. The picture was taken from the very top of the stadium with a wide-angle lens so that Billy Graham could be seen preaching to the thousands of people in attendance that night.

As I looked at the picture, my mind immediately went back to the crusade. I thought about the night and the memory of my mom and me at the event. Almost simultaneously, something in the picture caught my attention—a young girl and her mother sitting just three rows in front of the person who took the photograph. The bows in that young girls hair were very recognizable, and the young mom was most definitely the mother I had looked at my entire life. You see, sitting at the top of War Memorial Stadium listening intently to Billy Graham proclaim the message of Jesus Christ were my mom and I.
I could not believe it! Something that took place 13 years earlier that I never knew was captured on film was waiting for me on my first day of seminary—probably the day I felt my weakest and most unsure. As I looked at the picture in disbelief, the Lord held

me there and said some pretty amazing things. First, the Lord reminded me that He always has His eyes on His children, so there is never a need to feel lonely, rejected, or abandoned. Second, the Lord reminded me that He had a plan for my life and that He would use all of the hurts and pain for His glory. Third, I was impressed that just as He was with Billy Graham to accomplish His pleasing will in his life, He would be with me to accomplish His pleasing will in my life.

I cannot express the turning point that event represents in my life. For the first time, the pain, the questions, and the hurt began to take a back seat to the work of redemption God could and would perform. To this day, I get chills just thinking about how God meets us at our greatest need and lovingly draws us to Himself. God did not have to provide that picture, but out of His grace HE DID! Today, a copy of that picture sits in a very special place in my home. The picture reminds me that God has a perfect plan, and even when times are tough, God is working, and He is perfecting us in order to accomplish His glory.

God's Perfect Will--- An Example from Your Life

Now it is your turn. Thinking back over your life, please describe an event that in the initial stages you did not recognize as significant until you realized God was preparing you for a later, God-sized situation in your life.

_____

_____

_____

_____

Conclusion

Dear friend, the event you just described is the perfect will of God at work in your life. Please take a few minutes and praise God as you commit to view your life from His perspective, not your own.

_____

_____

_____

_____

_____

Reflecting His Glory

Week 7: "...Then you will be able to test and approve what God's will is—his good, pleasing and perfect will."

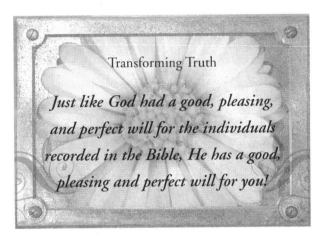

Transforming Truth

Just like God had a good, pleasing, and perfect will for the individuals recorded in the Bible, He has a good, pleasing and perfect will for you!

Day 4: Testing and Approving God's Good, Pleasing, and Perfect Will

During the last two weeks, we have studied the final phrase of Romans 12:2. Please read Romans 12:2 and underline the last portion of the verse.

Do not conform any longer to the pattern of this world, but be transformed by the renewing of your mind. Then you will be able to test and approve what God's will is—his good, pleasing and perfect will. (Romans 12:2)

The concept of God's good, pleasing, and perfect will challenges each of us to view God's will from His biblical perspective, not our own. In our study we saw God's good, pleasing, and perfect will in the lives of Paul, Ruth, and Peter. Today we will turn our attention to *our* lives and ask, "Lord, how do I know your good, pleasing, and perfect will for me?"

Do you desire to know God's good, pleasing, and perfect will in your life?

Dear friend, please hear this truth. Just like God had a good, pleasing, and perfect will for the individuals recorded in the Bible, He has a good, pleasing, and perfect will for you. Amazingly, many believers in Christ live their entire lives and miss this wonderful truth. Let's not miss this one. Join me as we pray.

Dear Lord,

We praise You! O Father, we proclaim Your wonder and Your worth. Today as we study Your truth, we thank You for Your faithfulness to speak. Lord, give us ears to hear and hearts to obey. In You we find all that we need, because in You, we find You. Thank You for life, redemption, meaning, and purpose. As we near the completion of our study of Your Word, please write Your truth on our hearts. Lord, to You be all the glory. In Jesus' name, amen.

Testing and Approving God's Will in Your Life

The process of recognizing God's will in our lives occurs as we test and approve. Please review Romans 12:2 at the top of the page and circle these words. The phrase *test and approve* come from the single Greek word *dokimazo*. *Dokimazo* means "approved, tested, to test, try, prove, scrutinize, discern, distinguish, approve, the process of testing a thing to ascertain whether it be worthy to be received or not."[65]

 As you look at the meaning of ***test and approve***, which word or words help you to grasp this concept better and why?

Testing and approving are not simple, but this process plays a necessary role in the believer's life. As we walk with the Lord, we naturally come to forks in the road—decisions that call us to go one way or the other. We must have a plan that allows us to filter the decisions of life through God's thought process.

 Currently, how do you test and approve God's will for your life?

For me, testing and approving prove to be challenging tasks. When presented with several choices, I wonder, "Lord, how do I know Your specific will for my life? How do I scrutinize, discern, distinguish, approve, or test something in order to ascertain its worth?" Decisions ranging from "insignificant" to "grand" daily present opportunities for us to test and approve God's will in our lives. When we make the choice to test and approve God's will, we reflect the glory of Christ to a world that desperately needs to see that Jesus determines the course for our lives.

For this reason, we must know how to test and approve God's good, pleasing and perfect will. Today, we will examine this process as we merge the information from the last two weeks of study to produce a step-by-step guideline for testing and approving God's will for our lives.

Step 1: Recognize the Authority of the Word of God

Let's think back to our study on God's *good* will where we discovered the importance of God's holy Word. From the apostle Paul's life we saw that God's good will often produces reassurances from the Bible in the form of a specific word or promise to claim.

As we think about the process of testing and approving, the importance of the Word of God takes on a new dimension. **This is true because the first step in testing and approving God's will comes as we recognize the authority of the Word of God.** Very simply, anything God calls you to do will line up with the precepts of His holy Scriptures. Therefore, knowing, understanding, and applying the Word of God is critical in determining His good, pleasing, and perfect will for life.

A dear sister in the faith once challenged me as she led a women's conference for my home church. During the conference, my sister stated that any time her children came to her for direction or advice, she asked one simple question, "What does the Bible say about that?" This simple question convicted me on many levels. First, the conviction came in regard to how often I try to solve my children's problems instead of teaching them how to go to the Bible, which provides help for every situation they face. Second, I was challenged to take a hard look at my life and evaluate how much of the Word I knew and how much of the Word I was applying in my daily walk with God. Much of the information that I presented in Week Five on Bible study and Scripture memory came as a direct result of examining my life and knowing that I needed to discipline myself to know more of God's Word.

How about you? Does the question, "What does the Bible say about that?" convict you? If so, please explain.

_____

_____

Please look up Psalm 19:7-11 and list every benefit of knowing and applying the Word of God in your life.

_____

_____

From Psalm 19:7-11 we discover the following benefits of knowing God's holy Word:

- Our souls are revived
- We are made wise
- We experience joy in our hearts
- We see things in a different way
- We are warned when in dangerous territory
- Reward comes into our lives as we obey.

The six things listed above are not only benefits but also necessary tools that help us test and approve God's good, pleasing, and perfect will. As we desire the good, pleasing, and perfect will of God, we must accept the paramount role the Word of God plays in the process. Apart from God's Word, we have no hope of distinguishing between God's path and the world's path.

Do you see the value of the Word of God in testing and approving God's will for life? Please explain.

_____

_____

_____

Step 2: Allow the Holy Spirit to Examine Our Attitudes and Actions

When we studied God's _pleasing_ will, we discovered the importance of our actions and attitudes. From the life of Ruth, we looked at how godly living positioned Ruth to know the pleasing will of God. As Ruth pleased God, God's pleasing will became evident in her life. Our actions and attitudes play an important role in our lives and must be examined on a daily basis.

Today as we think about the process of testing and approving God's will for our lives, our attitudes and actions once again come to the forefront of our discussion. As we come to those situations that call us to make important decisions, we must stop and take inventory of our hearts as well as of our previous actions to determine if sin is present in our lives. Because sin lessens the sense of God's presence in a believer's life, sin must be dealt with before life decisions are made. Like Ruth, we have choices, and the choices at times are life altering. If you and I fail to invite the Holy Spirit to check our hearts, we miss the valuable step of determining who or what is motivating us. **Therefore, the second step in testing and approving the will of God is allowing the Holy Spirit to examine our hearts as well as our actions.** When sin is uncovered, we must confess and repent. Confession involves recognizing that our attitude or action was wrong. When you confess that something is wrong you come into agreement with God by saying, "God you are right. I am wrong." Repentance involves turning from our attitude or action and embracing God's view on the sinful areas of our lives.

Before you make an important decision in life, do you stop and ask the Lord to search your heart for sin?

_____

If not, are you open to adding this step into your decision-making process?

_____

Please look up Psalm 139:23–24. What was David asking God to do?

_____

_____

_____

In Psalm 139:23-24, David asks God to search him, know him, test his thoughts, uncover the sinful ways of his life, and lead him down the right path. This cry from David becomes the perfect example of the second step in the testing and approving process. "Lord, look inside of me and uncover the sin. Lord, lead me in Your way, not my own."

What can you learn from David's plea?

_____

_____

_____

From David's request I learn the value of God searching and testing me. Often in life, I voice a simple prayer: "Lord, shine Your bright light into every dark corner of my soul and uncover the sin hidden in my heart." As this prayer has become a discipline in my life, I have been overwhelmed by God's faithfulness to honor this simple plea.

As God through His Holy Spirit reveals sin, I am challenged to confess the sin and turn from it. Once I have confessed and repented, I am better prepared to make important decisions in life. Why? Because I can hear His voice more clearly when my heart is clean before Him.

Step 3: Recognize God's Work in the Circumstances of Life

When we studied God's *perfect* will for our lives, we learned the value of God working in and through the circumstances of life to bring each of us to a place of perfection (remember that meant completion) in Him. The experience of Peter and his incredible journey to the home of Cornelius followed by his impact in the Jerusalem Council is a wonderful example of God's work in the circumstances of life.

Now we turn our attention to the third and final step in the process of testing and approving God's will. **This step involves examining the previous work God has performed in our lives in order to determine correct future steps.** This step represents nothing more than remaining teachable over the course of our lives as we view our time on this earth as a journey towards our heavenly home. As this attitude defines our lives, we stop compartmentalizing our lives and allow God to use anything and everything from the past for His glory. Peter did just that—he allowed God to use wisdom gained from a past experience to provide a spiritual reference for future decisions.

As you and I test and approve God's will for our lives, we must display the same openness. As we live on this earth, we can intentionally allow God to use every situation and circumstance—even the painful hurts from the past—to teach, lead, guide, and direct us to reflect His glory.

I cannot tell you how often I use this principle when I come to important decisions. When faced with several options, I begin to go through the recesses of my mind and ask, "Lord, what have you taught me in the past? What situation, circumstance, or lesson has prepared me for this time?" If I discover a lesson, I allow that experience to impact my decision. How? The lesson becomes an affirmation of God's work in my life. The reason for this approach is simple—this life is not a life of chance. We serve a God who works continually on our behalf.

Please look up Philippians 2:13 and write the verse in the space below.

_____

_____

_____

According to Philippians 2:13, who is working in our lives and why?

_____

_____

Clearly, God is constantly at work in our lives. He does not take breaks or enjoy a few days of vacation. No. God is at work. He is moving and will continue to move. Why? God's plan is working towards an end goal. That goal will be realized when Jesus Christ returns and we will be changed into His image. What an awesome God we serve! Are you wondering, "God, are You there? Do You see me? Do You know what is going on down here?" Take heart and claim the truth found in His Word—God is at work, and He has not forgotten you! Why don't you take a few minutes and praise God for His work in your life. Don't forget all the wonderful things He has taught you in the past and all the incredible things He is teaching you in the present. Remember how all of that is preparing you for the future.

_____

_____

_____

_____

Just for a quick review, please write the three steps in the testing and approving process.

- _____

- _____

- _____

The next time you come to a fork in the road, I challenge you to walk through these three steps as you prayerfully consider God's good, pleasing, and perfect will in your life.

Conclusion

Following our study of God's good, pleasing, and perfect will, do you sense that your focus has changed regarding the will of God?

_____

_____

_____

_____

What lesson sticks out as a life-changing one regarding God's good, pleasing, and perfect will?

_____

_____

_____

_____

As you test and approve God's good, pleasing, and perfect will, do you feel better equipped to make important life decisions?

_____

_____

_____

_____

Please close with a word of prayer expressing your desire to know His good, pleasing, and perfect will for your life.

_____

_____

_____

_____

Reflecting His Glory

Week 7: "…Then you will be able to test and approve what God's will is—his good, pleasing and perfect will."

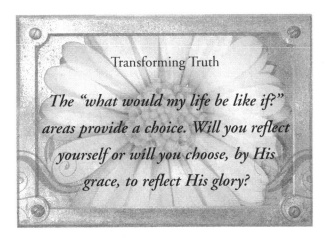

Transforming Truth

The "what would my life be like if?" areas provide a choice. Will you reflect yourself or will you choose, by His grace, to reflect His glory?

Day 5: Offering our Lives—Holy and Pleasing to Him

You made it to the last day of our study! Wow! Can you believe it? Over the last seven weeks we studied the topic *Reflecting His Glory*. This study took us from the Old Testament to the New Testament. We looked intently at Romans 12:2 and discovered valuable tools to help us in the process of *reflecting the glory* of Christ. In the space below, please write Romans 12:2. (Use your memory!)

_____

_____

_____

From the beginning, the goal of *Reflecting His Glory* was clear—to **place ourselves in a position to reflect the glory of Jesus Christ in every area of life**. As our study nears completion, I wonder if you made progress? Have you forsaken conformity to this world and embraced spiritual transformation?

Please take a few moments and journal your thoughts below.

_____

_____

_____

_____

_____

My sweet sister, I pray that God used this study to equip and challenge you to reflect the glory of Christ. I pray that you know more of Christ today than when you began. I pray that your desire to look like Christ, act like Christ, and ultimately reflect Christ has intensified as our study unfolded. Today we will conclude our study by looking at one final passage of Scripture, as well as at one final question for life. Before we begin, please take a moment and open our time in God's Word with prayer. You may journal your prayer below.

Dear Lord,

_____

_____

_____

_____

_____

Offering our Lives to Him

I trust you were able to write Romans 12:2 from memory. I know you read this verse at least forty times over the past seven weeks! The verse just prior to Romans 12:2 provides insight into how we can accomplish the clear call of Romans 12:2. Please look up Romans 12:1 and write it in the space below.

_____

_____

_____

_____

Romans 12:1 states, "Therefore, I urge you, brothers, in view of God's mercy, to offer your bodies as living sacrifices, holy and pleasing to God—this is your spiritual act of worship." Three crucial elements are presented in Romans 12:1; they impact our ability to *reflect the glory* of Christ and ultimately enable us to accomplish the call recorded in Romans 12:2. The elements are: **a bold reminder, a clear instruction**, and a **powerful reason**. Let's look at each.

1. **A bold reminder:** The bold reminder recorded in Romans 12:1 states, **"Therefore, I urge you, brothers, in view of God's mercy..."** In this reminder, Paul urged the believers in Rome to remember God's mercy in their lives. The use of the word *urge* conveys the intensity of Paul's thoughts on this matter.

   In your own words, please define *urge*.

   _____

   _____

   _____

The word *urge* found in Romans 12:1 "is used for every kind of call to a person which is intended to produce a particular effect."[66] When Paul urged the Romans to view their lives through the lens of God's mercy, he was calling the Romans to a point of action.

How would it change your perception to daily view your life through the lens of God's mercy?

_____

_____

_____

For me, viewing my life through the lens of God's mercy changes my perception much like putting on a pair of tinted glasses. Although I see the same things that I saw prior to wearing the glasses, they do not look the same. Tinted glasses change the appearance, which means I see things from a different perspective or point of view. I am always amazed at how this works. When I look at my life through the lens of God's mercy, my attitude becomes one of gratitude for God's amazing work in my life. I remember that the air I breathe is a gift from God. The mind I possess is a result of His work in my life. The body I occupy, although aging every day, is an incredible loaner from Him. You see, viewing life through the lens of God's mercy changes everything and ultimately calls for a response, which is clearly explained in our second point.

2. **A clear instruction:** In response to God's mercy, Paul issues a challenge—*a clear instruction*—to the believers in Rome. In Romans 12:1 Paul challenges them **"to offer your bodies as living sacrifices, holy and pleasing to God."** This is the heart of the teaching found in this Scripture. Let's break it down phrase by phrase in order to gain the full meaning of this verse. Next to each phrase please describe in your own words what the phrase means.

• **to offer**

_____

_____

When I think about the phrase *to offer*, I think about giving something freely and with no expectation of return.

• **your bodies**

_____

_____

The phrase *your bodies* teaches what we are to offer to God. What I love about this phrase is that it is all encompassing. Our bodies not only include our hands and feet but also our hearts and minds.

• **as a living sacrifice**

_____

_____

Two words jump out of the phrase *as a living sacrifice*. The first word—*living*—sets the stage for the second. Clearly, if we are living, we are alive. We are walking around this earth and breathing air. The second word provides the instruction as to how we should walk and breathe. We are to be living, breathing *sacrifices*. Among other things, a *sacrifice* is something that no longer controls itself.

• **holy and pleasing to God**

_____

_____

The words *holy and pleasing to God* provide further instruction as to how we are to offer our lives as a living sacrifice. The word *holy* means "separated from ordinary or common usage and devoted to God."[67] The word *pleasing* means "that which God wills and recognizes."[68] We live as a living sacrifice when we live a life that is different from what this world expects and that focuses on what God desires and recognizes.

3. **A powerful reason:** The *powerful reason* we should want to offer our bodies as a living sacrifice is recorded in Romans 12:1: **"...this is your spiritual act of worship."**

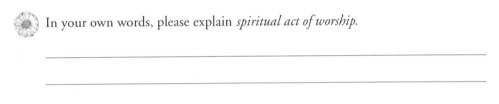

In your own words, please explain *spiritual act of worship.*

_____

_____

_____

The very heart of worship is giving everything we have to God. This giving process includes our fears, anxieties, wishes, hopes, desires, and dreams. As we give God everything, we display our deep sense of gratitude and trust in His ability and desire to care for us. With that said, let's ask ourselves one final question.

One Final Question to Consider

Proof of our willingness to offer our bodies as living sacrifices, holy and pleasing to God, can be measured in one simple question—a question that has life-altering potential. At least, this question altered the course of my life. The question is, **"What would my life be like if...?"**

For just a moment, voice this question out loud. Although you may not fully understand what this question means, I want to ask you to trust me regarding the relevance of this question. This question holds a major key to *reflecting His glory.* I believe as we ask ourselves this question, we discover the incredible potential to walk daily in the freedom we have in Christ.

Each of us possesses an area (or two, or three, or four) that keeps us from *reflecting His glory.* These areas of unwillingness must be turned over to the King of Kings and Lord of Lords if *reflecting His glory* will ever be a reality in our lives. Recently the Lord challenged me with this truth. "Andrea, you will never truly reflect Me until you have given Me everything." Ugh—that hurt. More than anything, I desire to reflect Him. However, my flesh also desires to remain in control. Because of these dueling desires, the Lord challenged me to imagine my life free from the control I so desperately seek. This challenge came to me in the form of the question, "Andrea, what would your life be like if…?"

As soon as the Lord asked this question, I started brainstorming, listing everything in my life that I so desperately sought to control. As I wrote, my eyes were opened to all the areas where I fail to reflect Him. My list was long and truly overwhelming. But praise God, I do not have to tackle my list alone!

The "what would my life be like if…?" areas included:
- "What would my life be like if…I stopped <u>being selfish</u> and really **put others first?"**
- "What would my life be like if…I stopped <u>worrying about our finances</u> and **trusted God to provide**?"
- "What would my life be like if…I stopped <u>trying to control True Vine Ministry</u> and **let it become God's**?"
- "What would my life be like if…I stopped <u>being so fearful</u> and **sought to live by faith**?"
- "What would my life be like if…I stopped <u>living based on my emotions and feelings</u> and truly **lived my life based on the Word of God**?"
- "What would my life be like if…I stopped <u>trying to force friendships to work in my life</u> and instead **allowed God to bring people in and out of my life** for His glory?"
- "What would my life be like if…I stopped <u>trying to prove myself to everyone</u> and **trusted God to be God**?"

As I read the list over and over again, I realized that within each statement, two choices were available—mine and God's. My choice is represented with the <u>underline</u> and God's choice is represented in **bold**. As I read, I felt a sense of hope, knowing that by God's grace His choice could become a reality in my life. I felt a tangible sense of excitement as I knew God was challenging me to reflect Him in the areas I desperately sought to control. Today, the Lord and I are making progress—and for now, that is good enough.

 How about you? Take a moment and ask the Lord to show you the "what would my life be like if…" areas in your life. Don't forget to <u>underline your choice</u> and **bold God's choice**.

- _____

- _____

- _____

- _____

- _____

- _____

- _____

Dear friend, do you want to know what keeps you from *reflecting His glory*? You just wrote the answers! Each "what would my life be like if...?" area becomes an area of control that causes you to reflect yourself rather than your Lord. Today, I hope you are experiencing a sense of hope, as you know that God is granting you the wonderful opportunity to imagine your life free from the chains that currently bind you.

Please take a moment and journal a prayer of thanksgiving as well as a cry for help regarding each "what if?" area in your life.

_____

_____

_____

_____

_____

_____

Conclusion

Spiritual progress occurs as we daily offer our "what if?" areas to God. This means that when we want to control, we surrender; when we want to hold back, we give; and when we want to live for ourselves, we choose to live for Him. This daily resolve provides a path for you and me to heed the words of Romans 12:2.

Over the last seven weeks, we have studied Romans 12:2. This verse has provided our road map as we sought to forsake conformity and embrace spiritual transformation. One last time, let's take a look at this important verse and see the spiritual truths it teaches.

- **Do not conform any longer to the pattern of this world:** In Week One, we were challenged to identify areas of sin in our daily lives—areas where we live in conformity to the world's pattern of success. Once sin was identified, we were called to turn from sin and seek the face of God.
- **But be transformed**: In Weeks Two, Three, and Four, we were presented with a clear definition of spiritual transformation. Four key elements of this process were introduced—a significant change in form, real spiritual growth, differentiation, and changes in habitat and habits.
- **By the renewing of your mind**: In Week Five, we were taught practical ways to renew our minds. The spiritual disciplines provided tangible ways to put renewing into practice. We focused on renewing via Bible study, Scripture memory, journaling, worship, meditation, giving, praying, and fasting.

- **Then you will be able to test and approve what God's will is—his good, pleasing and perfect will**: In Weeks Six and Seven, we were encouraged to seek God's good, pleasing, and perfect will from His biblical perspective, not our own. This focus helped us to broaden our view of God's good, pleasing, and perfect will for our lives and provided a clear way to test and approve God's will.

As you read the above recap of Romans 12:2 and the ways this verse challenged us to dig deep into God's Word, I trust the Holy Spirit gave you a new sense of clarity of the depth of teaching found in this verse. If so, please share your thoughts.

_____

_____

_____

In the space below, please express your desire for Romans 12:2 to continually challenge the way you live your life on this earth.

_____

_____

_____

I know my desire is for Romans 12:2 to daily call me to forsake conformity to this world and embrace spiritual transformation. As I forsake conformity (which is sin) and embrace transformation, I will look like, act like, and reflect more of Jesus Christ in my life. Renewing my mind will play a vital role in this process as I make the choice to daily seek God for who is He. Once my eyes are clearly on the Lord, I will have the God-given ability to know His will and purposes for me. My response to knowing God's will must be surrendering to the One who has given me everything I need for life. Wow! What wonderful truths are found in Romans 12:2—truths that enable you and me to reflect the glory of Jesus Christ!

As our study comes to an end, I want to challenge you to allow the truths taught in Romans 12:2 to shape the rest of your days on this earth. I believe this will happen if you make a plan to keep this verse in your heart and on your mind. I challenge you to place a copy of Romans 12:2 where you will see it every day. Then, ask a close friend to hold you accountable to the teachings set forth in this verse. As you take on this challenge, you can know that you will daily seek to live by the truths of God's Word instead of the shifting standards of this world. Please know that you are not taking this journey alone. You have a fellow sojourner in me—and, by God's grace, we will make it safely home.

Well, sister, I hope you know how much I love you. More importantly, I hope you know how much your heavenly Father loves you. Please allow me to pray for you one last time. May God bless you, my dear sister and new friend!

Dear Lord,

I praise Your Name! You and You alone are worthy to be praised. Thank You for the awesome journey represented in this study. Your faithfulness to speak to Your children reminds me of Your great desire to be intimately involved in the details of life. I want to pray specifically for my dear sister in Christ. Lord, may she reflect Your glory! Please plant Your Word of truth deep inside her heart. May she know the length, the depth, and the breadth of Your love. May she walk in the freedom that only You provide. May she forsake the things of this world and embrace the things of Christ. May she keep her eyes focused on heaven and long for the day when she will meet You face to face. Lord, keep her safe until we meet again. In the mighty, powerful name of Jesus I pray, amen and amen.

Endnotes

Chapter 1

1. *Zondervan Handbook to the Bible* (Grand Rapids, MI: Zondervan Publishing, 1999), 681.
2. Ibid.
3. Ibid.
4. Ibid.
5. Kenneth Barker and John R. Kohlenberger *III, Zondervan NIV Bible Commentary Volume 2: New Testament* (Grand Rapids, MI: Zondervan, 1994), 520.
6. Ibid.
7. Ibid.
8. Merriam-Webster's On-line Dictionary, "conform," September 24, 2007.
9. James Strong, *The New Strong's Exhaustive Concordance of the Bible* (Nashville, TN: Thomas Nelson Publishers, 1990), 28.
10. Ibid., 26.
11. Merriam-Webster's On-line Dictionary, "origin," September 24, 2007.
12. Merriam-Webster's On-line Dictionary, "pattern," October 30, 2007.
13. Bible Navigator Bible Software (Nashville, TN: Holman Interactive), *Strong's Greek and Hebrew Dictionary*, #1245. February 1, 2010.
14. Merriam-Webster's On-line Dictionary, "yield," September 24, 2007.

Chapter 2

15. Spiros Zodhiates, *The Key Word Study Bible* (Chattanooga, TN: AMG Publishers, 1996), # 3565, 2094.
16. Wikipedia On-line Encyclopedia, "Metamorphosis," September 10, 2008. http://en.wikipedia.org/wiki/Metamorphosis.
17. Robert Gundry, *A Survey of the New Testament* (Grand Rapids, MI: Zondervan, 1994), 306.
18. Zodhiates, *The Key Word Study Bible*. # 5922, 1686.
19. Merriam-Webster's On-line Dictionary, "corrupt," October 4, 2007.
20. Zodhiates, *The Key Word Study Bible*. # 391, 1586.
21. *Zondervan Handbook to the Bible,* 571.
22. Bible Navigator Bible Software. *Matthew Henry Concise Commentary,* Matthew 23:1–2, June 15, 2007.
23. Zodhiates, *The Key Word Study Bible,* # 59, 1574.
24. Ibid., # 5427, 1677.
25. Merriam-Webster's On-line Dictionary, "contained," September 10, 2008.

Chapter 3

26. Zodhiates, *The Key Word Study Bible*, # 201, 1581.

27. *Zondervan Handbook to the Bible,* 589.

28. Merriam-Webster On-line Dictionary, "differentiating," September 10, 2008.

29. David Alexander, *Eerdmans' Handbook to the Bible* (Carmel, New York: Lion Publishing, 1973), 522.

30. 4Him. "The Center of the Mark," September 10, 2008. http://www.stlyrics.com/songs/0-9/4him5140/thecenterofthemark793746.html.

31. Merriam-Webster's On-line Dictionary, "character," September 10, 2008.

32. Zodhiates, *The Key Word Study Bible*, # 3421, 1647.

Chapter 4

33. *The Baptist Hymnal,* "Revive Us Again" (Nashville, TN: Convention Press, 1991), 469.

34. *Little Book of Devotions,* (Nashville, TN: Freeman-Smith, LLC), Day 13.

35. Zodhiates, *The Key Word Study Bible,* #2997, 1640.

36. Bible Navigator Bible Software. *Strong's Greek and Hebrew Dictionary,* #2733, October 8, 2008.

37. Merriam-Webster's On-line Dictionary, "alloyed," September 10, 2008.

Chapter 5

38. Zodhiates, *The Key Word Study Bible*, # 364, 1585.

39. Zodhiates, *The Key Word Study Bible*, # 3364, 1646.

40. Bible Navigator Bible Software, *Strong's Greek and Hebrew Dictionary,* # 4146, September 10, 2008.

41. Richard Foster, *Celebration of Discipline: The Pathway to Spiritual Growth* (New York, NY: Harper Collins Publishers, 1978), 7.

42. Bible Navigator Bible Software, *Strong's Greek and Hebrew Dictionary,* # 1746, September 10, 2008.

43. Ibid., #353.

44. Bible Navigator Bible Software, *Barnes' Notes on the New Testament,* Ephesians 6:17.

45. Zodhiates, *The Key Word Study Bible.* # 1006, 1598.

46. Bible Navigator Bible Software. *Strong's Greek and Hebrew Dictionary,* #4729, October 8, 2008.

47. Ibid., #1820.

48. Ibid., #1459.

49. Ibid., #622.

50. Ibid., #2346.

51. Ibid., #639.

52. Ibid., #1377.

53. Ibid., #2598.

Chapter 6

54. Zodhiates, *The Key Word Study Bible*, # 2525, 1631.

55. Ibid., #19, 2049.

56. Ibid., # 9068, 1559.

57. Ibid., # 4409, 1662.

58. Ibid., # 2298, 1628.

59. Ibid., # 2879, 1517.

Chapter 7

60. *Zondervan Handbook to the Bible,* 252.

61. Merriam-Webster's Online Dictionary, "perfect," September 10, 2008.

62. Zodhiates, *The Key Word Study Bible,* # 5455, 1677.

63. Ibid., # 1507, 1610.

64. Ibid., #4151, 1659.

65. Ibid., #41, 1572.

66. Ibid., #2298, 1628.

Appendix 2

67. Campus Crusade International. "How To Fast Safely," September 10, 2008. http://www.ccci.org/growth/growing-closer-to-god/how-to-fast/03-how-tofast-safely.aspx.

68. Campus Crusade International. "How Long and What Type of Fast is Right for You?" September 10, 2008. http://www.ccci.org/growth/growing-closer-togod/how-to-fast/04-how-long-and-what-type.aspx.

Appendix 1

Scripture Memory

I challenge you to memorize Scripture. If you would like to take on this challenge but you are not sure where to begin, memorize the verses below. You will find some of the verses to be familiar because they were part of our study. These verses are taken from the New International Version of the Bible.

- "Do not conform to the pattern of this world, but be transformed by the renewing of your mind. Then you will be able to test and approve what God's will is—His good, pleasing and perfect will." Romans 12:2

- "So we fix our eyes not on what is seen, but what is unseen. For what is seen is temporary, but what is unseen is eternal." 2 Corinthians 4:18

- "How can a young man keep his way pure? By living according to your word." Psalm 119:9

- "I have hidden your word in my heart that I might not sin against you." Psalm 119:11

- "But seek first his kingdom and his righteousness and all these things will be added to you." Matthew 6:33

- "May the words of my mouth and the meditation of my heart be pleasing in your sight, O Lord, my Rock and my Redeemer." Psalm 19:14

- "If anyone would come after me, he must deny himself and take up his cross daily and follow me." Luke 9:23

- "We wait in hope for the Lord; he is our help and our shield. In him our hearts rejoice, for we trust in his holy name." Psalm 33:20–2

- "Set me free from my prison, that I may praise your name. Then the righteous will gather about me because of your goodness to me." Psalm 142:7

- "May those who fear you rejoice when they see me, for I have put my hope in your word." Psalm 119:74